THE BLACK VANGUARD

ORIGINS OF THE NEGRO SOCIAL REVOLUTION 1900-1960

Robert H. Brisbane

JUDSON PRESS
Valley Forge

THE BLACK VANGUARD

International Standard Book No. 0-8170-0441-6
Library of Congress Catalog Card No. 69-18900

Printed in the U.S.A.

THE BLACK VANGUARD

To
Kathryn
and
Phillipa

ACKNOWLEDGMENTS

AMONG THOSE WHO ASSISTED ME in producing this work, I wish especially to thank Dr. Stephen Henderson, of Morehouse College, and Mr. Miles Jackson, of Atlanta University. These colleagues read the original manuscript and made suggestions for its improvement and expansion. My thanks also to Mrs. Gaynelle Barksdale and the staff of the Trevor Arnett Library of Atlanta University, to Mrs. Brenda H. Scott and the staff of the West Hunter Branch of the Atlanta Public Library, and to the staff of the Moorland Library of Howard University.

My appreciation to Dr. Lester Granger for preparing a document for this study on his years as Executive Director of the National Urban League. I wish to mention Mrs. Eutavia Smith, of Atlanta; Miss Nora McNiven, of Atlanta University; and Mrs. Sylvia McAfee, of Morehouse College, all for assisting me in detail work prerequisite to publication.

Further, I give thanks to the Danforth Foundation who, through a generous grant to Morehouse College, help to make it possible for me and other members of the Morehouse College faculty to engage in meaningful and productive research and writing. And lastly to my wife, Kathryn, who in this, as in all of my other endeavors, has given me unfailing encouragement and assistance.

FOREWORD

It is less than a decade ago that John F. Kennedy won the Presidency. Some viewed his election as a mandate for change, but it could have hardly been so regarded in view of the very slim majority of the popular vote by which he won. Many things have changed drastically, nevertheless. We have witnessed, for example, some of the most profound changes in the outlook and status of Negro Americans that have ever occurred in the history of the United States. To be sure, the Kennedy and Johnson administrations did take a more active part in moving Negroes toward first-class citizenship than any of their predecessors. But the results were not very significant as far as drastic, even far-reaching, change was concerned. A real revolution did occur, but it was in the mind and attitudes and programs of Negro Americans themselves. The spirit of that revolution was characterized by a determination to achieve for themselves the equality that the nation had denied them for three centuries. They sat-in, marched, picketed, demonstrated, obstructed, and demanded; and, as resistance stiffened, they became more strident, more uncompromising, and even resorted to violence.

The humble and respectful requests of 1960 that were, for the most part, summarily rejected, would not satisfy them when graciously offered a few years later. The bitterness engendered by centuries of rejection all but alienated them and prompted them, in turn, to reject many of the nation's time-honored and venerated values. The new definition of first-class citizenship which they forged contained more about racial integrity and self-esteem than about the mythical melting pot and a common culture. It argued more for a specific share in the benefits of American life than for the theoretical rights about which they had been catechized for so long. It threatened more than it supplicated; and, unconsciously, it commended its new approaches to other dissidents, who seized on them with an avidity that frightened the more complacent, peace-loving citizens. How different our entire attitude is today toward social change from what it was only a brief decade ago!

One of the easiest of all possible things to do is to lose perspective during a period of rapid social change. This is understandable, for the agenda for change is so crowded and the work so preoccupying that there is little time for retrospection or reflection. It is also lamentable, for one important way of accelerating change is to see whether there is any experience that may assist in formulating a program or any foundation already laid on which to build. It is all-important for bystanders as well as participants to have some sense of the antecedents of change. The former may not be so alarmed when they discover, as is likely, that the changes of today are themselves a part of the past. The latter may find a new humility as they discover, as is also likely, that their struggle is part of a larger, ageless struggle and that their role is to continue it, even transform it, rather than to create it.

The black militants of today operate in an honorable and venerable tradition. Theirs is the spirit that moved the Negro soldiers during the Civil War, when they declined their meager pay rather than receive discriminatory pay. One sees it again when Negroes took the initiative in trying to enforce the Civil Rights Act of 1875, when the Attorney General of the United States dragged his feet and gave no evidence of interest in enforcing a federal law. Meanwhile, there was that hapless group of blacks who, in the same decade, staged a sit-in on the street cars of Louisville in the effort to break the stranglehold of segregation in that city. The spirit of bitter defiance of degradation was present in the efforts of scores of nineteenth century Negro scholars and writers who, with uncommon eloquence and felicity, denounced from the platform and in their writings the American laws, customs, and practices designed to dehumanize them.

It is in the first half of the twentieth century — appropriately called "A Half Century of Dishonor" as far as the status of Negro Americans was concerned — that we find the immediate origins of the current Negro social revolution. And it is these origins that Robert Brisbane has traced in great detail and with remarkable understanding. He recalls for us the memorable confrontation in 1914 of a militant Negro delegation with President Woodrow Wilson, who was a party to the reinstitution of segregation in every area of the federal establishment. The march in Boston in 1915 to protest the showing of *The Birth of a Nation,* a film that was a criminal distortion of the Reconstruction era, would warm the hearts of the most ardent militants of the present day. The silent protest parade in New York in 1917 to express outrage against the East St. Louis riot of 1917 was a remarkable demonstration of civilized restraint in the face of the most barbarous of crimes. Such acts revealed not merely imagination and creativity, but also a dramatic rejection of the status to which white Americans sought to relegate black Americans.

Perhaps the most important feature of Mr. Brisbane's delineation of the origins of the Negro social revolution is the variety of approaches and techniques that the early fighters for justice employed. There was the manifestation of pride of race that ran the gamut from the mass movement of Garvey's Universal Negro Improvement Association to the poignant expressions of "I am Somebody" in the Harlem Renaissance. There were the campus revolts at Fisk and Howard and the bitter and ultimately successful effort of a Negro dentist to destroy the white Democratic primary. The Jobs-for-Negroes campaigns, before and during the Great Depression, were as contagious as a winter virus, and their notable successes in the face of incredible obstacles reveal courage as well as determination on the part of the leaders and the rank and file.

The failure of these early efforts to achieve complete equality for Negro Americans tells us more about the depth and nature of white racism in the United States than it tells us about the weaknesses of the efforts themselves. That some of them lacked sophistication or even efficiency can hardly be gainsaid. But less strenuous efforts had won complete equality for other groups, if indeed others were required to make any efforts at all. Only against Negro Americans did the nation enact legislation and sanctify discrimination in order to keep a black man "in his place." Even in the face of such studied opposition and hostility, the current Negro social revolution can boast of a most respectable lineage. Mr. Brisbane has placed us very much in his debt by tracing this "family tree" and showing so clearly the origins of what is easily the most momentous social development of our time.

John Hope Franklin
University of Chicago

September, 1969

CONTENTS

THE BLACK VANGUARD

1 SETTLING THE NEGRO QUESTION

AFTER THE CIVIL WAR the grand task of clothing the Negro with civil and political rights was spurred on by the needs of practical politics and a political idealism which hung over from the heyday of Jacksonian Democracy. But the confidence of Radical Republicans and New England reformers about the Negro's fitness for the exercise of these rights was shared by only a small segment of the American populace and, least of all, their Southern brethren. For, given the ancient prejudices and new hatreds of the ex Confederates, any effort to erect political democracies in the conquered states upon the manhood suffrage of ex-slaves was doomed to miscarry. Picture the chagrin of Bourbon or clay-eater defeated, disfranchised, and forced to stand back while Negroes took control of state legislatures, went to executive mansions, and even sent one of their brethren to take the seat in the United States Senate left vacant by Jefferson Davis.

One can imagine the outraged response of the Southern whites. They were moved to magnify every mistake of the freedmen and to ignore or play down every laudable achievement. If the Radical Republicans could not be deterred from passing the Fourteenth and Fifteenth Amendments, a way was found to nullify them in the South — hence the Black Codes, the Ku Klux Klan, and even the mass murder of Negroes in the years immediately following 1868. The white South was determined to present the rest of the nation with a *fait accompli*. Beginning in 1868, therefore, the white South mounted what was in effect a counter revolution. The objectives were the complete and utter destruction of the black Reconstruction governments and the restoration of white Southern political rule under the banner of the Democratic Party. Since the blacks who took the trouble

17

to vote usually voted Republican, they were prevented from voting at all or they were forced to "cross Jordan" (vote the Democratic ticket). In Louisiana within a few weeks prior to the November general elections of 1868, some two thousand people, mainly black Republicans, were killed. Parts of the state were overrun by violence, midnight raids, secret murders, and open riots.[1]

> In the parish of St. Landry the Ku Klux Klan killed and wounded over 200 Republicans, hunting and chasing them for two days and nights through fields and swamps. . . . A pile of twenty-five dead bodies was found half buried in the woods. Having conquered the Republicans and killed and driven off the white leaders, the Ku Klux captured the masses, marked them with badges of red flannel, enrolled them in clubs, made them vote the Democratic ticket, and then gave them a certificate of the fact.[2]

In Tennessee the Klan, which had been organized in 1865, became so terroristic that Congress in 1871 appointed a joint committee to investigate it. This committee looked into conditions from April, 1871, to February, 1872, and issued a voluminous, twelve-volume report covering most of the Southern states. What it told was a tale of one bloody atrocity after another, usually against the hapless blacks but often against the white Yankee carpetbagger as well. In March, 1871, President Grant was petitioned for military aid to suppress the violence in South Carolina. Grant recommended legislation, and as a result the Ku Klux Klan Act of April, 1871, was enacted. It empowered the President to suspend the writ of habeas corpus and to seek destruction of the conspiracies against the Fourteenth and Fifteenth Amendments. Meanwhile, in North Carolina, Tennessee, and Texas, the writ had been suspended in the summer of 1870 by the governors, and in 1871 the dockets of the federal courts were filled with Ku Klux Klan cases. In all of these cases testimony was overwhelming, but conviction was impossible. President Grant declared that in some of the counties of South Carolina two-thirds of the whites were organized and armed.

Thus, in state after state the Ku Klux Klan and the Knights of the White Camelia swept back the black tide and redeemed the land for those they believed to be its rightful Caucasian masters. Tennessee, Georgia, Virginia, and North Carolina were "recaptured" by 1871 and Alabama, Texas, and Arkansas by the end of 1873. By 1874 only four states remained under Reconstruction government: Louisiana, Mississippi, South Carolina, and Florida. In July, 1874, representatives of all the secret organizations met in New Orleans and formed the White

League. "In less than sixty days after the formation of the New Orleans [headquarters] of the White League, it had spread to the furthest parts of the state, had before the end of the year 40,000 members, and was extending in all directions through the South." [3] In Mississippi a leading newspaper declared that the time had come for protective companies of private white militia to step forward. Governor Ames had the foresight to order sufficient copies of *Infantry Tactics* for them.[4] In South Carolina there were the semi-military and unofficial organizations of conservative whites known as "Rifle Clubs." Red-shirted and mounted, these men, in processions of a thousand and more, galloped through the streets of Columbia and Charleston screaming the "Rebel Yell" or singing the Confederate National Anthem "Dixie." These were the young "liberators" of the once proud South. By 1876 white rule had been restored in every ex-Confederate state save South Carolina and Louisiana, and black Republican rule in these was tenuous. Leaders of the white South were ready for a deal with the Northern Republican establishment, and with virtually all of Dixie in their pockets they could deal from a position of strength.

During this same period the primary interests of the non-Radical Republicans lay in things other than the Negro question. The men who financed the party's campaigns, paid its bills, and directed the writing of the rather innocuous and conservatively worded Republican Party platforms were primarily concerned with the promotion of financial and industrial capitalism in the United States. To this end they used both the Republican Party and the government of the United States. Indeed it was under their direction that between 1861 and 1875 the party, as well as the nation, was committed fully to the protective tariff system, a national banking structure, and free land and government aid to transcontinental railroads. During this period also the government adopted a "sound" money program.

Nevertheless, Republicans, and especially the Radicals, had no intention of tamely submitting to the violent undoing of their program in the South. Their answer to the Ku Klux Klan had been renewed military occupation of evacuated districts, the unseating of Democratic state administrations on the grounds of fraud, and a new crop of supervisory laws, the most important of which were the Force Acts of 1870 and the Ku Klux Klan Act of 1871. President Grant was reluctant to enforce these laws, and only once did he find it expedient to reestablish military rule on a large scale because he was aware that public opinion in the North would no longer support a drastic policy toward the South. Indeed in 1872 the split in the Republican Party was partly due to the Negro question. The splinter group known as the Liberal Party under the leadership of Horace Greeley promised a withdrawal of federal troops from the South and an end to the Southern problem. Grant was elected, but in 1874 the Democrats captured the House and the repudiation of Radical Republicanism was complete. Meanwhile, all the Southern states had been readmitted to Congress, and by the Amnesty Act of 1872 almost all Southern whites who were still disfranchised were restored to full political privileges. By 1876 the Republicans, like the Southern white Democrats, were ready for a deal.

Rutherford B. Hayes was inaugurated as President of the United States on March 4, 1877. Ever since that time American historians have been at odds over the exact conditions of the "Compromise of 1877" which allegedly handed the presidency to Hayes rather than to Democrat Samuel J. Tilden. The classical account of the Compromise runs along these lines: Sometime during the last two or three days of February, 1877, representatives of the two parties meeting in the Wormley Hotel in Washington, D. C., agreed that Hayes would be President in return for the prompt removal of federal troops from South Carolina and Louisiana by the new administration. As part of the deal also, the Southerners "promised that the rights of the Negro would be safeguarded and that there would be no bloody reprisals against political enemies." [5] In short, the Republicans were agreeing to the abandonment of the Negro in exchange for the peaceful possession of the presidency. Whether or not there was actually such a compromise, on April 10, 1877, President Hayes ordered the federal troops withdrawn from South Carolina, and on April 20 those stationed in New Orleans received similar orders. In September of 1877 Hayes and his family, along with several members of his cabinet, made a grand tour of the South. In Louisville, Kentucky, he was met by none other than the arch-Confederate Wade Hampton, who had come all the way from South Carolina to greet him. The President's party was escorted by mounted Confederate veterans, and all along the way he was greeted with the Rebel Yell. In Atlanta Hayes assured the none too enthusiastic Negroes in his audience that their "rights and interests would be safer if this great mass of intelligent white men were let alone by the general government." [6] For Negroes, if for no one else, this speech signaled the end of the game. The Republicans had cut bait. Negroes now looked toward the rising Peoples Party with new hope.

The Agrarian Revolt, or Populist Crusade as it is often called, first touched the South in 1874 with the establishment of the Southern Farmers' Alliance. This organization grew with amazing rapidity. Under various names branches appeared in state after state. Interstate and regional mergers were consummated until in 1889 the two most important coalitions in the South united as the National Farmers' Alliance and Industrial Union. The three million members included many middle-class planters and professional people from large cities; but, for the most part, the Alliance was a movement of the dirt farmers and "wool hats" of the back-country areas of the South. Naturally, Negro farmers eager to better their condition sought to join. They were refused, for even by the poverty-stricken poor whites the Negro was adjudged "too costly a sacrifice to 'white supremacy.'" [7]

But the fever of the progressive movement had struck the Negroes too deeply for them to sit by and watch. Hence, at Houston, Texas, in December, 1886, a few Negro farmers organized themselves into a group which became known as the Colored Farmers' Alliance.[8] This organization lost no time in making its existence known to the millions of Negro farmers in the South and West. A weekly publication known as the *National Alliance* was sent to Negro communities, and Negro as well as white representatives were sent to organize Negro farmers wherever they were numerous enough to form branches. Thus, by 1891 locals of the Colored Alliance had been established in Alabama, Florida, Louisiana, Mississippi, North and South Carolina, Tennessee, Virginia, and Kentucky. The Colored Alliance also organized co-operative exchanges for Negroes in such cities as Charleston, S.C.; Mobile, Alabama; New Orleans, Louisiana; and Houston, Texas.[9] A territorial alliance was also established among the Indians. By 1892 the membership of the Alliance totaled over 1,250,000.

The Southern Populists soon saw the potentialities of the Colored Alliance as an ally in their crusade. Indeed, as the dirt farmers and Bourbons battled, neither side could long resist the temptation to appeal for aid from the unwanted Negro. And in so doing, the agitators temporarily forgot the standing black challenge to white supremacy. For this one brief period in Southern history the rich and poor whites were opposing each other on the fundamental issues of economic and political supremacy. The Negro held the balance of power between the two groups of whites. For the 1896 elections in Louisiana, for instance, 130,344 Negroes registered as against 164,088 whites registered.[10]

Naturally, the greatest appeal to the Negro could be expected to come from the Populists. Since the great majority of Negroes were in some measure identified with agriculture, it seemed reasonable to hope that they would vote for the party that promised most to the farmers. In keeping with this spirit the Alabama People's Party in 1892 addressed the following remarks to Negroes:

> We favor the protection of the colored race in their legal rights and should afford them encouragement and aid in the attainment of a higher civilization and citizenship, so that through the means of kindness, fair treatment, and just regard for them, a better understanding and more satisfactory condition may exist between the races.[11]

But the gathering of the Negro vote did not prove to be as difficult a task as that of breaking down the racial antipathies of the poor whites. Thus, in the heat of the Agrarian Crusade, Thomas E. Watson, the Populist leader in Georgia, addressed the backcountry farmers:

> You might beseech a Southern white tenant to listen to you upon questions of finance, taxation, and transportation; you might demonstrate with mathematical precision that herein lay his way out of poverty into comfort; you might have him "almost persuaded" to the truth, but if the merchant who furnished his farm supplies (at tremendous usury) or the town politician (who never spoke to him except at election time) came along and cried "Negro rule!" the entire fabric of reason and common sense which you had patiently constructed would fall. . . .[12]

Watson's intelligent and matter-of-fact appeal to the Negroes of Georgia before 1896 won for him a wide following among Negro farmers in that state. On October 23, 1892, Watson and two thousand of his followers armed themselves and marched all night to a village to prevent the lynching of a Negro Populist.[13] After this, many Negroes regarded Watson as a "savior." As one of his biographers put it: "Tom Watson was perhaps the first native white Southern leader of importance to treat the Negro's aspirations with the seriousness that human strivings deserve." [14] Other white Populist leaders in the South were quick to learn from Watson. Thus, in Texas in 1891 white Populists elected two Negroes to the state executive committee.[15] Negro orators were sent to address white audiences, and Populist county officers even called Negroes to jury duty. In Tennessee and North Carolina in 1890 Negro candidates for Congress were nominated by white Populists and Negro Republicans. With the white Alliance in

Virginia refusing to cooperate with them, Negro Populists and Republicans bolted the regular Republican ticket in the election of 1890 and sent one of their own race, John M. Langston, to Congress. In South Carolina a Populist leader, Ben Tillman, was known to be a Negro-baiter, but in the election of 1890 Negro Populists and Republicans rallied to him in the belief that he represented a new party and a new deal for all dirt farmers. Tillman later became one of the Negroes' bitterest foes in the South.

After 1889 no Populist convention in the South and West was without delegates from the Colored Alliance. Negroes received ninety-seven seats at the St. Louis Convention in 1892. It appears, however, that only five out of ninety-seven Negro delegates arrived in time for the proceedings. Thus, Humphrey, the white leader of the delegation, sold the remaining ninety-two votes to another leader, who used them for his own purpose. The Negroes present became incensed and walked out of the convention in a body.[16] And in 1896 in the same city a Populist leader drew a round of applause with the remarks: "I tell you what we propose to do; we propose to wipe the color lines all off our politics." [17]

But, in spite of all their enthusiasm and their best efforts, the Southern Populists seldom received significant Negro support during elections. Negro voters were willing enough, but the Bourbon Democrats fighting for their political lives were determined to keep Negro Populists and Republicans away from the polls. Hence in the elections of 1892 and 1896 the Reconstruction pattern of Southern politics reappeared. The issue of white supremacy and Negro domination was dinned into the ears of the poor whites. Ballot boxes were hidden, stuffed, or destroyed to prevent Negroes from voting. And where Negroes could be neither intimidated nor bought by the Democrats, they were simply mobbed. In some sections in which Negroes considered it useless to attempt to vote, they were, nevertheless, counted as Democrats by the Democratic election officials.

With the elections of 1896 the high tide of the Agrarian Crusade was reached. After the defeat of William Jennings Bryan, the People's Party declined rapidly in significance throughout the country. The North remained under the control of Marcus A. Hanna's million-dollar Republican machine. And in the South the Bourbon Democrats had managed to beat back the challenge of dirt farmers and professional agrarians.

To the Southern Negro who had striven to aid a cause which

promised to lift him from his political and economic debasement the fadeout of the Populist Crusade was a calamity. Everywhere around him his bitterest enemies had regained control and were preparing to rid him for all times from Southern politics. Worse yet, the Democrats were joined by Populists who, overlooking fundamental causes, were blaming the Negro for their defeat. "The argument against the independent political movement in the South," wrote Thomas Watson in 1892, "may be boiled down to one word — nigger." [18]

If the Negro disfranchisement was to be swift and final, it must above all be "legal." For no later than 1890 the Republicans under Henry Cabot Lodge had attempted to pass a Force Bill to protect Southern Negroes in the exercise of their civil and political rights. Southern political leaders definitely were in a quandary. For the second time, however, the state of Mississippi was to show the way. The first "Mississippi Plan," which was originated during the Reconstruction period and followed generally in the South, prescribed brute force as a means of disfranchising Negroes. The second "Mississippi Plan" originated by that state in 1890 included a series of devices for the so-called "legal" disfranchisement of Negroes. The poll tax, a literacy test, and a property qualification requirement constituted the essentials of the plan. Mississippi incorporated these devices in its constitution in 1890, and by 1910 seven other Southern states had adopted all or some of these methods as a means of taking the Negro out of politics.

The clearest expression of the purpose of this second Mississippi Plan came from Carter Glass in a debate during the Virginia Constitutional Convention of 1901-1902:

> Discrimination! Why, that is precisely what we propose; that, exactly, is what this convention was elected for . . . the elimination of every Negro voter who can be gotten rid of, legally, without materially impairing the numerical strength of the white electorate. . . . It is a fine discrimination, indeed, that we have practiced in the fabrication of this plan.[19]

An example of the effectiveness of the new device was demonstrated in Louisiana in the brief period of four years. In the election of 1896 in that state 130,344 Negroes registered, but by 1900 this number had dwindled to 5,320, a drop of almost 96 percent.[20] Unbound elation now prevailed among demagogues such as Ben Tillman, Hoke Smith, and Thomas Watson, who now became Negro-baiters. With the outright repeal of the Fifteenth Amendment selected as the next objective of the white South, Governor James K. Vardaman of Mississippi addressed the following remarks to an audience in April, 1907:

> How is the white man going to control the government? The way we do it is to pass laws to fit the white man and make the other people (Negroes) come to them. . . . If it is necessary every Negro in the state will be lynched; it will be done to maintain white supremacy. . . . The XV Amendment ought to be wiped out. We all agree on that. Then why don't we do it? [21]

To the white citizens above the Mason and Dixon line the plight of the Southern Negro was rapidly declining in importance as a national issue. For as the din of the Agrarian Crusade subsided, the attention of the North was focused upon the noisy conflict raging between industrialists and the rising trade unions. Moreover, the attitudes of Northern intellectuals and leaders toward the race problem were increasingly conditioned by the new economic and sociological doctrines of the age, doctrines which supplied scientific bases for the ever widening belief in white superiority.

If by 1890 it had become clear to the American Negro that he could not expect to obtain justice and fair play through the regular political processes of the national and state governments, it would soon become equally clear to him that he could not expect much more from the courts of the land and especially the United States Supreme Court. At the close of the Civil War it seemed clear to the Radical Republicans that without the intervention of the federal government the Southern states would by legislative restrictions strip the newly freed Negro of most of the ordinary rights and immunities of free citizens. To meet this situation the Fourteenth Amendment was proposed by Congress to place the civil rights of the Negro upon a firm basis by authorizing the national government to step in and protect him against actions by his own state government. The states were forbidden to take life, liberty, or property without due process of law or deny to anyone the equal protection of the law. The amendment defined United States citizenship in terms which included the Negro, and the states were forbidden to make laws abridging the privileges and immunities of that citizenship.

Negroes were not involved in the first case to come before the Supreme Court under the Fourteenth Amendment. But since the protection of Negro rights was avowedly the purpose of the amendment, the Court could hardly avoid the issue. Nevertheless, but few people could have been prepared for the hatchet job performed on the Negro aspects of this law by the high tribunal. In its decision in the *Slaughter-house* Cases the Court effectively disabled those provisions of the amendment which vested individual rights with federal protection. Justice Miller asked the question:

> Was it the purpose of the fourteenth amendment, by the simple declaration that no State should make or enforce any law which shall abridge the privileges and immunities of *citizens of the United States,* to transfer the security and protection of all the civil rights . . . from the States to Federal Government? . . . was it intended to bring within the power of Congress the entire domain of civil rights heretofore belonging exclusively to the States?" [22]

Answering his own questions Justice Miller states: "We are convinced that no such results were intended by the Congress which proposed these amendments, nor by the legislatures of the States which ratified them." [23]

Ruthlessly applying the logic of the decision in this case, the Court between 1873 and 1883 struck down virtually every congressional enactment designed to protect the rights of the ex-slave. It emasculated the privileges and immunities clause and hobbled the due process and equal-protection-of-the-laws provisions of the Fourteenth Amendment. The most pervasive of its decisions in this connection was given in the Civil Rights cases. The Civil Rights Act of 1875 made it a crime and a civil wrong for any person to deny to any other person "the full and equal enjoyment of the accommodations, advantages, facilities and privileges of inns, public conveyances on land or water, theatres and other places of public amusement. . . ." [24] The cases arising under this law involved several different incidents: the denial to a Negro of a seat in the dress circle of a theater in San Francisco; the refusal by a conductor on a passenger train to allow a Negro woman to travel in the ladies' car of the Memphis & Charleston Railroad; the denial of hotel accommodations to Negroes in Kansas and Missouri; and the mistreatment of a Negro in the opera house in New York City. That only one of these cases originated in the South was evidence of the widespread nature of the Jim-Crow mind in America. Nor was it of less significance that none of the defendants in the criminal cases was represented by counsel before the Court. Presumably they were all pretty well convinced beforehand that the Court would rule in their favor.

In ruling the Civil Rights Act unconstitutional the Court declared that the Thirteenth Amendment was not applicable, since racial discrimination was not involuntary servitude, and the Fourteenth Amendment gave Congress no authority to prevent racial discrimination by private individuals.

The best rebuttals to these contentions were delivered by Justice Harlan. In a blistering nearly forty-page dissenting opinion he argued that common carriers and those who operate inns and places of amusement are not private persons. On the contrary, he asserted that they carry on businesses under state authority, subject to public controls and are in a very real sense agents of the state. This association with and dependence on the state brings them within the prohibiting language of the due process and equal protection clauses.[25]

Plessy v. *Ferguson* is easily the best known of all Supreme Court cases involving the issues of the segregation of the races. It was, however, the keystone rather than the cornerstone of the American institution of apartheid. Cornerstone honors must be reserved for the decision in the Civil Rights cases. Although the issues in the *Plessy* case are so well known they hardly need retelling, a short review of them will be helpful. The legislature of Louisiana had passed in 1890 a statute providing

> that all railway companies carrying passengers in their coaches in this State, shall provide equal but separate accommodations for the white, and colored races, by providing two or more passenger coaches for each passenger train, or by dividing the passenger coaches by a partition so as to secure separate accommodations. . . .[26]

A fine of $25 or twenty days in jail was the penalty for sitting in the wrong compartment. On June 7, 1892, Homer A. Plessy, an extremely light-skinned Negro, was riding in the white compartment of a train running between New Orleans and Covington, Louisiana. When Mr. Plessy refused to move to the Negro compartment after ordered to do so, he was arrested.

As opposed to the circumstances in the Civil Rights cases, where private individuals were the defendants, the discrimination involved in the *Plessy* case was clearly state action and as such was a prima facie violation of the Fourteenth Amendment. But the Court did not agree. In ruling against Plessy the Court held the Louisiana statute to be a "reasonable" regulation within the meaning of the Fourteenth Amendment. "We consider the underlying fallacy of the plaintiff's argument to consist in the assumption that the enforced separation of the two races stamps the colored race with a badge of inferiority. If this be so, it is not by reason of anything found in the act, but solely because the colored race chooses to put that construction upon it." The Court could not accept the argument "that social prejudices may be overcome by legislation, and that equal rights cannot be secured to the Negro except by an enforced commingling of the two races." "Legislation," it insisted, "is powerless to eradicate racial instincts or to abolish distinctions based upon physical differences. . . ." [27] Loren Miller accuses the Court in this decision of smuggling "Social Darwinism into the Constitution." [28] But more than this, the Court had breathed life into the mythical shadow of Jim Crow and had clothed him with the dignity and protection which the word "person" in the Fourteenth Amendment had intended for the Negro. Justice Harlan's historic dissent in the case may be best summed up in one of the paragraphs therefrom:

> The arbitrary separation of citizens, on the basis of race, while they are on a public highway, is a badge of servitude wholly inconsistent with the civil freedom and the equality before the law established by the Constitution. It cannot be justified upon any legal grounds. [29]

The American Negro was destined to be straitjacketed by legal segregation for almost sixty years before Justice Harlan's dissent would become the rule of law.

The turbulent political conflicts in the South had long kept Northern investments in that section of the country to a minimum. Almost any program designed to bring peace and order and at the same time allow a profitable exploitation of Southern resources was certain to be supported by most Northern business interests. The fact that "peace and order" was synonymous with white rule could mean but little in the balance.

To the practical consideration of the Southern race problem by the Northern industrialists must be added the rationalizations offered by the doctrine of Herbert Spencer. The dominant ideology of *laissez-faire* could allow no more protection to the Southern Negro than it did the Northern white laborer. If the Negro found himself in a subjugated position in the South, indeed in the entire country, this was because he was the weakest, and as such he deserved no higher position in American society. According to the leaders of the business community, the law of the survival of the fittest regulated each man's place in the social scale.

But if Social Darwinism offered little sanctuary to the hopes of the American Negro, the naked dogma of Nordic supremacy offered far less. Worse yet, this doctrine was finding ready listeners in the Northern part of the United States. Originally brought to this country by American scholars who had studied under anthropologists in German universities, the doctrine of J. A. de Gobineau and his followers was soon to be found in American history textbooks as the basic explanation of Anglo-Saxon supremacy in the United States. Professor Herbert B. Adams, of Johns Hopkins University, took the lead in popularizing this racist dogma, which was echoed by the historian John Fiske in his *Excursions of an Evolutionist.* John W. Burgess, of Columbia University's faculty of political science, drew out the implications of the theory of white superiority for American and world history.[30] It was the conviction of Professor Burgess that "the Teutonic nations are the political nations of the modern era" and that the "duty has fallen to them of organizing the world politically." Failure to do so would be "not only mistaken policy, but disregard of duty." [31]

By the end of the nineteenth century a great many prominent Americans, including some who were formerly pro-Negro, abandoned the black man's cause in face of what seemed to be mounting evidence of his biological and cultural inferiority. The opinions of some of these people, as summed up by Professor Paul Buck, of Harvard University, follow:

1. The mass of Negroes are unfit for the suffrage. — R. W. Gilder, A. D. Mayo, and the Englishman James Bryce.
2. The only hope for good government in the South rests upon the assured political supremacy of the white race. — Edward Atkinson, E. L. Godkin, Carl Schurz, Charles Eliot Norton, C. D. Warner. . . .
3. The history of the Negro in Africa and America "leads to the belief that he will remain inferior in race stamina and race achievement." — Albert Bushnell Hart.[32]

Thus within two generations after emancipation, the black race in America had practically lost its fight for equality in every walk of American society. James Weldon Johnson, a young Negro poet and author just then reaching manhood, summed up the Negro's plight:

By 1900 the Negro's civil status had fallen until it was lower than it had been at any time since the Civil War; and, without noticeable protest from any part of the country, the race had been surrendered to Disfranchisement and Jim-Crowism, to outrage and violence, to the fury of the mob.[33]

White people were united as never before in their determination to compel the Negro to begin from the bottom. There was but one thing needed. Some black man with a voice capable of reaching the Negro masses must be found; he must tell them to abandon their futile fight and to attempt to improve themselves in strict accordance with the social and economic rule prescribed for them by the white South.

At the opening of the Atlanta Cotton States and International Exposition in Atlanta, Georgia, on September 18, 1895, a tall rawboned Negro school principal stepped forward on the rostrum to address the vast audience. This man was Booker T. Washington, who had already achieved some renown in the South, and those who invited him to speak knew what to expect from him.[34] At the very outset of his address Washington took the "ignorant and inexperienced" Negro race to task for beginning "at the top instead of at the bottom." Clarifying this statement, the Negro speaker went on to say that the Negro had attached greater importance to politics than he had to the acquiring of "real estate or industrial skill." Then asserting that it was in the South that the Negro was given his greatest opportunities, Washington warned the Negro against migration from Dixie. The absence of racial equality was no handicap to the Negro, for, as he put it: "In all things that are purely social we can be as separate as the fingers, yet one as the hand in all things essential to mutual progress." He linked the welfare of the Negro and the Southern white in this verse:

> The laws of changeless justice bind
> Oppressor with oppressed;
> And close as sin and suffering joined
> We march to fate abreast.

And lest there was doubt in some hearts as to the Negroes' continued devotion to the Southern whites, Washington gave these reassurances:

As we have proved our loyalty to you in the past, in nursing your children, watching by the sick-bed of your mothers and fathers, and often following them with tear-dimmed eyes to their graves, so in the future, in our humble way, we shall stand by you with a devotion that no foreigner can approach, ready to lay down our lives, if need be, in defense of yours. . . .[35]

If, as the press reported, Negro listeners cried and applauded at the conclusion of this speech, they must have done so in the emotion and excitement of the moment. For in comparison with the fighting remarks of former Negro leaders, this address smacked of an outright capitulation to the age-long demands of the South. In recounting the reactions of Negroes to his speech, Washington recalled that after

the first burst of enthusiasm began to die away, and the coloured people began reading the speech in cold type, some of them seemed to feel that they had been hypnotized. They seemed to feel that I had been too liberal in my remarks to the Southern whites, and that I had not spoken out strongly enough for what they termed the "rights" of the race.[36]

From the vast throngs of whites in the audience, the applause was deafening. One observer stated that ladies stood on their chairs and waved their handkerchiefs while men threw up their hats, danced, and whistled. Here at last was a "sensible" Negro. After that day Washington's fame spread like wildfire among Southern white leaders, and the contagion soon reached the North.

Before his famous address, Washington had enjoyed but a moderately successful career. Born a slave, he had worked his way through Hampton Institute in Virginia. Then in 1881, with thirty young Negro students, he founded a school to which the name of Tuskegee Institute was given. The rapid growth of this project was due to Washington's administrative ability as well as to his peculiar talent for raising funds among Southern white people. His career, therefore, fitted in well with the rags-to-riches stereotype of success in the United States. He was easily built up by the nation's press; in fact, he was literally hoisted from his modest beginnings to the position of the nation's most outstanding Negro.

Whether Washington actually subscribed to the opinions he voiced at Atlanta is difficult to ascertain; but in view of the fame they had brought him, he undoubtedly found it inexpedient if not impolitic to abandon them. Thus Washington hammered away on the same theme whether he was at a Harvard University commencement or an industrial convention in Alabama. The Negro was to drop his fight for political and civil rights and come to terms with the white South. Higher education among Negroes was not to be entirely abandoned, but since the Negro in the South was primarily a farmer, he should concentrate upon agricultural and industrial pursuits. Above all, the masses of Negroes should remain in the South for the reason that they were not "fitted to survive and prosper in the great northern cities." [37] And, if a Negro was mobbed and lynched occasionally in the South, it was because of the victim's "dense ignorance," [38] a condition which was to be eradicated by the establishment of more agricultural and industrial schools.

These institutions were particularly inoffensive to the South because of what one writer described as the "master and servant tradition" which they perpetuated. On the other hand, the fact that the industrially trained Negro artisan was banned from white labor unions did not greatly concern Washington. He considered the philosophy and tactics of trade unions too hostile to industry, and therefore, no movement for the Negro. As Washington put it, the Negro "does not like an organization which seems to be founded on a sort of impersonal enmity to the man by whom he is employed." [39]

This, of course, was the type of program which fitted in most admirably with the schemes for gradual improvement then being urged upon the black race. Washington was hailed as the "Negro Moses" throughout the country. His opinions were widely publicized and his patrons, which included philanthropists such as Andrew Carnegie, Jacob Schiff, and Julius Rosenwald, contributed hundreds of thousands of dollars to Tuskegee Institute. In time, it became difficult for any Negro college or institution to obtain funds from philanthropists if Washington withheld his approval. Illustrative of this point was the lesson driven home to John Hope during his first years as president of Morehouse College. Hope had been begging and beseeching Andrew Carnegie for funds to erect a much needed classroom and office building on the Morehouse campus. When no response was forthcoming from the great philanthropist, Hope apparently got the message — he was not going through the proper channels. As his biographer relates the outcome, Hope, upon the advice of Robert Russa Moton, turned to Booker T. Washington:

> Then, as if by magic, things began to happen. Carnegie made a gift; the General Education Board made a gift; the society in New York voted a large sum, and the future of a new building, Sale Hall as it was to be called, was assured. [40]

Sometime later Hope attempted to rationalize and explain this episode to his friend William E. B. Du Bois, an arch foe of Washington. Du Bois responded as follows:

> Of course I am sorry to see you as anyone in Washington's net. It's a dangerous place, old man, and you must keep your eyes open. At the same time under the circumstances I must say that frankly I do not see any other course of action before you but the one you took. In your position of responsibility your institution must stand foremost in your thought. One thing you must not, however, forget: Washington stands for Negro submission and slavery. Representing that with unlimited funds, he can afford to be generous and most of us must accept the generosity or starve. Having accepted it we are peculiarly placed and in a sense tongue-tied and bound. I may yet have to place myself in that position but by God I will fight hard before I do. [41]

This power and influence was the foundation of the famed "Tuskegee Machine."

With the election of Theodore Roosevelt to the presidency, Washington even became something of a political boss. Not only was he consulted on every Negro appointment, but his advice was also sought on the standing of several white men whom Roosevelt desired to reward with office.[42] During the administrations of Roosevelt and Taft, Washington became something of an unofficial "Secretary of Negro Affairs." In and out of the Capitol frequently, he was consulted on all matters of policy towards the race; and virtually no political appointment went to any Negro unless Washington approved. Washington also drafted or edited the sections of presidential speeches and papers dealing with the Negro. Thus, in 1908, President-elect Taft, grateful for Washington's assistance in writing the acceptance speech, sent word that he wished to consult Mr. Washington "'fully and freely on all racial matters' during his administration."[43] By 1905 Washington had achieved something of a press lord's domination over Negro publications. Where he could, he simply bought out already established newspapers. The New York *Age* was a case in point.[44] His control was secured by loans, advertising, printing orders, and political subsidies. His fief included at least one, and probably both, of the then existing Negro press associations.[45]

To ascertain the Negro's honest opinions and feelings toward Washington would be a difficult task. For racial antagonism in the South, as well as a thinly veiled hostility to the Negro, had made the Negro a reticent individual. Apparently, however, Washington had an immense popularity among Southern Negroes. Booker T. Washington Clubs were established in all parts of the South, and there was hardly a Negro home without a picture of the new black leader adorning its walls. But educated Negroes examined Washington's career with a deeper insight. One of them thus summed up the reasons for Booker T.'s fame within the race:

> Mr. Washington's following was at first very largely prudential and constrained; it lacked spontaneousness and joyance [sic]. He was not hailed with glad acclaim as the deliverer of his people. He brought good gifts rather than glad tidings. Many believed in him for his work's sake; some acquiesced rather than antagonize one who had gained so large a measure of public confidence; others were willing to co-operate in the accomplishment of good deeds, though they inwardly detested his doctrine; while those of a political instinct sought his favor as a pass key to prestige and place.[46]

Basically, Washington's philosophy and pattern of leadership were anachronistic. Though the crowning glory of the nineteenth century was the rise of the common man, a rise predicated upon the attainment of greater civil and political rights for the masses of workingmen throughout the world, Washington holds the unique distinction of having been one of the few leaders of his time to acquiesce in sub-citizenship for any important group of people. His maxims of self-help and self-improvement for Negroes and his dreams of a Negro bourgeoisie were an adaptation of the theories of free competition and economic individualism, which even in his day were being repudiated by the rise of great industrial combines. To a particular segment of the Negro intelligentsia, the spiritual heirs of Garrison, Phillips, and Lovejoy, Washington's speech was a bold bid to sell out the Negro race. Here was a public betrayal by an ex-slave himself of all those who had suffered and died in four years of the bloodiest war in the nation's history, a denial of the last hope of those millions of blacks who had endured thirty years of Reconstruction and post-Reconstruction bitterness and vengeance. As Washington's status as a race leader expanded, it cast a shadow, which to the Negro irreconcilables was the herald of a blackout for Negro rights in America.

2 THE FIRST MILITANTS

William Monroe Trotter—Du Bois and
the NAACP—The Urban League

ALTHOUGH MANY OF THE NEGROES in the South were willing to accept the advice of Booker T. Washington, those who had migrated to the North were not willing to submit to his philosophy. Among the more aggressive Negroes arose first individual voices and then organizations to challenge the bonds of prejudice and segregation which had been shackled upon their race. They were the first militants among the American Negroes of the twentieth century. William Monroe Trotter used every medium at his disposal, including the press, to attack Booker T. Washington. His protests were soon joined by those of the National Association for the Advancement of Colored People, led by William E. B. Du Bois, and finally the groups which coalesced in the Urban League joined in; all demanded full American rights for the Negro American.

1. WILLIAM MONROE TROTTER

William Monroe Trotter was born April 7, 1872, in Springfield Township, Rose County, Ohio. Sometime later his parents, James Monroe and Virginia Isaac Trotter, migrated to the east. During the Civil War the elder Trotter fought under the colors of Colonel Thomas Wentworth Higginson's famous Massachusetts company. Because of his valor, Trotter moved up through the ranks from buck private to lieutenant. James Trotter's interests, many and varied, ran the gamut from music to politics. In 1878 he published a work entitled *Music and Some Highly Musical People*.[1] Although he had long held a position of assistant superintendent of the registered letter department in the Boston post office, in 1883 he resigned in protest against the color line drawn in his and other federal agencies under the administration of President Chester A. Arthur. Carrying his protest even further, Trotter bolted the Republican Party in 1884 and campaigned for the Democrats. In recognition of his services Grover Cleveland appointed him recorder of deeds, an office which in the words of one contemporary was worth "seven thousand to ten thousand dollars per year and has much patronage attached to it." [2]

Young Bill Trotter, therefore, had little to want for in his youth and early manhood. He attended the best elementary schools; he lived in a "white" neighborhood and in general was looked up to by lesser Negro youths as a member of the snobbish and condescending "black aristocracy." But young Trotter had more to recommend him than his so-called class status. He possessed a brilliant mind. In 1890 he graduated from Hyde Park High School as president and valedictorian of his class. Entering Harvard College a year later, he won rank among the first four men in his class. He was selected to receive the famous Deturs, a prize of books annually awarded to a meritorious undergraduate in the College. As an upperclassman Trotter continued to pile up honors. In his junior year he was elected to Phi Beta Kappa and in 1895 he graduated *magna cum laude* with the A.B. and A.M. degrees.

The mark of the Puritan on Trotter began to develop during his days as an undergraduate. At Harvard he joined the crusade of the Prohibition Club and swore to "never" with the Total Abstinence League. What is probably more significant, young William could find no son of Harvard more worthy of veneration than the anti-slavery agitator and reformer *par excellence,* Wendell Phillips. For five or six years after his graduation, however, Trotter's life and activities displayed few, if any, signs of the monomania which was to seize him and dominate him so completely in later years. On the contrary, the young Negro intellectual engaged in what he termed a "certain mild activity" in local Republican Party politics in Boston, eventually becoming assistant registrar of voters in the city. In 1899 he married a young woman by the name of Geraldine Louise Pindell.[3] Financially independent of his father, Trotter managed to derive a comparatively lucrative income from his business as a real estate broker. He had, therefore, carved a niche for himself and seemed ready to settle down in it.

Those who expected Trotter to remain in this niche, however, were in for a rude awakening. For beneath the conventional exterior displayed by this young Negro, there was a seething discontent — a discontent with his lot and the Negro's lot. Trotter at heart was a sensitive, proud, and impatient young man. At Harvard he had met and mastered the best that the white world had to offer. Yet after graduation he had shared the experience of all Negroes in being shunted off the highroad of American life and relegated to what was then considered to be the obscurity and triviality of Negro America. This was a frustration for which no amount of success as a real estate broker in a Negro ghetto could compensate. On the other hand, Trotter, along with other young Negro intellectuals, was becoming increasingly appalled at the mounting power and influence wielded by Booker T. Washington. Indeed, Washington had become so powerful that his opposition was fatal to the careers of young Negroes. One contemporary observed: "Things came to such a pass that when any Negro complained or advocated a cause of action [different from Mr. Washington's] he was silenced with the remark that Mr. Washington did not agree with this." [4]

By 1900 Trotter and his close friend, George Forbes (an Amherst man of the class of 1895), had become angry young men — angry young *black* men. Booker T. Washington and the Tuskegee machine with all of its trappings must be brought down if at all possible. At the least, the Washington heresy had to be challenged, refuted, and discredited. To carry out these purposes Trotter and Forbes in 1901 decided to found a newspaper. With what might be interpreted as a call upon his patron saints for maximum inspiration, Trotter leased space on the same floor of the same building in which William Lloyd Garrison had turned out his *Liberator* and where Harriet Beecher Stowe's *Uncle Tom's Cabin* first had gone to press. The new publication became a weekly newspaper named the *Guardian.* Its motto was "for every right with all thy might," and it was dedicated to a relentless war upon the "compromisers" and "soft pedalers" inside and outside of the race. But whatever the *Guardian* might say in its motto or otherwise, its main preoccupation — and this for fifteen years — was Booker T. Washington. Thus, in 1905 Dr. Kelly Miller, a friend of Trotter, wrote the following:

> Through the influence of *The Guardian,* Mr. Trotter has held together and inspirited the opposition to Mr. Washington. His every utterance leads to the Cato-like refrain — Booker T. Washington must be destroyed. [5]

Washington, on the other hand, remained neither oblivious nor impassive to the campaign mounted against him by the *Guardian.* [6] Privately he used every means at his disposal to muzzle Trotter and Forbes. He initiated two lawsuits against the *Guardian* in order to bankrupt it. When these attempts failed, he tried the tactic of buying the paper out. Finally, following the tactics of his big business mentors, Washington decided to subsidize a competitor of the *Guardian*, the *Boston Colored Citizen*, and this in a city which could barely support one Negro weekly newspaper.[7] However, there were already about a half dozen Negro newspapers that Washington was subsidizing or owned outright. These included the New York *Age*, the Washington *Colored American*, *Alexander's Magazine*, and the Washington *Bee*.[8]

Up until the summer of 1903 Trotter and Washington had battled each other from a distance, but due to the aggressiveness of Trotter's nature, inevitably he sought a direct confrontation. Thus, in mid-July of 1903 Trotter and Forbes journeyed to Louisville, Kentucky, to attend the National Convention of the Afro-American Council which up to this time was the largest and most prestigious Negro organization in the country. Trotter and Forbes intended to interrupt the sessions by incessantly demanding recognition and by introducing resolutions which they knew this group would not consider or adopt. Most of all, Trotter wanted to engage Washington verbally. But the chairman of the conference was the able and skillful friend of Booker T. Washington, T. Thomas Fortune. Fortune mercilessly wielded the power of the chair to bridle and suppress Trotter and Forbes.[9] They did not get the confrontation which they so earnestly desired, and in their frustration they returned to Boston to await another opportunity.

This chance came some two weeks later with the occurrence of the so-called Boston Riot of July 30, 1903. As it happened, the Boston branch of the Negro Business League in the spring of 1903 had engaged Booker T. Washington to address the local Negro citizens. The affair was well publicized in the city, and plans were made to give Washington a reception in keeping with his importance. For the occasion of Washington's address Trotter and Forbes organized a group of about thirty people whom they supplied with questions with which to interrupt Washington's speech. These people were well distributed among the audience.[10]

The police apparently knew of Trotter's plans, for the first attempt of one of his followers to heckle Washington was speedily ended with the removal of the heckler.[11] A few minutes later, however, Trotter arose and began to ask a number of questions of the speaker. When Trotter was seized by the police, a general din arose in the audience, and the meeting broke up in confusion. Subsequently, Trotter and one of his companions were fined fifty dollars and sentenced to thirty days in prison. The importance of this incident arose from the wide publicity it received, especially in the Negro press. Because Trotter was a notorious enemy of Washington, several Negro newspapers seized the occasion to highlight the feud. The result was that an ordinary incident was magnified into a riot by headlines like this:

BOOKER T. WASHINGTON'S SPEECH
SIGNAL FOR SERIOUS RIOT [12]

Trotter now became something of a martyr to the Negro radicals.

Leading this latter group was Trotter's friend and former schoolmate, William E. B. Du Bois. Du Bois was at that time probably the most outstanding Negro scholar in the United States. He had received his A.B. and A.M. degrees from Harvard University, and in 1895 had won his doctorate with a thesis which became the first number of the famous Harvard Historical Series. If anything, Du Bois was more opposed to Washington's doctrine than was Trotter. But, unlike his friend, Du Bois during these years managed to keep his opposition on a level above vehemence and name calling. In his *The Souls of Black Folk*, published in 1903, Du Bois subjected Washington's leadership to a dignified yet withering attack, while at the same time restating the Negro's post-Civil War demand for political and social equality.[13] The immense popularity of this work made Du Bois the number one adversary of the group at Tuskegee Institute.

The news of Trotter's imprisonment, in the summer of 1903, reached Du Bois at Atlanta University, where the latter was conducting classes in sociology. Like Trotter's other friends and followers, Du Bois became incensed. He did not entirely exonerate Trotter, but as he put it, "he [Trotter] was an honest, brilliant, unselfish man, and to treat as a crime that which was at worst mistaken judgment was an outrage." [14] It was here that Du Bois decided to abandon his efforts to improve the Negro's condition by "scientific study." This procedure was too laborious and too feeble in results. By this study Du Bois had planned to chart the major aspects of Negro group life from decade to decade and thus provide "an increasing body of scientifically ascertained fact, instead of the vague mass of the so-called Negro problem." [15]

Direct political and social action was to be the new strategy. Hence only three weeks after the Boston incident, Du Bois issued a call to Negroes in seventeen different states to meet near Buffalo, New York,

from July 11 to 13, 1905. The avowed purpose of the meeting was to
bring about "organized, determined, aggressive action" on the part
of men who believed in Negro freedom and growth.[16] The aims of
the group were listed as follows:

1. To stop the curtailment of the Negroes' political rights.
2. To urge the Negroes to vote intelligently and effectively.
3. To push for civil rights.
4. To organize Negro business cooperation.
5. To build schools and increase interest in Negro education.
6. To open up new avenues of Negro employment and strengthen the hold
   on that already obtained.
7. To distribute information with regard to the law of health.
8. To bring Negroes and labor unions into mutual understanding.
9. To study Negro history.
10. To increase the circulation of honest unsubsidized newspapers and peri-
    odicals.
11. To attack crime among us all by civilized agencies.[17]

Actually, however, this meeting was called to assemble the most capable and outstanding opponents of Booker T. Washington and to plan
methods of counteracting his doctrines. However, Dr. Kelly Miller
asserts:

The platform of the movement contained nothing new, and its dynamic was
derived from dissent. It was merely a protest against American color discrimination based upon Mr. Washington's alleged acquiescence. Many of the sub-
scribers to the new movement had not, up to that time, been known for their
activity in behalf of the race, and espoused the cause as a "cult" with all the
wonted zeal and intolerance of new converts.[18]

Of the number of men invited, twenty-nine attended. Another meeting was held in January, 1906, and the group at this time adopted the
name of the "Niagara Movement." Little or no notice was taken of
this group during the first few months of its existence; but as the
public became aware of the movement's membership and the implication of its platform, which among other things included demands for
full social and political equality for the Negro, opposition began to
rise on all sides. *The Outlook,* which was known to be friendly to
Booker T. Washington, complained:

The Niagara Movement does not aim to urge negroes to fit themselves for the
requirements of the suffrage as laid down in the Southern States; but endeavors
to force the Southern States, chiefly by appeal to the Federal Congress, to
abandon their suffrage requirements; it does not use its efforts to see that accommodations in cars for blacks are as good as those in cars for whites, but
demands the abandonment of race separation. . . .[19]

In spite of the best efforts of Du Bois and Trotter, the Niagara

Movement never became more than an annual round table conference of young Negro intellectuals. Without funds or permanent organization, the group was never properly equipped for the task it was known to have selected for itself. Booker T. Washington was too strongly entrenched in the favorable opinion of the country, backed as he was by the white press and several white philanthropists. Moreover, Washington began plotting the destruction of the Niagara Movement from the very day of its inception.[20] He planted spies and informers within the group and actually sought to encourage dissension and division.[21] And through the use of his considerable influence over the editors and publishers of Negro newspapers, he was able to effectuate at least a partial blackout of news of the Niagara Movement within the Negro press.[22]

Most damaging to the future of the movement, however, was the schism which began to develop between Du Bois and Trotter. At the second annual conference of the Niagara Movement in 1906 they quarreled over the wording of a resolution; during the following year Du Bois threatened to resign unless the organization ruled against Trotter, who wanted to fire one of the officers for personal reasons.[23] The matter was smoothed over, however, and Du Bois remained with the movement. Nevertheless, relations between the two men cooled perceptibly, and after the final demise of the Niagara Movement in 1910 they saw practically nothing of each other.

For reasons which will be discussed later in this work, Trotter maintained a distance between himself and the group of his erstwhile associates and friends who were laying the foundations of a new organization to be known as the National Association for the Advancement of Colored People. In 1908 he and a few of his more militant associates founded a new movement known first as the National Independent Political League and later as the National Equal Rights League.[24] Its initial objective in 1908 was the defeat of William Howard Taft in his bid for the presidency. By 1914, however, the League had become what everyone knew it would become — a medium for the propagation of Trotter's personal brand of militancy and a foil in his losing struggle against Washington. Avoiding the South for obvious reasons, Trotter traveled throughout the western parts of the country and managed to establish several branches of the League. But, self-centered and too much the personal operator, Trotter failed to maintain any reasonable communications with the League's local chapters. He really had no program, and he clearly lacked the qualities necessary to lead and direct a national movement. As a result the League, unmourned, went to its final reward in 1921.

But if Trotter could not quite direct the whole battle of Armageddon, he was more than qualified to mount a charge. Trotter was the first Negro activist to employ tactics of group confrontation and group protest to achieve the race's aims. A half century later these techniques, refined and improved, would be known as "sit-ins" and "marches." In April, 1915, David W. Griffith's *Birth of a Nation*, the filmed version of Thomas Dixon's *The Clansman*, opened in Boston. Trotter tried to no avail to get Mayor James M. Curley to ban the film. Thus, on the night of April 17, some five hundred Negroes with Trotter in the vanguard arrived at Tremont Theater and demanded to buy tickets. The manager insisted that the house had been sold out and that people had bought tickets in advance of the opening. Rejecting this statement as an unmitigated lie, Trotter directed his followers to remain on the scene. As a result the manager put in a hurried call for the police. The upshot was the immediate arrest of a half dozen people, including Trotter and a white activist named Joseph Gould.[25] A few hours later nine other persons were arrested.

On the following day, under Trotter's leadership, throngs of Negroes and sympathetic whites attended a double mass meeting at the historic Faneuil Hall. Trotter solemnly called for a march on the State House for the next day. And thus on April 19, 1915, the first Negro "march" for the rights of the race took place. More than one thousand Negroes marched through the streets of Boston and to the State House. They waited outside while a committee of Negroes conferred with Governor David I. Walsh.[26] But this was just the beginning. A Boston municipal court ordered the theater to cut the most objectionable scenes but refused to ban the film outright. However, the cause was one which was widely publicized and widely supported, especially by a number of prominent whites. For his own reasons Booker T. Washington moved in to support Trotter. On May 21 Governor Walsh signed into law a new censorship measure, but when a new board of censors refused to close the show, the Trotterites went back into the streets. Finally in August the showing of the *Birth of a Nation* came to an end. After this time films which were objectionable to Negroes were by gentlemen's agreement kept out of Boston theaters.

Probably the most widely publicized event in Trotter's tumultuous career was his confrontation with President Woodrow Wilson. On November 12, 1914, Trotter and a delegation of Negroes were led into the presence of President Woodrow Wilson, who had agreed to hear protests against the continuation of segregation in federal bureaus. In speaking for this group, Trotter abandoned all formalities and bitterly assailed the President for this latest insult to the race. Redfaced, yet managing to suppress his anger, Wilson retorted "that never since he had been in office had he been addressed in such an insulting fashion." After nearly one hour of an interview which had been originally scheduled for only fifteen minutes, Wilson directly rebuked Trotter for the aggressiveness of his speech.[27]

With the passing of Booker T. Washington in 1915, the Boston *Guardian* trained its fire upon Robert Russa Moton and other heirs to the Tuskegee machine with the same consistency and mercilessness as it had done with their master. Nevertheless, the death of Washington left the editorials of the *Guardian* with a certain hollow ring. After all, Trotter had spent the better part of fifteen years engaged in an indecisive, if not a losing, struggle against the Washington heresy. After 1915 Trotter encountered increasing difficulties in retaining his reputation as a recognized race leader. His activities, once considered important and courageous, began taking on a bizarre hue. In 1010 the U. S. Department of State refused to grant Trotter a passport to go to Paris for the purpose of presenting a petition to peace conferences on the Negro question in America. Undaunted, Trotter made his way to Europe serving as a cook on a steamship.[28] He filed several petitions with the peace conferences, but his importance as a race leader had clearly declined. Mainly this was due to the times and the leadership preferences of the race. The great majority of the Southern Negroes continued to abide by the Washington compromise. Northern Negro allegiance was divided between two newly risen leaders. The radical intelligentsia paid homage to Dr. W. E. B. Du Bois, and the radical rank and file hailed the new messiah, Marcus Garvey. Alongside of these two new figures, Trotter's stature shrunk to that of a mere pygmy.

As a champion of the Negro's cause, Trotter made his most effective contribution in the years between 1901 and 1915. After this time his activities constituted hardly more than a postscript to a hectic career. The Boston agitator continued to ascend the public rostrum, but his declamations were drowned out by the mounting din of a new Negro nationalism, one which he had done much to precipitate, but which he could not hope to lead or to control. In truth he inspired more than he led. In the opinion of one of his famous contemporaries, Trotter could not work, except alone; and, although there were numbers of people who subscribed to his opinions, he lacked capacity to weld his followers into a form that would give them any considerable group effectiveness.[29]

Trotter was without doubt the spiritual father of the twentieth century Negro protest movements. His weekly, the *Guardian,* if by nothing but its consistent chauvinism, forced the Negro press to sound a stronger note for the Negro's rights. He was the founder of the National Equal Rights League, but more important than this, his activities led to the birth of other protest movements of greater significance and permanence. In 1903 he jarred the brilliant Du Bois loose from the latter's attempt to improve the Negro's lot by "scientific study." Thereafter, Du Bois swam in the mainstream of national Negro affairs. More than any other Negro of his generation, Trotter devoted himself unselfishly and passionately to the welfare of his people. No suffering left him unmoved; no oppression escaped his condemnation.

The zealousness with which he fought for race's rights earned for him from his enemies and from some of his friends the label of fanatic. But Trotter was no mere fanatic, nor reformer, nor agitator. In truth, his was the first clear voice of black militancy to be heard in the twentieth century.

2. DU BOIS AND THE NAACP

Unlike the Niagara Movement, the National Association for the Advancement of Colored People (NAACP) was not organized by Negroes but by white people. These included muckrakers, social and political reformers, suffragettes, and some who, like Oswald Garrison Villard and William Lloyd Garrison, Jr., were donning the mantles of their abolitionist forebears. Since 1900 these people had been watching the Grandfather Clause erase the Negro's political rights in the Southern states. They had also seen and protested bitterly against the spiraling rate of lynching in the country. And as the first decade of the century slipped by, it became apparent to them that something more than disorganized protests had to be mounted if the Negro was to be helped at all.

The incident which brought them into concerted action occurred in the summer of 1908. During August of that year a race riot flared up in Springfield, Illinois, the home of Abraham Lincoln. This was the one hundredth anniversary of the birth of the famous President. With thousands of Negroes entering the town to visit his shrine, the dormant prejudices of the white citizenry were aroused. A mob containing some of the town's "best people" raged for two days, killing and wounding scores of Negroes, and driving thousands out of the city. What made the event particularly reprehensible was *where* it occurred. Many indignant friends of the Negro published articles in magazines on the subject. Among them was one in the *Independent* by William E. Walling entitled: "Race War in the North." Walling was a Southerner who had spent many years in Russia working in the cause of revolutionists. In his article, he described the Springfield riots and then went on to ask what group of citizens would come to the aid of the Negro.[30]

Walling's pleas probably evoked the sympathy of many people, but the first person to answer them was a young white social worker and descendant of an abolitionist by the name of Mary White Ovington. For many years Miss Ovington had lived and worked among Negroes. In 1906 she took part in the barefooted pilgrimage conducted by the Niagara Movement to John Brown's grave at Harper's Ferry. During the first week of January, 1909, Miss Ovington and a young Jew, Dr. Henry Moskovitz, met with Walling in a little room of a New York apartment and laid the foundation of the group which would become the NAACP.[31]

The next move obviously was to bring the organization to the attention of Negroes and whites who could and would help to establish it. In so doing, the little group contacted Oswald Garrison Villard, owner of the *New York Post*. Villard was enthusiastic. Grandson of the great liberator, William Lloyd Garrison, Villard was an abolitionist by inheritance. Since his youth he had been concerned with the plight of the people his forebears had labored so hard to free.[32] Thus, Villard agreed not only to use his newspaper but also his personal influence to help obtain a large attendance at a meeting or a conference. To this end, he drafted a Lincoln's Birthday "Call" which was sent to a host of prominent people throughout the country for their signatures. Among those who signed were Jane Addams, Ray Stannard Baker, Professor John Dewey, Dr. William E. B. Du Bois, William Lloyd Garrison, Jr., the Rev. John Haynes Holmes, William Dean Howells, J. G. Phelps-Stokes, Lincoln Steffens, Lillian D. Wald, and Rabbi Stephen S. Wise. In substance the "Call" directed attention to the alarming deterioration of the Negroes' condition in the United States, the institutionalization of segregation and discrimination, the wanton lynching and brutalization of blacks everywhere, the denial of virtually all political and civil rights to them, and finally the obvious indifference of white America to the entire problem.[33]

The National Negro Conference, which was the outgrowth of the "Call," convened in the Charity Organization Hall in New York City on May 31 and June 1, 1909. Cooper Union was the site of the evening mass meetings. Although the term "racism" had not entered the national vocabulary, what it meant and what it implied in all of its ugly manifestation was the main theme of the conference. White America's attitude toward the Negro had begun to calcify. Hardly anyone, including many Negroes themselves, bothered to challenge the commonly accepted notions of Negro inferiority and bestiality. Hence, this conference was significant and unique if only because it brought together a group of scientists and scholars, predominantly white, who were the first in this century to refute and reject the general thesis of white Anglo-Saxon racism.[34]

During the final session of the two-day conference, Trotter and his colleague, the Reverend J. Milton Waldron, apparently attempted to impale the new organization even as it was being born. Villard and others at this session, which carried on until midnight, had been attempting to put together a body of resolutions which would summarize the thinking of the conference. Trotter and Waldron, with ill-concealed hostility, harangued and talked and challenged the wording of almost every resolution put to the body. Villard was to say later that Trotter and Waldron conducted themselves "very badly," and he told them at the close of the meeting that their "wrangling" had been "unbearable." [35] In truth, Trotter had opposed the new organization even before its inception. For one thing Trotter was a "loner" and not an organization man. Nor could he relish the prospect of his image being dimmed by such luminaries as Du Bois and the prominent whites in the new group. Finally, he foresaw that the new group would adopt a definite policy of conciliation toward Booker T. Washington. On the other hand, there was ample reason for dislike and distrust of Trotter among participants at the conference.[36] His reputation as an agitator was national, and meetings which he attended were too frequently marked by disruptions. In the end Trotter did not join the new movement. In fact, after the first conference, Trotter was no longer welcome among the group, and his name was pointedly omitted from the list of the Committee of Forty which formally founded the National Association for the Advancement of Colored People.[37] Ironically, it was Trotter, rather than Washington, who was the first to attack the new civil rights organization openly. Editorials in the *Guardian* remained hostile to the NAACP for some years after its founding.[38]

The name "National Association for the Advancement of Colored People" was officially adopted at the second conference in May, 1910. The first officers of the group were: Moorfield Storey of Boston, president; William E. Walling, chairman of the executive committee; John E. Milholland, treasurer; Oswald Garrison Villard, disbursing treasurer; Frances Blascoer, executive secretary; and William E. B. Du Bois, director of publicity and research. The platform adopted was practically identical with that of the Niagara Movement. At this time it was considered extremely radical, demanding equality in civil, educational, and voting rights.[39]

Within five years after its founding, the NAACP had spread about the country through fifty-four branches, nine locals, and four college chapters. Its membership had risen to approximately ten thousand. Long-range objectives were formulated annually at the national conferences held in different cities.[40] But the actual direction of the Association's business took place at its national office in New York City. In the main, the organization never lost its interracial background; but as the directorship fell increasingly into the hands of Negroes, the NAACP came to be characterized as a Negro protest organization. It was the first of many such organizations to arise in New York City during the ensuing decades.

None of the original or the later members of the NAACP's ruling hierarchy was ever drawn from the ranks of radicals. The program and tactics of the Association were zealously kept within the bounds of respectability. At times, of course, the group was branded as radical by those who resented its militant demands for Negro equality and rights. But the Association was careful never to espouse anything but the "American way of life"; it challenged only the sub-citizenship status of the American Negro. Much importance was placed on the need of cultivating the *prestige* of the Association. For this reason expediency and opportunism were always important elements of policy.

This approach ruled out violence of any kind or even crusades as remedies for the Negroes' ills. But the full power of the organization would be placed behind any effort to gain for the Negro any additional measure of civil or political rights. In the matter of justice in the courts of law, the Association early disavowed any intention of becoming a legal aid bureau for Negroes. It would, however, attempt

to gain legal redress for Negroes whenever the injustice was particularly flagrant or when it involved more than one black man. Nor
was there to be any full-scale attack on the Southern system of segregation and discrimination. As Dr. Myrdal points out, "The Association
has often accepted segregation, and in fact, has sometimes had to
promote further segregation, while it has been pressing for increased
opportunity and equality within the segregated system." He evaluates
these tactics as "the principle of opportunism, but also the integration
of opportunism into the [Association's] long-range aims. . . ." [41]

From the beginning the presence of Du Bois gave the organization
its real meaning to most Negroes and to many whites. "By 1914,
[however], there were thirteen Negro members on the Board of
Directors, most of whom were veterans of the Niagara Movement." [42]
Du Bois' greatest efforts were exerted through the *Crisis*, the organization's monthly journal, which was founded in 1910. [43] It became immensely popular in a short time. When Du Bois first assumed his new
task, he was informed that his "activities would be so held in check
that the Association would not develop as an organ of attack upon
Tuskegee." He soon overrode these instructions, for in his opinion:
"Here was an opportunity to enter the lists in a desperate fight aimed
straight at the real difficulty; the question as to how far educated
Negro opinion in the United States was going to have the right and
opportunity to guide the Negro group." [44]

In time Du Bois conceived his mandate to be even broader than
this. By 1913 he was claiming what virtually amounted to proprietary
rights over the *Crisis*. To many observers the *Crisis* was indeed Du
Bois' domain — a separate department in the Association. Du Bois
once declared "that the magazine was 'the only work' in the organization 'which attracts me.'" [45] Between 1913 and 1915 frequent conflicts developed between Du Bois and various officials of the Association. The most protracted and eventful of these was the one between
Du Bois and Villard. [46] Like many white liberals of the time Villard's
attitude toward Negroes was compassionate, benevolent, and a bit
patronizing. Deep down in his heart, he, like many of his brethren,
probably did not entirely escape the thought that there just might
be something (if not very much) to the commonly accepted notions
of Negro inferiority.

On the other hand Du Bois was by no means the easiest man to get
along with. In spite of, or because of, the tremendous respect his
brilliance earned him, he was arrogant and haughty. He was not

easily approached or generally liked. J. Saunders Redding quipped that "Negro and white people — and not just inconsequential people either — complain that they must be introduced to Du Bois time after time, because only the fifth or sixth introduction seems to 'take' with him." [47] With respect to his running conflict with members of the Association's board, Du Bois believed the members to be simply guilty of race prejudice. He suggested that dissension within the Association's executive office would be ended if separate white and Negro divisions were established. Sometime later he stated in a *Crisis* editorial:

> I thank God that most of the money that supports the N.A.A.C.P. comes from black hands; a still larger proportion must so come, and we must not only support but control this and similar organizations and hold them unwaveringly to our objects, our aims and our ideals. [48]

The issue was clearly drawn: How responsible to the board was Du Bois to be, and how much actual influence over the *Crisis* was Du Bois to have? The Association's leaders believed that they had a clearer understanding of the Association's needs than did Du Bois. Villard, as chairman, believed that he had the right to control Du Bois and the *Crisis*. But Du Bois refused to consider himself as Villard's subordinate. [49] Bitter and frustrated, Villard resigned the chairmanship. Saddened by Villard's resignation, Mary White Ovington wrote to him:

> I am sick at heart over it. . . . it means a confession to the world that we cannot work with colored people unless they are our subordinates. And everyone who believes in segregation will become a little more convinced that he is right. [50]

The conflict between Du Bois and Villard continued in a minor key. In the end Villard could not prevail. The *Crisis* was a black journal, edited by a black man and primarily for black readers.

As Du Bois' star began to rise, that of Booker T. Washington and his famed Tuskegee machine began to fade. By 1912 alterations within the power structure of the Republican Party had resulted in a drastic curtailment of Washington's influence. Once a power in party councils, he was now only barely tolerated and rarely consulted. Indeed, in their bitter competition for white Southern support, Roosevelt and Taft virtually sounded as though they had never heard of Booker T. Washington. The election of Woodrow Wilson in 1913 brought a final and complete end to Washington's power in national politics. A good many of the Negro federal officeholders who were being sacked by

the Wilson administration had been "Booker T.'s" men. Another element of his power slipped away when the administration of the
Julius Rosenwald Foundation funds for the advancement of rural elementary education for Southern Negroes was transferred from the
Tuskegee staff to a separate office of administration in Nashville. His
dominance over the Negro press was showing unmistakable signs of
erosion. The Topeka *Plaindealer* ventured that Washington's program
was all right for the South but not for the country as a whole. "We
think," it said, "you will finally come to realize that it is not only
wealth and education that are needed by the Negro — but a little manhood and courage to go along with it." [51] As the decade advanced,
metropolitan Negro newspapers could count on circulation and advertising to provide the income which ten years previously had originated in Tuskegee.

More important, as the shadow of racial discrimination lengthened
in the nation, Washington was increasingly impelled to make obei-
sances in the radicals' direction. And while he continued to pretend
that Du Bois was a non-person, he was careful to maintain an open
and frequently used line of communication with Oswald Garrison
Villard and other prominent members of the NAACP. Shocked in
1913 by the evident malevolence of President Wilson's racial policies,
Washington wrote to Villard, "I have never seen the colored people
so discouraged and bitter as they are at the present time." [52] In 1915
he publicly supported Trotter and other Negroes of Boston in the
controversy involving the film *Birth of a Nation.*

Booker T. Washington died in 1915. But even before his death his
philosophy was showing signs of erosion. For one thing, the social
context to which his doctrines were shaped was rapidly changing.
The continued success of his brand of leadership required, above all,
an inert and docile Southern Negro population. Indeed, his most often
repeated advice to the Negroes of Dixie, "Cast down your buckets
where you are," was being rejected. At the beginning of World War I
in Europe, hundreds of thousands of Negroes were finding it un-
profitable if not dangerous to stick to Washington's admonition. For
one thing, by 1910 the boll weevil was advancing eastward across
the Mississippi. In its slow trek to the Atlantic coast few Southern
states were spared. The destruction was terrible. In many places,
particularly in Georgia and South Carolina, farms and plantations
were permanently abandoned. For the millions of Negroes depending
solely upon cotton culture for a livelihood, this catastrophe left but

two alternatives: migration or slow starvation. The following letter
was sent by a Negro minister in Alabama to a Northern friend:

> Doubtless you have learned of the great exodus of our people to the north and
> west from this and other southern states. I wish to say that we are forced to
> go when one thinks of a grown man's wages is [sic] only fifty to seventy-five
> cents per day for all grades of work. He is compelled to go where there is better
> wages and sociable conditions, believe me. When I say that many places here
> in this state the only thing that the black man gets is a peck of meal and from
> three to four lbs. of bacon per week, and he is treated as a slave. As leaders we
> are powerless for we dare not resent such or to show even the slightest dis-
> approval. Only a few days ago more than 1000 people left here for the north
> and west. They cannot stay here. The white man is saying that you must not go
> but they are not doing anything by way of assisting the black man to stay. As a
> minister of the Methodist Episcopal Church (north), I am on the verge of
> starvation simply because of the above conditions. . . .[53]

The poor economic conditions of the Southern states were not
alone responsible for the unprecedented migration of Negroes to the
North and West. After the outbreak of World War I, America began
to shut its doors to the European immigrant. This caused the drying
up of a labor source upon which Northern industry had long depended. The demands of war production impelled industries, therefore, to turn to the great reservoir of Southern Negro labor. Soon
agents were sent South to arrange for the shipping of Negro laborers
to Northern industrial centers.

> It is impossible to estimate the influence of agents, both white and Negro, sent
> out by Northern industries. . . . Not only were there agents with specific prom-
> ises of jobs and money to pay the railroad fare of Negroes . . . but there were
> rumors of agents who did not exist. . . .[54]

To the thousands of black folk, the possibilities of good jobs, decent
living conditions, and the "rights" made the North seem like the promised land. Negroes also moved to the North to seek better educational
opportunities because there they had access to better schools than
in the South.

> Many Negroes also felt they could no longer tolerate the subordinate and
> restricted position. Both the fact and the myth of Northern equality played a
> role in stimulating some Negroes to go North.[55]

After 1915, therefore, it was a common sight in Southern cities and
seaports to see Negroes squeezing into boxcars and steamship steer-
ages on their way North.

Upon reaching the Northern or Western city of his destination,
the Negro migrant underwent a mental transition. His racial attitude
was swiftly hammered into conformity with a new pattern. He was

instructed by the Negro press, his associates, and sometimes even his minister to drop all trappings of "Uncle Tom." He was to fight either alone or in groups any time he was attacked by whites. He was to take advantage of the ballot and to protest against any infraction of his civil or legal rights. To most Negroes the transition came easily as they strove to integrate themselves unobtrusively into the new environment. Others, however, were hasty or "bumptious" in the enjoyment of their new freedom and quickly repaid any mistreatment from whites. In the North after 1915, however, the major cause of race friction was the white workman's fear of Negro competition for jobs. This fear was aggravated by the Negro's tendency to break strikes because of the antipathy of labor unions to him and his willingness to accept lower wage scales than white workers. The race riots which occurred throughout the country during and after World War I were the logical outcome of the economic competition between black and white laborers.

Because of its activities during this period of rising race tension and conflict in Northern cities, the NAACP earned the name of "watchdog" over Negro rights. For reasons of policy as well as limitation of funds and facilities, the Association accepted cases on a selected basis. But even with this restriction the number of actions in which the organization participated was phenomenal. Legal actions were conducted by a legal department established in 1913. For difficult or important litigation, however, the Association often retained distinguished attorneys. Publicity was also an important aspect of its activities. In the *Crisis* Du Bois, of course, kept up his constant battle for Negro rights.

The Association also acted as a clearinghouse for information on all known instances of injustice to Negroes. Factual data were supplied to the Negro and white press. By these means the Association kept its activities before the public. For the period beginning in 1912, most of the work of the NAACP can be included under three headings:

1. The fight for civil and political rights
2. Efforts to obtain legal redress for Negroes
3. The campaign to outlaw lynching in the nation

The fight to obtain a greater measure of civil and political rights for Negroes was begun on a broad front as early as 1912. Largely under the instigation of Dr. Du Bois, the Association adopted the tactics of using the Negro vote in the North as bait for promises from political parties.

In addition to the Democrats and the Republicans, in 1912 a third party, the Progressives, led by ex-President Theodore Roosevelt emerged. It was this latter group whom the NAACP at this time sought to entice. Dr. Du Bois diligently composed the following proposed plank for inclusion in the Progressive (Bull Moose) Party's platform:

> The Progressive Party recognizes that distinctions of race or class in political life have no place in a democracy. Especially does the party realize that a group of 10,000,000 people who have in a generation changed from a slave to a free labor system, re-established family life, accumulated $1,000,000,000 of real property including 20,000,000 acres of land, and reduced their illiteracy from 80 to 30 per cent, deserves and must have justice, opportunity and a voice in their own government. The party, therefore, demands for the Americans of Negro descent the repeal of unfair discriminatory laws and the right to vote on the same terms on which other citizens vote.[56]

This was taken to the party's convention at Chicago. There, the officials of the Association, Jane Addams, Joel Spingarn, and Dr. Henry Moskovitz, worked in vain for its adoption. Roosevelt, eager to attract white Southern votes to his new party, turned it down flatly. In addition, the Bull Moose convention refused to seat most of the Negro delegates.[57]

Faced with this undeniable rebuff, the NAACP now made a move which caused many raised eyebrows among Negro and white politicians. The Democratic Party was now to be supported by all Negroes who had the ballot. This was, again, largely Du Bois' work. No effort was made to insert a plank in the Democratic platform, but Bishop Walters of the African Zion Church went to see Woodrow Wilson, the Democratic candidate, in October, 1912, and received from him the following promise:

> Should I become President of the United States, they [Negroes] may count upon me for absolute fair dealing, for everything by which I could assist in advancing the interest of their race in the United States.[58]

With this statement on record the Association thus summed up its position in the *Crisis* for November, 1912:

> We sincerely believe that even in the face of promises disconcertingly vague, and in the face of the solid caste-ridden South, it is better to elect Woodrow Wilson President of the United States and prove once for all if the Democratic party dares to be Democratic when it comes to black men. It has proven that it can be in many Northern States and cities. Can it be in the nation? We hope so and we are willing to risk a trial.[59]

It is, of course, impossible to know to what extent the NAACP's position influenced the Negro electorate. Du Bois offers this statement:

We estimated that in the North a hundred thousand black voters had supported Woodrow Wilson in 1912, and had been so distributed in strategic places as to do much to help his election.[60]

If this was so, however, there were soon to be at least a hundred thousand disappointed Negroes in the United States. With Wilson's election, Southerners began demanding segregation in Washington streetcars and other public facilities, the dismissal or downgrading of Negro civil servants, and the outright firing of prominent Negro officeholders. A hate group known as the National Democratic Fair Play Association held mass meetings and distributed printed matter demanding the immediate segregation of Negroes in the federal bureaus and agencies. One handbill declared:

Deserving white girls in this City . . . have appealed to us from nearly every Government Department where they are compelled to work alongside of a greasy, ill-smelling negro man or woman; that sometimes, where a negro is in charge or control of that Bureau, Division, or Office, those poor girls are forced to take dictation from, be subservient to, bear the ignominy and carry the disgrace of the taunts, sneers or insults of such negroes.[61]

And on April 11, 1913, at a cabinet meeting the Wilson administration did not oppose the policy of the segregation of the races in federal bureaus and agencies throughout the country.[62] Consequently, Postmaster General Albert S. Burleson and William G. McAdoo, Secretary of the Treasury, who directed the only departments with any significant number of Negro employees, began immediately to introduce and enforce segregation in offices, shops, toilets, and lunch rooms. In addition they made a clean sweep of Negro political appointees in the South and permitted local postmasters and collectors of internal revenue either to downgrade or dismiss Negro civil service workers. Especially hard hit were venerable Negro officeholders who had received their appointments under past Republican administrations.[63]

Meanwhile, Villard had been hounding Wilson in an attempt to get him to repudiate the new departure. "He tactfully suggested that the segregation policies might have been introduced on the initiative of subordinate officials." [64] On July 23, 1913, however, Wilson thoroughly disillusioned his anxious petitioner. He wrote Villard that segregation had been initiated in several departments and had been carried out with the approval of several prominent Negroes for the purpose of removing the friction — or rather the discontent and uneasiness — which had prevailed in many government departments. Wilson insisted that this was not a movement against Negroes. He believed that "by putting certain bureaus and sections of the service in the charge of Negroes we are rendering them more safe in their possession of office and less likely to be discriminated against." [65]

Badly let down by a man whom he had greatly admired, Villard directed that an official protest of the NAACP be released to the Associated Press. It was entitled *A Letter to President Woodrow Wilson on Federal Race Discrimination*. The public response to this complaint, especially from Northern white liberals, was uproarious. The Wilson policy was denounced as "cruel, unjust and contrary to the spirit and the institutions of this country." [66] The *New York World* declared:

> Whether the President thinks so or not, the segregation rule was promulgated as a deliberate discrimination against negro employees. Worse still, it is a small, mean, petty discrimination, and Mr. Wilson ought to have set his heel upon this presumptious Jim-Crow government the moment it was established. [67]

However, in spite of these reactions and the somewhat heated and emotional confrontation of the President by Trotter during the next year, the policy of segregation was continued and even accelerated during the remainder of Wilson's first term. During the election campaign of 1916 the Association, thoroughly disenchanted with Wilson, considered offering its support to Charles Evans Hughes, the Republican candidate for President. The board wrote Hughes a letter wanting to know his position on the Negro question, but Hughes was apparently not interested in bidding for the Negro vote. He simply acknowledged the board's letter and did not even bother to answer a telegram from Du Bois requesting an answer in time for the November issue of the *Crisis*. Rebuffed and ignored, Du Bois came out for Hughes anyway. [68]

By 1918 segregation and discrimination in federal bureaus in Washington had become established policy. Applicants for civil service positions were being required to file photographs of themselves. Inquiries about the reason for this requirement at first brought only evasive answers. Cornered, the Civil Service Commission gave assurance that measures were being taken to prevent the requirement from being used to discriminate against Negroes. "Nevertheless, [the Association soon learned] of Negroes, who having passed civil service examinations, were directed by telephone to report for duty, only to be informed upon reporting that an error had been made and that there were no vacancies." [69] Segregation was extended to the Senate lunchroom in the Capitol and even to the galleries of the Senate chamber. Indeed, segregation even invaded the restaurant and lunchroom of the Library of Congress. The Association used every ounce of its power to reverse the trend but to no avail. Washington was in the hands of racist white Southerners, and night had fallen on the city.

When the United States declared war on Germany in April, 1917, there were at least five anti-war people on the NAACP's board. They were Villard, Lillian D. Wald, Mary White Ovington, Jane Addams, and John Haynes Holmes. The Association as a whole was neither pacifist nor pacifist oriented. In general it accepted the war, but as yet it had formulated no board policy on the issue of the Negro and the war.[70] To remedy this situation the Association sounded the call for a general Negro conference to be held in May of 1917. The meetings were attended not only by members from NAACP branches but also by delegates of other Negro organizations. With Du Bois playing a major role, the conference in its resolutions promised to support the war effort; but it also demanded the right of Negroes to train as fighting men under Negro officers, the end of lynching, the repeal of segregation ordinances, the abolition of the Jim-Crow railroad car, and equal civil rights in public institutions. Du Bois played a role also in the staging of the first Negro protest march in New York City.[71] This was the "Silent Protest Parade" of July 28, 1917, when about ten thousand Negroes silently marched down Fifth Avenue to the sound of muffled drums. James Weldon Johnson, an eyewitness, described it as "one of the strangest and most impressive sights New York has witnessed."[72]

As the NAACP continued to shape up its policy toward the war, news burst upon the nation of the "Houston Affair." On the night of August 23, 1917, a battalion of the Negro Twenty-Fourth Infantry allegedly shot up the city of Houston. Seventeen white persons and two Negroes were killed. The soldiers were stationed at Camp Logan in Houston, Texas. Martha Gruening, who investigated the incident for the NAACP, asserts that the shootings were in retaliation for the repeated and aggravated assaults committed against the black troops by the white Houston police.[73] The findings of the United States Army's investigation, however, were much different. Those who were condemned as guilty received what many felt to be excessively harsh sentences. Sixty-three men were court-martialed, thirteen of whom were, in December, 1917, summarily hanged without the right of appeal under a law which, in the view of some observers, applied only to troops in battle. In a second court-martial fifty-one men were sentenced to life imprisonment, five were given long prison terms, and five others condemned to death. In an effort to save the lives of the men who were condemned but not yet executed, the NAACP in February, 1918, dispatched James Weldon Johnson to Washington to intercede with President Wilson. Johnson carried with him a petition bearing twelve thousand signatures asking the President to commute the death sentences. Before the sentences of the court-martial had been reviewed, eleven more men were condemned to die. Wilson ultimately commuted ten of the death verdicts to life imprisonment.[74]

It was undoubtedly the "Houston Affair" plus innumerable reports of injustices to Negro soldiers that caused Du Bois to adopt a hard line against the United States government during and after the summer of 1917. When the NAACP board tacitly accepted segregated army training camps, Du Bois, confronted with a *fait accompli*, remained noncommittal. But in bitter, strident editorials in the *Crisis*, he condemned alternately the President, the Adjutant General, and the Secretary of War for the continual whitewashing of Army injustices to black troops. At its June, 1918, conference the NAACP board ordered Du Bois to tone down his attacks upon the government and to present only the facts and constructive criticism. The board appointed a legal consultant to review the contents of the *Crisis* before publication.[75]

As the weeks and the months of the conflict wore on, Du Bois not only abated his attacks on governmental policy, but he began to examine the war and the social forces it released in terms of their usefulness in effectuating an improvement in the race's future in American life. He began to feel that after fifty-four years in the wilderness, the tide would turn and the Negro would see the walls of prejudice crumble before the onslaught of common sense. And so in his famous "Close Ranks" editorial in the *Crisis* of July, 1918, he wrote:

> We of the colored race have no ordinary interest in the outcome. That which the German power represents today spells death to the aspirations of Negroes and all darker races for equality, freedom and democracy. Let us not hesitate. Let us, while this war lasts, forget our special grievances and close our ranks shoulder to shoulder with our own white fellow citizens and the allied nations that are fighting for democracy. We make no ordinary sacrifice, but we make it gladly and willingly with our eyes lifted to the hills.[76]

The "Close Ranks" editorial came as a surprise and a shock to Negroes throughout the country. A leading militant journal, the *Messenger*, had already suggested that Du Bois and others like him go

to France if they were so anxious to make the world safe for democracy. The *Messenger* "would rather make Georgia safe for the Negro." [77] The Washington, D.C., branch of the Association held a special
meeting at which Du Bois was denounced for abandoning the traditional NAACP position.

Shortly after this, word was leaked to the press that Du Bois had
been offered a commission with the Intelligence Bureau of the General Staff of the Army in Washington, D.C. Du Bois' duties would
be to act as a one-man grievance board for disenchanted and unruly
black troops.[78] Eager to accept the appointment, Du Bois went before
the NAACP board proposing that it retain him in control of the *Crisis*
while he was serving in the Army and pay him his salary as editor
as well. The board turned him down.[79] The Negro press again went
after his scalp — they charged that the War Department had captured
the *Crisis* so that the publication would support the racist policies
of the government. As a result of this tempest the Army quietly withdrew its offer to Du Bois.

Since its inception it had been the intention of the Association
to institute and follow up test cases on laws which appeared to violate
the civil and political rights of Negroes. One of the most outstanding
of such laws was the so-called "Grandfather Clause" used widely in
the Southern and border states to disqualify Negro voters. The essential features of this device were two: First, the establishment of a
rigorous educational qualification (in some states a property qualification) drastic enough to permit the disfranchisement of most Negroes.
Second, a provision that the qualification need not be met by those
who were legal voters in 1866, or who were lineal descendants of such
legal voters.

In 1913 the NAACP managed to persuade the Solicitor General of
the United States to challenge the constitutionality of the Oklahoma
version of this law. When the case[80] was heard in the Supreme Court,
the counsel for the NAACP, Moorfield Storey, was given permission to
file a brief *amicus curiae* on behalf of the Association.[81] In June,
1915, Chief Justice Edward D. White read a decision which declared
the Grandfather Clause to be in violation of the Fifteenth Amendment.
This was the first in a long line of great civil and political rights cases
the Association would win in the federal courts for its client, the
American Negro.

In 1916 the NAACP was again before the Supreme Court. This
time it was fighting to outlaw municipal ordinances enforcing resi-

dential segregation upon Negroes. Beginning in the city of Baltimore in 1912, this practice of ghettoizing the Negro soon spread to northern and western cities. When the city of Louisville, Kentucky, passed such an ordinance in 1914, the NAACP was ready to carry the fight through to the high court. The case, *Buchanan* v. *Warley*,[82] reached the Supreme Court in 1916 with lawyers who were representatives of the Association arguing for the plaintiffs. The case was reargued before the Court in 1917.

In its decision the Court held the Louisville ordinance contrary to due process because of undue interference with property rights. The effect of this decision was somewhat weakened by a later case, *Corrigan* v. *Buckley*.[83] After hearing the argument in this case that a restrictive covenant in a deed or conveyance of real estate which provided that the property should never be leased or sold to a Negro did not violate the due process clause, the Court dismissed the case for lack of jurisdiction. All in all, however, the NAACP was highly successful in its battle before the Supreme Court. This success was to continue in later years, especially in its cases involving the Texas white primary laws.

Probably the most solid of the Association's accomplishments was the work, begun in 1912, to prevent or to redress injustice to Negroes in the lower courts of the land. From the beginning this activity was carried on by the local chapters as well as by the national office. In numerous cases the lawyers of the organization were instrumental in saving Negroes from unequal treatment by the courts, sometimes getting them acquitted when they were sentenced, or in danger of being sentenced, on flimsy evidence; sometimes getting death penalties or other severe penalties reduced. Often the Association was successful in fights to prevent the extradition of Negroes from Northern to Southern communities when the likelihood of obtaining a fair trial for the Negroes could be shown to be doubtful. In other instances, police brutality, third-degree methods of forcing confessions, and peonage have been challenged with success.

In the latter part of January, 1921, Henry Lowry, a Negro, shot and killed a white man and his daughter at Nodena, Arkansas. Lowry escaped but was captured by officers of the law. These officers surrendered him to a mob. The mob chained him to a log and lynched him. A part of the account of the lynching was given in the Memphis, Tennessee, *Press* in its issue of January 27, 1921, by one of its special correspondents who was an eyewitness:

More than 500 persons stood by and looked on while the Negro was slowly burning to a crisp. A few women were scattered among the crowd of Arkansas planters, who directed the gruesome work. . . . Not once did the Negro beg for mercy despite the fact that he suffered one of the most horrible deaths imaginable. . . . Even after the flesh had dropped away from his legs and the flames were leaping toward his face, Lowry retained consciousness. . . . Once or twice he attempted to pick up the hot ashes and thrust them into his mouth to hasten death. Each time the ashes were kicked out of his reach by a member of the mob. . . . Words fail to describe the sufferings of the Negro. Even after his legs had been reduced to the bones he continued to talk with his captors, answering all questions put to him. . . .[84]

This incident was not unique; the NAACP had dealt with a number of cases equally atrocious and had tried through publicity and protest to make them the means of arousing the conscience of the nation against this evil. Indeed, since its inception each issue of the *Crisis* gave a total of lynchings by states in which they had occurred. Every lynching or attempted lynching was reported. And on several occasions the Association sent representatives, usually white, to the scene of a mob action to secure the facts. From 1910 to 1915 the number of lynchings in the country showed a steady decline. On the other hand, the brutality and sadism involved in these crimes were increasing. Group lynchings, or so-called race riots, in which the casualties were predominantly Negroes showed a steady rise during and after World War I.

The worst of these riots occurred in East St. Louis, Illinois, on July 2, 1917. For almost the entire day a mob of white citizens raged through the Negro quarters, literally setting everything on fire.[85] The cause of the riot was reported by the Attorney General of Illinois as follows:

The excuse assigned by the mobs for the riot was the murder of two policemen the night before by a mob of negroes. (The negroes were beaten up by the whites during the day before the riot, and rumors of a massacre were carried to the negroes, causing them to arm and become disorderly.)[86]

Actually, however, the temper of the whites had long been aroused as a result of the large number of Negro laborers being imported into town from the South by labor agents. The results of the disturbance as summarized by the Attorney General were:

Eight whites were killed. . . . Many — over 100 — negroes were shot or beaten up, or both. . . .
Over 250 buildings were burned. In some instances entire blocks in the negro district were completely consumed.[87]

Ironically enough, the East St. Louis authorities held a group of

Negroes responsible for the riot. The NAACP secured a staff of lawyers headed by Charles Nagel, Secretary of Commerce under President Taft, for their defense. Funds were raised for the relief of those who had been made destitute by the riot.[88] In 1919 the Association sponsored over two thousand public meetings against mob violence, and it held a national conference in New York City against lynching and raised over twelve thousand dollars to finance a national anti-lynching campaign. The greatest efforts of the Association, however, were directed toward congressional action to make lynching a federal crime. Many petitions and protests were sent to the House and Senate, some begging for, some demanding, a law. Not until 1921, at the opening of the Sixty-seventh Congress, was the federal legislature persuaded to act. On April 11 of that year, Congressman Leonidas Dyer, Republican of Missouri, introduced a bill (H.R. 13), "to assure persons within the jurisdiction of every state the equal protection of the laws and to punish the crime of lynching; . . ." [89] The bill would inflict a heavy fine upon any county in which a lynching occurred, requiring part of the money to be given to the victim's relatives. The measure was referred to the Judiciary Committee and reported out favorably on October 20.

The indignation of the Southern members of the House was intense. They were determined to block passage of the bill. Every known tactic and every opportunity to keep the bill from coming to a vote were used. On the other hand, the NAACP, backed by a host of organizations and newspapers, directed the fight for its passage. Money was used liberally. Congressmen were deluged with telegrams and letters. The Association kept a lobbyist, James Weldon Johnson, on the scene to speak to the Representatives and to supply them with needed information. The Anti-Lynching Bill came to a vote on January 26; and in spite of such opposition, it was passed by a vote of 246 to 101.

The excitement and celebration which resulted among Negroes all over the nation was a bit premature, for the Senate had yet to consider the measure. The bill was referred to and reported out favorably by the Senate Judiciary Committee. On November 27 it was brought up for consideration. Within a few minutes after this move, a group of Southern senators managed to gain the floor and began the threatened filibuster. These senators vowed to hold the floor until adjournment if that were necessary to defeat the bill. On December 2 the Republican leaders agreed to withdraw it.

Naturally this unexpected outcome was disappointing to the NAACP as well as to Negroes in general. Nevertheless, it was an education in congressional politics. Johnson, the Association's lobbyist for the bill, thus summed up the fight in the Senate:

> The filibuster was not met by any determined aggression on the part of the Republicans. . . . The majority leaders seemed to feel that they would have done their duty and cleared their own skirts when they allowed the Southern Democrats to "put themselves on record" and in doing so, assume responsibility for the failure of the measure.[90]

The fight over the Dyer Anti-Lynching Bill in Congress was followed by a decided improvement in race relations throughout the country. Lynching continued to decline. The NAACP maintained its fight against the evil but did not sponsor another anti-lynching measure until 1934.

After 1922 the NAACP began to lose prestige rapidly among Negroes. Indeed, the *Crisis*, which for some years had been a self-supporting publication, began to fall off in circulation. There were several reasons for this change in fortune, but much of the blame can be attributed to the Association itself. For one thing, the program of the Association had become much too narrow. For while most Negroes were willing to concede the importance of the fight for civil and political rights, they felt that race leadership should also direct the fight in the economic arena. This the Association would not do.[91] In defense of the NAACP's position Myrdal wrote that the Constitution and the entire legal system of the nation supported the Negro in his struggle. Many liberals in the South as well as the North would aid in a fight for justice, but would resist more radical economic changes.[92]

The white members of the board were drawn from the respectable bourgeois stratum of society. Their interest in the Negro problems was motivated by a sense of "fair play" and a desire to see the Constitution fulfilled. They wanted the Association to keep its skirts free of the grime and bitterness of economic strife. The Negro members of the Association took their cues from their white associates. In the main, they were cautious, racially-minded liberals, and not infrequently forthright reactionaries. The intellectual myopia with which they were afflicted was thus described by Du Bois:

> The bulk of my colleagues saw no essential change in the world. It was the same world with the problems to be attacked by the same methods as before the war. All we needed to do was to continue to attack lynching, to bring more cases before the courts and to insist upon our full citizenship rights.[93]

In addition to this, the Association did not have a mass basis. In its zeal to remain respectable, the Association made it a policy to place its branches and chapters under the guidance of the upper-class Negroes. To some extent this was a good practice, but the weakness in it was that not infrequently these so-called upper-class Negroes were light-skinned mulattoes who felt themselves superior to the black rank and file. Under these circumstances it was difficult for the blacks to really take the Association to their bosom. The NAACP voiced a part of their protest, but it turned a deaf ear to others.

3. THE URBAN LEAGUE

When the Committee on Urban Conditions Among Negroes in New York City was established in 1910, there were more than ninety thousand Negroes living in all boroughs of the city. Two-thirds, or some sixty thousand, of these resided in Manhattan. Brooklyn had the second largest number of Negroes. These were largely the descendants of the frightened blacks who had fled Manhattan's bloody draft riots of 1863. The big black ghetto of Harlem, as it would later become known, did not then exist. Negroes were concentrated in an area on the lower west side known as "San Juan Hill." In the main, they were menials — employed in such capacities as maids, butlers, cooks, elevator operators, waiters, busboys, and common laborers. These were low-level, low-paying, "nigger jobs" but they offered stable, steady employment to the race.[94]

Between 1910 and the outbreak of the war in Europe, however, the lot of the Negro in New York changed drastically. In the decade between 1901 and 1910 over six million immigrants from eastern and southern Europe landed on American shores and the bulk of these newcomers remained where they landed in New York City. Penniless, unskilled, and generally illiterate, the desperate white immigrant was willing to accept any employment, menial or otherwise, at rates even lower than the lowest paid Negro. To make matters worse the Negro population itself expanded almost daily by a steadily mounting inmigration of illiterate and unskilled blacks from the impoverished rural areas of the South. As unemployment of Negroes arose, social conditions among them deteriorated. Nor did the America of 1910 provide the veritable "emporium" of welfare benefits that came to exist a half century later. There were no unemployment benefits, social security, or aid for dependent children or unwed mothers. Indeed, there was virtually no public welfare at all. The vast federal welfare structure that we know today would not be built until after the Great Depression. State and local communities were still in the experimental stages of public welfare. The one available source of assistance to the needy was public charity, but there was little of this for Negroes. The result was an alarming increase among Negroes of petty crimes, juvenile delinquency, and prostitution.

As early as 1905 the steadily worsening conditions of the Negro in New York City began to attract the attention and concerns of a few of the members of the white business and professional groups of the city. During that year, William H. Baldwin, then President of the Long Island Railroad and head of the General Education Board, called a conference at his home of Negro and white leaders for the purpose of doing something positive and constructive about the Negro problem. As a result of this conference the Committee for Improving Industrial Conditions of Negroes in New York City was formed in 1906. Mary White Ovington and Oswald Garrison Villard were members of this group. During the next year Mrs. Frances Kellor, a worker among white female immigrants, called a similar conference to discuss the worsening condition of Negro women in the city. Out of this conclave came the League for Protection of Colored Women. The two organizations worked hand in hand for four years. Then in 1910 Mr. Baldwin called a third conference of all groups working to aid the Negro. This meeting produced the Committee on Urban Conditions Among Negroes.

A year later the leaders of the three groups did the only sensible thing; they merged themselves into a single organization, thenceforth known as the National League on Urban Conditions Among Negroes. The first president was Professor Edwin R. A. Seligman, of Columbia University. Two years previously Professor Seligman had participated also in the founding of the NAACP. Probably the most enthusiastic member of this group was George E. Haynes, a young Negro social worker in New York City. It was Haynes who persuaded Eugene Kinkle Jones to leave his post as a high school teacher in Louisville, Kentucky, and to take a position with the new organization. Becoming the League's first full-time secretary in April, 1911, Jones remained with the organization for the rest of his active life.

For its first year the League operated on a budget of $8,500; and during this time the organization confined itself to travelers' aid work in New York City, Philadelphia, Baltimore, and Norfolk. A branch was established in Nashville, Tennessee, for the training of students from Fisk University in social work. Basically, the League, like the NAACP, was an interracial body. Its governing board sitting in New York City was composed of Negro and white members, all of whom were drawn from the middle class. Sincere and honest though it was in its efforts to aid the race, the League was unknown among the black masses except by those who were referred to it for assistance.

The directors of the League's policy, of course, knew that the basic problem for Negroes was unemployment. Faced with the undisguised antipathy of labor unions and the hard crust of employer indifference, the League, realizing that it was unable to solve the problem alone, concentrated upon assisting Negro people in education, home and community situations, and recreation. In every locality in which a branch of the League was organized, trained social workers were sent out to make case studies of the Negro needs. The advent of World War I gave the League a new function. With the bars against Negro labor lowered temporarily, the League was in every industrial center the only group properly organized to supply the thousands of Negro workers suddenly demanded by local plants. From 1914 to 1917, therefore, Urban League branches became emporiums of Negro labor.[95]

After the war, employment opportunities for Negroes dried up almost as quickly as they had opened in 1914. This should have been expected by the race and at least by Negro leaders. Unfortunately, however, the race, buoyed by temporary prosperity during the war, became unreasonably optimistic about the future. Naturally, the inevitable reversion to the status quo was thus made all the more bitter and unbearable. This was the situation after 1918. Urban League officials in branches throughout the country daily greeted thousands of Negro callers with the frustrating remark — no jobs today.

Aside from returning to domestic service or accepting charity, the Negro worker had another, if somewhat infrequent, alternative — strikebreaking. Spero and Harris give some of the historical bases for this practice among Negroes in the following:

> The Negro's willingness to break the white man's strike is partly traceable to his slave time distrust of white labor and his dependence on the white master class. Primarily, however, the Negro's availability as a strike breaker has been due to his complete ignorance not only as to what a strike or a union was, but even of what a factory was. Most of the colored labor used to break strikes came straight from the farms without any previous industrial contacts. When these ignorant farm hands heard the leaders of their own group, such as the minister or politician whom they were accustomed to respect, counsel

them to beware of the white man's union and remain loyal to the employer, the word naturally carried more weight than that of the white unionist asking them to quit their jobs.[96]

In addition to the above there were other important reasons why Negroes were not too reluctant to break strikes. First, at the beginning of the century strikebreaking was not held in the abhorrence that it is today. White workers crashed the picket lines as much as, or more than, did Negroes.[97] Indeed, the picket line did not become really sacred until after 1935. Secondly, the Negro had little reason not to break a strike. Whether he did so or not, he was still barred by every important union in the country. Also there did not seem to be any immediate promise or prospect that the iron anti-Negro rule of the unions would be broken. Thirdly, if it is argued that the Negro strikebreaker was impairing what future opportunity he might have to join unions, it must be pointed out that, given the Negro laborers' miserable conditions, the immediate benefit was primary. Strikebreaking was dangerous, but it paid Negroes higher wages than they had ever received. On the other hand, if a strike was broken or a union crippled, the Negro strikebreaker stood a chance of gaining steady employment with the plant involved.

The position in which the above situation placed Urban League policy makers was far from enviable. Should the League throw down the gauntlet to the lily-white unions, encourage strikebreaking, and supply Negro scabs wherever and whenever they were needed? Or should the organization refuse to refer laborers to strike-bound plants as well as to educate Negroes in the fine points of trade-union practices? There was no neutral position in this quandary, for a refusal to refer or supply Negro scabs would appear, at least, to be a pro-union position. At the annual meeting of the League in 1919, Eugene Kinkle Jones gave what was purported to be the official stand of the organization in the matter. He stated that while the League upheld the principle of organized labor and collective bargaining, in those instances when unions excluded colored men, the Negro might be justified in taking a job as a strikebreaker.[98]

This statement did little to clarify the League's position. In fact, it was but an awkward attempt to straddle the issue. Perhaps the League knew what it meant, but it could have hardly expected unlettered Negro laborers to solve this riddle. As time passed, however, the strategy underlying the League's position became clearer to observers. The national League was to take a pro-union stand, while the locals which were practically autonomous anyway were to be allowed to adapt their policies to the situations prevailing within their respective areas. Thus, in 1918 and 1920, the National Urban League sent resolutions to Samuel Gompers asking for a movement to bring Negroes into A.F. of L. unions.[99] In 1925 the League offered

> to raise one-half of the salary of a competent Negro who would work under your [William Green's] direction in trying to smooth out the relationship between colored workers and the various component national and international organizations. . . .[100]

Green politely replied that the A.F. of L. could not pay its share of the salary of such a staff member.

While the national body was seemingly holding to its pro-union position, several of the local branches of the League in large industrial areas were moving in the opposite direction. Indeed, the liaison between these locals and management became so close that the locals could only be considered as sources of cheap Negro labor for non-union plants and of strikebreakers in cases of emergency. In Detroit, where the Urban League supplied more than half of the Negro labor supply, the Employers' Association financed the League's industrial department and paid the full salary of the industrial secretary.[101] It is not hard, therefore, to understand why this local League freely furnished Negro strikebreakers in the Detroit metal trades' strike of 1921. To one plant, in fact, the industrial secretary personally delivered over 150 strikebreakers, "marching them past pickets who were afraid to attack so large a group" of men. After delivering his men, the secretary "left the plant, unnoticed, by a side exit." [102]

In Newark, New Jersey, the Urban League local in 1923 actively recruited Negroes all over the city in response to a plant's request for strikebreakers. Spero and Harris state that the League on this occasion even "allowed the company the temporary use of its secretary to keep tab on the efficiency of [its Negro] labor." [103] While this pattern was followed more or less by League branches in many areas, the Chicago branches engaged in the most intense anti-union activity. In giving his reasons for opposing a strike at a plant at which Negroes were employed, the industrial secretary of this branch wrote the following:

> Since the company has in the past advanced Negroes from the status of common laborers to semi-skilled and skilled positions, the probability is that they will continue to do so. In talking with the company officials, I have been assured that they will continue this policy and that the loyalty on the part of the Negro workers will be rewarded.
> Therefore . . . if the Negro supports the A. F. of L., he will probably wind

up by finding himself definitely excluded from the best jobs, and if the A. F. of L. organizes the industry, introducing a closed shop, the companies will no longer be able to continue their policy to employ Negroes to offset collective bargaining, and the incentive for the employment of Negroes will be lessened.

On the other hand, if the Negro exercises his position as a minority group and plays the management against the remaining workers, he will get more thereby. I would go further and even suggest Negroes go in as strike-breakers, provided they were retained when the strike was over.[104]

The hard lines of Urban League strategy appeared in sharp focus in 1926. In Chicago at this time, the newly organized Brotherhood of Sleeping Car Porters was beginning its decade-long struggle with the Pullman Company for recognition as the bargaining agent for the thousands of Negroes in that company's employ. Since the Brotherhood was the first Negro union to challenge a large company, the struggle rapidly became a "cause" to the race. Aware of the importance of even a show of race loyalty, the national League through Eugene K. Jones publicly endorsed the Brotherhood's fight.[105] The question was immediately raised as to whether Mr. Jones and his associates in the national League knew of the amicable and profitable relations between the Chicago local and the Pullman Company. The company, however, remained silent until its contribution to the Chicago League became due. Then it inquired whether "Mr. Jones was speaking for the whole Urban League or merely expressing his personal viewpoint." Chicago League officials hastened to assure the Pullman Company that the national Urban League officials handled only national questions. Chicago was directing its own policy. Satisfied, the company then sent its usual stipend.[106]

In order to prevent hindsight from unduly prejudicing one's opinions toward the thinking of Urban League officials, it is necessary to reemphasize that the League, as well as other Negro protest and betterment groups, was simply shaping its own strategy and tactics to the social context in which it was operating. In the midst of conflicting social and economic allegiances no black leader dared to attempt to wed his followers to any belligerent in the struggle unless definite advantages were to be forthcoming from the coalition. Of course, the Negro race like other groups had its idealists. Educated in white universities or indoctrinated by white sects, they struggled to retain the larger view of issues. Yet, but few of them ever climbed to a position of leadership in the race until they had paid lip service, at least, to the primacy of the Negro question.

The anti-labor union activity of the Urban League branches was seldom condemned by the orthodox Negro leader, and for the very good reason that the League was merely practicing what he was thinking. On the other hand, the League won the plaudits of Negroes as well as whites for the work it was doing for the race outside of the employment field. Its activities extended to virtually all types of social service to Negroes. Branches throughout the country established vocational training and guidance centers, day nurseries, baby clinics, and child placement centers. Pregnant Negro girls and illiterate Negro mothers were given needed instruction. The League branches even established schools for domestics and janitors in order to improve the earning ability of these groups. Some of the most sterling work performed by League agencies was in the field of juvenile delinquency. In addition, the League supplemented parole supervisors, assisted Negro girls appearing in court, and fought an unceasing war against commercialized prostitution in Negro ghettos.

By 1929 national Urban League branches had been organized in all the chief cities in the United States. The $8,500 expended in 1911 was dwarfed by the $450,000 used in 1929. News of the League's activities was broadcast through its monthly publication, *Opportunity*. Few people denied that the League was doing a splendid job as a whole. And yet the attitude of the Negro masses towards this organization was virtually the same as that which was held toward the NAACP. To the Negro migrant these organizations were still too new and too distant. What he longed for in leadership was the warm emotionalism of the Methodist or Baptist minister whom he had left behind in Dixie. To some extent this longing was gratified in the Negro churches mushrooming in the Northern cities. What remained of this desire was exploited to the hilt by the new agitators competing for the race's loyalty.

3   1919: THE LONG BLOODY SUMMER

BY ALL ODDS the summer of 1919 was the bloodiest and most brutal period of interracial disorder and violence in American history. Although the disorders of the so-called "long hot summer" of 1967 produced much greater property loss and social dislocation, the total of eighty-three people who died during the 1967 disorders pales in significance alongside the approximately four hundred Negro and whites who were killed in 1919. If in 1967 it was the Negro who precipitated the nationwide disorders, the "race war" of 1919 was marked by the naked aggressiveness and malevolence of the white American. Perhaps, as suggested by the *New Republic,* the white mobs were driven by a will to lynch. If so, these were social orgies of cruelty in which certain classes in the community expressed their hatred of a race they considered to be inferior, their contempt for the law, and their sense of Anglo-Saxon superiority.[1] Perhaps — but there did exist more direct and immediate causes.

Foremost among these in 1919 was the presence of tens of thousands of semiskilled and unskilled Negroes in a labor market that no longer needed them. Competition between Negroes and whites for the few available jobs frequently erupted into bloody incidents. Most of the Negro labor was nonunion and, as such, it presented a continual threat to the job security of white union labor. There was ample evidence that big business was manipulating the white and Negro labor forces in such a manner as to keep the costs of labor at a minimum. This was a dangerous game.

The racial tensions of 1919 were heightened also by the acute shortage of housing for both low-income blacks and whites. The black ghettos already filled by the vanguard of the great migration could

71

no longer contain the steady stream of newcomers from the South. The Negro population of Manhattan, which prior to 1914 was easily contained in a section of the West Side, had so expanded by 1919 that it was rapidly transforming Harlem into the nation's largest black metropolis. Chicago's South Side was following close behind. In almost all cases the areas of the new black ghettos in the Northern cities had until recently been occupied by low-income whites. With the coming of the Negro these whites in many cases had moved out to the fringes of the black ghetto. In such instances they constituted a buffer between the white middle class on one side and the pressing blacks on the other. A tinderbox situation was the inevitable outcome.

The racism that had been historically characteristic of white Southern mores was exacerbated during and immediately following the war. For one thing the migration was seriously depopulating the South at a time when field hands and common laborers were desperately needed James Weldon Johnson states:

> I witnessed the sending north from a Southern city in one day a crowd estimated at twenty-five hundred. They were shipped on a train run in three sections, packed in day coaches, with all their baggage and other impedimenta.[2]

In order to halt this exodus, the whites in some communities held meetings and conferences with Negroes. Other communities, such as Wilmington, Delaware, offered outright inducements, such as better schools and other public facilities to keep the Negroes at home. Even the federal government entered the picture when Secretary of the Treasury William G. McAdoo issued an order through the United States Railway Administration restraining any one from prepaying the transportation of a Southern Negro who wished to come North. By and large, however, Southern planters and industrialists resurrected archaic legislation from slavery and reconstruction days in an effort to break the back of the migration.

A major responsibility for the sadism and brutality of the riots of 1919 must be attributed to the Ku Klux Klan. This "new" hooded order had nothing in common with the Klan of Reconstruction days but a name and a purpose to "keep the nigger in his place." Its formation in Atlanta, Georgia, in 1915 was influenced by the film *The Birth of a Nation,* which had opened up in the city. The Klan made little progress during its first two or three years, but with the coming of peace it flourished like the green bay tree. By 1920 the Klan had established a chapter in almost every sizable city in the United States, and dues-paying members numbered in the hundreds of thousands.

The typical Klansman was a lower middle-class Anglo-Saxon. His education was minimal and his views on life were further narrowed by his fundamentalist creed. In the North he was a migrant. Wherever he worked, his wages were below average, his tasks often menial, his responsibilities slight, and his opportunity for advancement remote. In short, he was just one level above the "nigger." Life seemed to offer him little dignity or personal significance. He felt that he had but one redeeming asset — he was white. The Klansman hated and despised Jews, Catholics, and foreigners, but he reserved a special venom for the blacks. He viewed the Negro as a mental pygmy, incapable and unwilling to perform any but the lowest tasks and always anxious to prey upon the purity of white women. In the words of one Klansman: "The Negro, in whose blood flows the mad desire for race amalgamation, is more dangerous than a maddened wild beast and he must and will be controlled." [3]

Herbert J. Seligmann once stated that the American Negro before World War I was the despair of radicals, even liberals. He was typically the "good old darky," a pathetic personality compounded of servility, docility, and gratitude. He had been spiritually crippled by a "Reconstruction mentality" and to a large degree "tranquilized" by Booker T. Washington's philosophy. In short, he was, as Mary White Ovington so aptly dubbed him, half a man. But in the five-year period between 1914 and 1919 a "new" Negro appeared. The combination of the great migration and the entrance of the United States into the war had wrought a significant change in the race. The new Negro was new in the literal sense that he was the product of a generation that had grown to adulthood during and since the war. He was comparatively sophisticated and definitely militant. He was a veteran either of the battlefields of France or of the racial conflicts in the great metropolis. He would not panic in the face of violence, nor would he flee in terror before a white mob. He would stand and fight for his rights.

With a Southern Democratic administration in power, Negroes could not expect protection from the federal government. They had seen local government abdicate before the lynch mob — they had seen brutality reign unchecked save for their own efforts to counter it. They had taken the measure of the white press and had made due note of its hostility. Indeed, one observer commented that probably never before in the history of the country had there been more distrust of American white men by Negroes than after the world War. [4]

The despair felt by the race at ever obtaining justice in white America was amplified by Du Bois in mid-1919.

> A League of Nations is absolutely necessary to the salvation of the Negro race. Unless we have some supernatural power to curb the anti-Negro policy of the United States and South Africa, we are doomed eventually to *fight* for our rights. . . . [The League] will be open to the larger influences of civilization and culture which are ineffective in the United States because of the prevailing barbarism of the ruling classes in the South and their overwhelming political power.[5]

Probably nowhere was the new militancy more vividly reflected than in the editorials and columns of Negro newspapers. In 1919 the Negro press had moved a long way from that day and time when Booker T. Washington could virtually silence any black journalist. Indeed, even before his death in 1915, the Negro press had been baying at his heels. It kept a watchful eye on the race's leadership and was quick to sound the tocsin upon any sign of treachery or betrayal. At a conference called by the War Department in 1918 to secure their support for the war, thirty-one Negro editors solemnly called the government's attention to the anomaly of lynching and mob violence in a nation purportedly fighting to make the world safe for democracy. By 1919 much of the Negro press had run the gamut from mild conservatism to extreme radicalism and chauvinism. Editorials proclaiming the new mood gravely warned those who would trample on the race's rights that the new Negro was ready to lay down his life in the struggle for liberty.

At any other time these utterances, menacing as they might have sounded, would probably have been shrugged off as the fulminations of a few disgruntled and upstart Negro radicals. In 1919, however, the situation was quite different. The Western world was then scarcely recovering from the shock of the Bolshevik successes in Russia. Communists, anarchists, and syndicalists had to walk warily. Even the most mildly intemperate statement was labeled "sedition." Attorney General A. Mitchell Palmer, pressing for the passage of a federal sedition act, quite naturally kept newspapers under surveillance. In his voluminous report to Congress in 1919 on syndicalism and anarchism in the United States, Attorney General Palmer included a section entitled "Radicalism and Sedition among the Negroes as Reflected in their Publications." The report cited practically every Negro magazine and newspaper in New York as having been seditious at one time or another. The Negro press was charged with having had an "identification . . . with such radical organizations as the International Workers of the World and an outspoken advocacy of the Bolsheviki or Soviet doctrines. . . ." As to the general tone of the Negro press the report stated:

> In all the discussions of the recent race riots there is reflected the note of pride that the Negro has found himself, that he has "fought back," that never again will he tamely submit to violence or intimidation. The sense of oppression finds increasingly bitter expression. Defiance and insolently race-centered condemnation of the white race is to be met with in every issue of the more radical publications. . . . The Negro is "seeing red" and it is the prime object of the leading publications to induce a like quality of vision upon the part of their readers.[6]

Lastly, the report warned that the editors of these journals were men of education and that their opinions could not be dismissed as the "ignorant vaporings of untrained minds."

Early in 1919 the NAACP published a study entitled *Thirty Years of Lynching in the United States: 1889-1918*. During that period "Judge Lynch" had taken a toll of 3,224 unfortunate souls. In one section entitled *Special Features of Lynchings* the report noted that a considerable number of the victims had been burned alive, others were tortured before death, and some had been beaten to death or cut to pieces. Sixty-one women had been among those lynched. Most atrocious of all was the week's orgy which ran from May 17 to 24, 1918, in Brooks and Lowndes Counties in Georgia. Of the half dozen people lynched on this occasion one of these was an eight-month pregnant woman, Mrs. Mary Turner. An account follows:

> Her ankles were tied together and she was hung to the tree, head downward. Gasoline and oil from the automobiles were thrown on her clothing and while she writhed in agony and the mob howled in glee, a match was applied and her clothes burned from her person. When this had been done and while she was yet alive, a knife, evidently one such as used in splitting hogs, was taken and the woman's abdomen was cut open, the unborn babe falling from her womb to the ground. The infant, prematurely born, gave two feeble cries and then its head was crushed by a member of the mob with his heel. Hundreds of bullets were then fired into the body of the woman, now mercifully dead, and the work was over.[7]

If the lynchings of 1919 were not so numerous as in some previous years, there were ample indications that they were definitely becoming openly sanctioned instruments of regional and local policy. A major purpose was to deter or discourage militancy or self-assertiveness especially among younger Negroes. As such, lynchings began to take on the air of a public rite planned and programmed and with public attendance encouraged. Public officials claimed that they were powerless to prevent such actions even when clear notice was given in the press of the intentions of the mob. Thus, "lynch law" became a hideous mockery, indeed, of that revered principle of Anglo-Saxon justice: due process of law.

The race war, i.e., the major riots of 1919, extended through the period May 10 to September 30. And while some members of the race, especially the brethren of the cloth, advised caution and solemnly beseeched the Negro to place his faith in God, others of a more militant disposition were ready to man the barricades. Thus, the young Claude McKay in mid-July penned a battle cry:

> If we must die, let it be not like hogs
> Hunted and penned in an inglorious spot,
> While round us bark the mad and hungry dogs,
> Making their mock at our accursed lot.
> If we must die, O let us nobly die,
> So that our precious blood may not be shed
> In vain; then even the monsters we defy
> Shall be constrained to honor us though dead!
> O kinsman! we must meet the common foe!
> Though far outnumbered, let us show us brave
> And for their thousand blows deal one death-blow!
> What though before us lies the open grave?
> Like men we'll face the murderous, cowardly pack,
> Pressed to the wall, dying, but fighting back![8]

In discussing the race war of 1919 some historians chronicle as many as twenty-five race riots, but any such count would have to include a number of brief interracial clashes and expanded lynchings. But in terms of the impact on the nation as a whole, only seven racial confrontations need be discussed. These were the four smaller ones which occurred in Charleston, South Carolina; Longview, Texas; Knoxville, Tennessee; and Omaha, Nebraska — and the three major riots which took place in Washington, D.C.; Chicago, Illinois; and Phillips County, Arkansas.[9]

Charleston: Trouble in this city began on Saturday night, May 10, when two white sailors for no apparent reason shot and killed a Negro civilian. When news of the incident was broadcast, a considerable portion of the city was turned into a battleground between white sailors and Negro civilians. Hundreds of sailors moved into the Negro district capturing, beating, and shooting several Negroes along the route, looting shooting galleries for rifles and ammunition, and sacking Negro-owned stores. Although many were unarmed, Negroes kept up a steady sniper fire against the sailors. The Marines arrived to reestablish order in the city. The casualties were two Negroes killed and seventeen wounded; seven sailors and one white policeman wounded.[10]

Longview: Longview was an east Texas cotton town of five thousand people, 30 percent of whom were Negroes. Race relations in the town had always been tenuous. The situation grew worse when Dr. C. P. Davis organized the Negro Business Men's League for the purpose of preventing the exploitation of the Negro cotton farmer by local whites. Davis also organized Negro cooperative stores for the same purpose. But the direct cause of the trouble in Longview grew out of the lynching in a nearby town of a young Negro who had allegedly raped a white woman. In carrying the story the Chicago *Defender,* which was distributed locally, claimed that the woman had actually been in love with the Negro and was despairing because of his death. Infuriated Longview whites attributed the story to a local Negro schoolteacher named Samuel L. Jones. On July 11 a mob hunted Jones down and beat him almost to death. Then they ordered him out of town.

Jones took refuge in the home of his friend Dr. Davis. Anticipating trouble, Davis called together a number of the members of his Business League. These men brought their weapons with them.

> Close on midnight the mob came down the street. Four white men mounted the back porch and called for Jones to come out. Not until he was sure that their plan was to rush the house did Dr. Davis open fire. In the violent scrimmage which followed no colored men were killed, but it is reported that the manager of the Kelly Plow Works admitted the death of eleven white men.[11]

In its retreat the mob set fire to a number of Negro homes and shops, including Dr. Davis' office. On July 12 the Texas Rangers restored order in the town.

Knoxville: Racial troubles erupted in this city on August 30 when a young Negro who had been accused of murdering a white woman was moved for safekeeping to Chattanooga. Not believing that the Negro had been removed, a mob stormed the jail for the purpose of lynching the prisoner. When it was turned back by the National Guard, the mob turned to looting hardware stores and pawnshops for pistols, rifles, and knives. The next morning a crowd of about one hundred armed whites moved toward the Negro district but were met with gunfire from Negroes who had erected barricades. When twelve hundred National Guardsmen rushed to the scene and began to advance against the barricades, the Negroes opened fire on them. Two white troopers died as a result of the skirmish. Along with white civilians the Negroes ultimately gave up their arms and by nightfall order was restored.[12]

Omaha: As in the case of Knoxville, just a month before, a white mob in this city demanded that the local authorities turn over to them a Negro accused of raping a white woman. When the mayor refused, he was dragged at the end of a rope for half a city block. He was on the verge of being hanged from a trolley pole when the police cut the rope and rushed him to the hospital. The mob then moved to the jail, beating and stomping any Negro who happened to be in the crowd. After seizing the accused Negro, the mob shot him, hanged him, burned his body, and hung it in the public square.[13]

Washington, D.C.: On Saturday, July 19, the *Washington Post* headlined the story of the raping of a young white woman by several Negroes. The girl in question was the wife of a man in the naval aviation department. Two hundred white sailors and marines then proceeded to lynch two Negro suspects who had been released by the police for lack of evidence. The contingent then moved on to the Negro district where they were stopped by gunfire from street barricades. These events set off a bloody black-versus-white conflict that continued virtually unabated in the city for four days. Whenever a white mob caught a Negro in the downtown area, he was lucky to escape with his life. Negroes, on the other hand, were mobbing white men caught in their areas. Automobiles were manned by armed Negroes and were used as "armored cavalry" in lightning attacks on white neighborhoods. Whites soon adopted the same tactic. At least one running fight was reported between Negroes and whites in two such automobiles. On the 22nd of July the disorders subsided, and a series of protracted investigations was begun to discover the causes.[14]

Chicago: The Chicago "race war" was anticipated and expected many months before it actually occurred. Shortly after the outbreak of the war, Negro migrants began pouring into the city by the thousands. With the old Black Belt unable to contain them, Negroes began to move into white neighborhoods. "Block-busting" began to pay high dividends to greedy real estate dealers. The subsequent interracial hostility produced an ever mounting number of bloody clashes between Negroes and whites in the city. One such incident ignited the "race war." On Sunday, July 27, at a lake-front bathing beach a Negro boy was knocked off a raft by a white boy and was drowned. Negroes moved in on the whites, and bloodshed erupted. The investigation which ensued revealed the all-too-complex nature of Chicago's social ills,[15] but the casualty figures of the riot spoke for themselves. During the six-day period thirty-eight were killed. The total of wounded and injured for Negro and white exceeded five hundred.[16]

Phillips County, Arkansas: During the summer of 1919 the Negroes of Phillips County organized themselves into a farmers' union, the purpose of which was to emancipate themselves from the veritable state of peonage in which they were being held by the white landowners in the county. On the night of October 2, they were holding a meeting in a little church at Hoop Spur in an effort to raise the fee of a Little Rock firm of white lawyers, which they had hired to take their case. The meeting was fired into by a sheriff and his deputy. In the eruption that ensued the deputy sheriff was killed and the church was burned to the ground.[17] A county-wide reign of terror was then begun against Negroes. James Weldon Johnson reports: "Between two hundred and three hundred Negroes were hunted down in the fields and swamps to which they had fled, and shot down like animals. Many of them had no idea of what the trouble was about."[18] In accordance with common policy the full blame for the bloody episode was placed upon the Negro population. "Seventy-nine Negroes were indicted and brought to trial at Elaine, Phillips County, Arkansas, on charges of murder and insurrection. The trials were held in the presence of an armed mob, and the jury quickly brought in verdicts condemning twelve to death and sixty-seven to prison terms ranging from twenty years to life."[19] The NAACP took up the case and fought it for five years. Ultimately, the twelve Negroes condemned to die were freed and the sixty-seven others released from jail.[20]

If it is true that the peace treaty of Versailles of 1919 brought the real end of nineteenth-century Europe, it is equally true that 1919 signaled the fade-out of the post-Reconstruction period in America. The racial pattern of this period had depended almost entirely upon the maintenance of the status quo in the South. But the boll weevil, the great war, and the great migration had conspired to destroy this status quo, and the events of 1919 rode in the wake of this destruction. With migration, or the imminence of it, a new threat, the white South would have to temper its brutality against its Negro labor force. Hence, the number of lynchings in the ten-year period between 1919 and 1929 was reduced by 90 percent. In the North, 1919 did not mark the end of a period so much as it heralded the beginning of one. This section of the country would witness the rise of the sprawling black ghetto with all of its attendant social maladies. The North would have to learn to deal with an incipient Negro militancy that would perennially threaten to erupt into a race war. And some of the more thoughtful among the middle-class whites in the cities would accurately read the portents of that year and look toward the rising new peripheral communities. The flight to suburbia would not yet begin, but it would be charted for the future. In spite of their other preoccupations in 1919, American Negroes found time to scrutinize the credentials of a new messiah — short, black, and silver-tongued — Marcus Garvey.

4 THE ERA OF MARCUS GARVEY

IN DECEMBER, 1920, a scant four years after Marcus Garvey had taken up his abode in the Negro ghetto of New York City, an authoritative New York periodical commented upon him as follows:

> The most striking new figure among American Negroes is Marcus Garvey. His significance lies in the fact that he embodies and directs a new spirit of independence among the Negroes. Whatever may happen to his grandiose schemes of finance and politics, he is the best point at which to study what is going on inside the heads of the ten million colored people in the United States. They are doing and thinking many things that are unsuspected by the public at large.[1]

Marcus Garvey, Jr., was born on August 17, 1887, in the sleepy little town of St. Ann's Bay in Jamaica, British West Indies. He was the youngest of eleven children. His father, Marcus, Sr., a master printer by trade, was typical of the lower-middle-class blacks on the island. Proud, somewhat arrogant, and with little formal education, he was forever parading his self-acquired erudition. In proper Victorian style he ruled his household in an authoritarian manner — his word was law. He was "Mr. Garvey" to everyone, even to Sarah his wife, and to his children. He was also a stubborn man, not very much given to compromise or give-and-take. Hence, in a series of disastrous court cases he managed to lose every parcel of land he owned except the plot upon which the Garvey homestead stood. The mother of the household, Sarah, was a woman of striking beauty, somewhat retiring, and very religious. Young Garvey went to her with his problems.

As a boy the younger Garvey received an adequate elementary education in the schools at St. Ann's Bay. He may have also received additional training through a pupil-teacher course provided by the Jamaican educational system. Garvey later claimed to have received a higher education at Birkbeck College, now University of London, but his assertion is open to some doubt. Edward D. Cronon in his biography of Garvey states:

> The records of Birkbeck College, now a part of London University, were partly destroyed in the London blitz of 1940 and unfortunately do not indicate definitely whether Garvey was ever a student or what courses he attended. The registrar of the college believes, however, that Garvey may have attended law classes as an occasional student in 1912 and 1913.[2]

In Kingston, Jamaica's capital, at the age of fourteen Garvey had become apprenticed to his godfather to study the printing trade. He learned his trade well, and at the age of twenty he had become a master printer. But for an incident that occurred at Kingston, Jamaica, when he was twenty-two years of age, he might have never left the island. In 1909 a strike was called at one of the largest printing establishments in Kingston. Garvey was a foreman at this plant. Anxious to prove to himself that he was a leader of men, he disregarded the conventional allegiance to the management and joined the strikers. The men elected Garvey to lead the walkout. He did his job efficiently, organized public meetings, and for the first time demonstrated those extraordinary oratorical talents which were soon to win for him so much acclaim. The employers finally broke the strike and fired Garvey.[3]

During the next year Garvey secured employment at the government printing office, and in his spare time he edited a periodical known as the *Watchman*. He also found time to organize a political organization, the National Club. When both of these ventures failed, Garvey set out on an odyssey which took him to several other West Indian islands and to Central and South America. In Costa Rica Garvey's uncle aided him in securing a job as timekeeper in one of the banana plantations of the United Fruit Company. Here he was shocked at the repressive conditions under which the blacks labored on the steaming plantations. Garvey later observed his people working under similar conditions in Ecuador and other places he visited. Depressed and sickened, yet resolute, he finally returned to Jamaica. Two years later he sailed for London.

The two years spent in London after 1912 were quite possibly the most decisive period in Garvey's life. In this city the young provincial West Indian with his troubled but blurred sense of Negro rights met the members of other darker races who also had their grievances against the Caucasian.

These men — followers of Ghandi [sic], Mustapha Kemal Pasha, Dr. Sun Yat Sen, Saad Zaghlul, and Ibn Saud — had definite, clear-cut programs to follow. Garvey heard such slogans as "India for the Indians" and "Asia for the Asiastics" [sic]. He became interested in the condition of the African Negro as a result of discussions with the followers of Chilembwe of Nyasaland and Kimbangu of the Congo. As a result of these experiences Garvey's vision broadened considerably.[4]

He realized that what he had once considered a local problem of West Indian and Central American Negroes was in reality an international problem for the blacks, and as such, required an international solution. He saw, too, that no other darker races were demanding rights within, nor attempting to become a part of, the Caucasian society. Instead they were demanding lands that were historically theirs. Black men, Garvey concluded, must do the same. They must cease their futile beating upon the stone walls of Western race prejudice and look homeward — homeward to Mother Africa. Out of such meditations Garvey fashioned his gaudy, but effective, program of Pan-Africanism — the slogan of which was soon heard on the lips of countless blacks — "Africa for the Africans at home and abroad." Garvey became interested in the conditions of Negroes in America through reading Washington's *Up from Slavery*. This broader knowledge of the problems of the Negro added a new dimension to Garvey's thinking. As he describes it:

> ... my doom — if I may so call it — of being a race leader dawned upon me. ... I asked: "Where is the black man's Government?" ... "Where is his President, his country, and his ambassador, his army, his navy, his men of big affairs?" I could not find them, and then I declared, "I will help to make them."[5]

On July 15, 1914, Garvey sailed from Southampton bound for his native island of Jamaica. The dreams of a continent-wide African Empire fired his imagination. He saw before him "a new world of black men, not peons, serfs, dogs and slaves, but a nation of sturdy men making their impress upon civilization and causing a new light to dawn upon the human race."[6] Back in Jamaica, Garvey immediately founded an organization to which he gave the impressive name of "The Universal Negro Improvement Association and African Communities (Imperial) League." The purpose of this organization was to unite "all the Negro peoples of the world into one great body to establish a country and Government absolutely their own."[7] Garvey wrote to Booker T. Washington in America telling him of the new organization and his plans. The sage of Tuskegee responded with an invitation to Garvey to come to the United States for a speaking tour.

Pan-Africanism was, indeed, on the march. Garvey was soon to discover, however, that Jamaica was not the place to begin his empire building. The natives on the island would have none of it. Garvey complained:

> I really never knew there was so much color prejudice in Jamaica, my own native home, until I started the work of the Universal Negro Improvement Association. . . . Nobody wanted to be a Negro. "Garvey is crazy; he has lost his head." "Is that the use he is going to make of his experience and intelligence?" — such were the criticisms passed upon me. Men and women as black as I, and even more so, had believed themselves white under the West Indian order of society.[8]

In 1916, therefore, Garvey sailed for the United States in search of more fertile soil for his plans.

The ferment in race relations and the rising nationalism among Negroes during and after World War I have been described in other parts of this book. These were the conditions which gave Garvey his greatest chances for success in America, for in a sense black America was waiting for him. Garvey's first public appearance in the United States was in the role of a soapbox orator on the streets of Harlem in the company of some of Harlem's first Negro demagogues and chauvinists. Late in 1916 Garvey took an extended trip throughout the country visiting and speaking in thirty-eight states.

By 1917 he was already achieving some acclaim as an orator as demonstrated by the size of his street-corner audiences. But in June, 1917, Garvey got his first big opportunity to establish himself as a man to be reckoned with. At a large mass meeting in a Harlem church Garvey was recognized by the chairman, who invited him to say a few words. Garvey, however, said more than a few words. James Weldon Johnson thus describes the event: "The man spoke, and his magnetic personality, torrential eloquence, and intuitive knowledge of crowd psychology were all brought into play. He swept the audience along with him."[9] After this occasion Garvey's fame in New York grew by leaps and bounds, and his self-confidence rose accordingly. Garvey now decided that the time was ripe for him to try the Universal Negro Improvement Association on the American Negro. His stature as a race leader had risen swiftly in New York City. His doctrines were hailed in America, whereas they had been laughed at and rejected in Jamaica. Hence, he began to highlight the aims and ideals of the Association. The word "black," long used as an epithet even by jet black Negroes themselves, was to be dignified. Garvey insisted that all men of African blood must refer to themselves as black men rather than as Negroes or colored men. The Negro's past in Africa, as little as was then known or thought of it, was to be glorified. Garvey instructed the members of his race:

> Negroes, teach your children that they are direct descendants of the greatest and proudest race who ever peopled the earth; and it is because of the fear of our return to power, in a civilization of our own, that may outshine others, why we are hated and kept down by a jealous and prejudiced contemporary world.[10]

Above all, the Negro was to cease his futile beating against the solid walls of American race prejudice. If the white man claimed this nation as his alone, then by all means give it to him.

> The professional Negro leader and the class who are agitating for social equality feel that it is too much work for them to settle down and build up a civilization of their own. They feel it is easier to seize on to the civilization of the white man and under the guise of constitutional rights fight for those things that the white man has created. Natural reason suggests that the white man will not yield them, hence such leaders are but fools for their pains. Teach the Negro to do for himself, help him the best way possible in that direction. . . .[11]

These were Garvey's words. To such Negro leaders as W. E. B. Du Bois and Robert R. Moton, the successor to Booker T. Washington, Garvey was simply ridiculous. A. Philip Randolph considered Garvey to be a nuisance who represented the views of the ignorant Negro immigrant only. Nevertheless, Garvey's insight into the mind of the American Negro was keener than that of his critics. Moreover, he was well aware of the many complexities existing within the race itself. Like any intelligent agitator, he was able to turn an intended insult into a compliment. Thus, if he had hailed from the mudsill of Jamaican society, he was only the better qualified to lead the great masses of Negroes who were from the mudsill of American society. Of the greatest value to Garvey's agitation in America, however, was the description written of him by W. E. B. Du Bois in which Garvey was pictured as "a little, fat black man, ugly, but with intelligent eyes and a big head."[12] Garvey used this description of himself time after time to demonstrate that the greatest enemy of the blacks in America was not the white people, but the mulattoes or light-skinned Negroes such as Du Bois. Indeed, it is hardly an overstatement to say that much of Garvey's success can be attributed to the existence of the color-caste system not only between the whites and blacks, but that existing within the Negro race itself.

Since the days of slavery the mulatto or light-skinned Negro had enjoyed a position in America much below that of the whites generally, but substantially above that of the blacks or near-blacks. Myrdal has described how, under slavery, the "fair-skinned house girls were more frequently used as mistresses" by the planters, thus mothering successive generations of even whiter offspring. These mulatto off-spring were often freed by their fathers, or given the opportunity to work out their freedom. Once in the free society, these light-skinned Negroes were able to obtain a status educationally, econom-ically, and socially superior to the blacks.[13] With the passing of slavery the mulattoes retained and even expanded their position above the black rank and file. Superior education and culture qualified them to fill all positions of leadership in the race. Economically they consti-tuted the backbone of the Negro bourgeoisie. Within two generations after emancipation, they had erected a color-caste system within the race somewhat analogous to that prevailing in India.

The color standard prevailed in practically every walk of Negro life in America. Until the advent of Marcus Garvey, leaders con-sidered it impolite to attack or even to refer to this color-caste system. One reason might well have been that many of these leaders were themselves mulattoes. In any case, the distance between the leader-ship and the black masses led to frustrations, envy, and bitterness ripe for exploitation by a black leader. The traditional Negro leaders like Du Bois argued that to emphasize racial differences would only heighten the tension between the races.[14] In response Garvey an-swered that Du Bois and the NAACP were advocating a racial amal-gamation that would wipe out both the black and the white races.[15]

Garvey's first two attempts to establish his organization in Harlem proved abortive. On each of these occasions petty Negro politicians joined the Association and attempted to use it for their own purposes. When Garvey objected, these men succeeded in disrupting the group. Finally, at the request of some of the members Garvey placed himself in sole charge of his organization. He had the Universal Negro Im-provement Association (UNIA) incorporated and provided it with a regular meeting place and two secretaries. He then went out to speak on the street corners of Harlem at night to attract members. The re-sults of his efforts are described by Garvey himself as follows:

In three weeks more than 2,000 new members joined. . . .
The organization . . . grew by leaps and bounds. I started The Negro World. Being a journalist, I edited this paper free of cost for the Association, and worked for them without pay until November, 1920. I traveled all over the country for the Association at my own expense and established branches until in 1919 we had about thirty branches in different cities. By my writings and

speeches we were able to build up a large organization of over 2,000,000 by June, 1919. . . .[16]

While few of Garvey's observant contemporaries agree with his account of the startling rise of the UNIA, by 1919 the *Negro World* had become the most widely read Negro weekly in America, if not in the world. Garvey, of course, used the paper as a medium for the expression of his personal opinions and biases. But, in addition, this weekly carried news articles and editorials on Negroes throughout the world. A Spanish-language section was published for the benefit of Negroes in South and Central America. Primarily, the *Negro World* was devoted to the building up of the black man's pride. Its most often used slogan was "Up You Mighty Race." Several European nations took the precaution of banning the *Negro World* in their African colonies. Garvey states: "In certain places the punishment to be seen with a *Negro World* was imprisonment for five years, some life imprisonment and in French Dahomey the penalty was death."[17]

By 1919 Garvey was already the most talked about Negro in the world. His attacks upon the whites and mulattoes, his championing of the black and pan-black ideals, indeed, his naked chauvinism constituted the ingredients for the type of racist ideology which was yet to have its day in Europe. Many Negroes, however, were ready to accept any doctrine or ideology which helped to raise their self-esteem. Garvey received invitations from every obscure Negro hamlet in America. Unsolicited contributions poured into the office of the UNIA from Negroes everywhere, all wanting to get the African Empire started as soon as possible.

The potentialities of his organization now began to dawn upon Garvey. He had not counted upon such an overwhelming response from Negroes. Moreover, they were beginning to ask for something more concrete than plans and speeches. Hence, in June, 1919, Garvey announced to his followers that the UNIA would shortly establish a merchant marine to engage in trade among Negroes all over the world. This was the famous Black Star Line. Garvey incorporated this new venture on June 27, 1919. The first announced capitalization was $500,000, which was later raised. 100,000 shares of stock were to be sold at five dollars a share.[18]

Many of Garvey's critics immediately denounced his new plans as a scheme to defraud the public. Others held that Negroes by themselves were too poor to sustain a fleet of ships. Late in 1919, in the midst of these speculations, Garvey calmly announced that the

UNIA had acquired its first ship. The boat was the S. S. *Yarmouth,* a thirty-two year old coasting vessel bought for $168,500 and re-commissioned the S. S. *Frederick Douglass.*[19] If Garvey's critics were dumbfounded, his worshipers were uncontrollable in their joy. Here was proof that Garvey was sincere, that he meant to carry out his promises. The *Frederick Douglass* was given a new coat of paint, repaired, and staffed with an all-black crew from captain to messmen. Claude McKay thus describes the first weeks during which the ship was docked on the Hudson River:

> There was a wild invasion of Harlem by Negroes from every black quarter of America. Hordes of disciples came with more dollars to buy more shares. The boat was moored at the pier with its all-Negro crew. And the common people gladly paid half a dollar to go aboard and look over the miracle. Loudly talking and gesturing, they inspected the ship, singing the praises of Marcus Garvey.[20]

The membership of the UNIA now reached proportions unheard of for a Negro organization. Garvey claimed that by August, 1920, four million people paid dues in the association. Du Bois, on the other hand, asserted that the membership was probably less than three hundred thousand. It is generally believed, however, that the UNIA had about a half million dues-paying members and an additional four million sympathizers all over the world. The possibility of establishing the African Empire now began to seem real, even to Garvey. Thus, early in 1920, he issued a call for a convention of Negroes from all parts of the world to meet in New York City from the first to the thirty-first of August. The UNIA hastily took title to three apartment houses to be used as offices and purchased the foundation of an unfinished Baptist church which was covered over for use as a meeting center.

During the last days of July, African tribesmen (some in their native dress), Negroes from other countries, as well as some representing the forty-eight states, enthusiastically greeted each other in Harlem on what was for them a momentous occasion.[21] In the month that followed, these delegates solemnly labored at plans for the establishment of a Negro state in Africa. The convention finally adopted a "Declaration of Rights of the Negro Peoples of the World" containing sixty-six articles, a universal anthem, and an African tri-color of red, black, and green. Garvey was designated His Excellency, the Provisional President of Africa.[22] The name of the anthem was "Ethiopia the Land of Our Fathers." Following is the first stanza:

Ethiopia, thou land of our fathers,
Thou land where the gods loved to be,
As storm cloud at night suddenly gathers
Our armies come rushing to thee.
We must in the fight be victorious
When swords are thrust outward to gleam;
For us will the vict'ry be glorious
When led by the red, black and green.[23]

And since the logic of an all-black state called for a black God, the convention set up the African Orthodox Church. The Reverend George Alexander McGuire, a well-known Episcopalian priest in Boston, abandoned his pulpit in 1920 to join the Garvey movement. During the following year in services conducted by the high clergy of the Greek Orthodox Church, McGuire was consecrated as the first archbishop of the African Orthodox Church.[24] The convention apparently was not certain as to whether it wanted a monarchy or a republic, for in addition to its president, it created an African court, as well as a hierarchy of African nobles.

At the conclusion of the convention Garvey and his delegates staged the largest and, as some thought, the most bizarre parade ever to be held in Harlem. An eyewitness thus describes the procession:

> His Excellency, Marcus Garvey, Provisional President of Africa, led the demonstration bedecked in a dazzling uniform of purple, green, and black, with gold braid, and a thrilling hat with white plumes. . . . He rode in a big, high-mounted black Packard automobile and graciously, but with restraint becoming a sovereign, acknowledged the ovations of the crowds that lined the sidewalks. Behind him rode His Grace, Archbishop McGuire, in silk robes of state, blessing the populace. Then, the Black Nobility and Knight Commanders of the Distinguished Order of the Nile followed, the hierarchy of the state, properly attired in regalia drawn from a bold palette. Arrayed in gorgeous uniforms of black and green, trimmed with much gold braid, came the smartly strutting African Legion; and in white, the stretcher-bearing Black Cross nurses. Then came troops of kilt-clad Boy and Girl Scouts, trailed by a multitude of bumptious black subjects.[25]

The capstone of these festivities was a mass meeting held that evening at Madison Square Garden. The *New York Times* estimated the attendance at twenty thousand persons.[26] The highlight of the affair, of course, was an address by Garvey. His eloquence was torrential. Lashing out right and left at the Negro's "enemies," Garvey touched off a frenzy of applause with these remarks:

> We are striking homeward toward Africa to make her the big black republic. And in the making of Africa the big black republic, what is the barrier? The barrier is the white man; and we say to the white man who dominates Africa that it is to his interest to clear out now, because we are coming, not as in

the time of Father Abraham, 200,000 strong, but we are coming 400,000,000 strong and we mean to retake every square inch of the 12,000,000 square miles of African territory belonging to us by right Divine.[27]

Resolutions were passed and messages sent to the United States Government officials, to the Empress of Ethiopia, and to the President of Liberia. A message of sympathy and support was also dispatched to Eamon DeValera, Provisional President in Exile of the Irish Republic. Because of the Irish struggle for independence, this message was duly noted in the London newspapers.

After 1920 Garvey's place of leadership among millions of Negroes was established. Most observers agreed that he was assured of continued mass support as long as his objectives were reasonable and obtainable. But many feared the eventual collapse of Garvey's program for the establishment of an African state. For even while Garvey and his followers were drawing their blueprints for nationhood, the peace conferences of Europe were busy recarving the Dark Continent. Some of the African mandates and colonies constituted the most valuable possessions of the European nations to which they belonged. Nothing short of war could change the map of Africa. It was childish, therefore, for a mass of unarmed and powerless Negroes, no matter what their numbers, to think of marching from "Cape to Cairo" and driving every white man into the sea. This wishful thinking, of course, was inspired by Garvey. His critics called the idea a "fraud."

Indeed, it was difficult to believe that a man credited with Garvey's intelligence could have believed in the "pipe dream" with which he intoxicated his followers. It was common talk among "smart" Negroes that Garvey was merely using "Back to Africa" as a propaganda line or smoke screen to conceal more practical objectives. Garvey never paid too much attention to the business ventures started by the UNIA. In the main these schemes were the progenies of other minds in the association. Garvey was primarily concerned with his position as leader of the Negro race, and as such he ranked himself in importance with the heads of established governments. There is no evidence that Garvey ever abandoned one iota of his belief in the possibility of establishing his black republic. One is left to speculate, therefore, as to whether Garvey was either unwilling or unable to see the gigantic flaws in his main plan, for nowhere does one encounter an intelligent and objective consideration of the "Empire." "Manifest Destiny" for the Negro was forever shrouded in bombast, exaggeration, and demagoguery.

Nevertheless, the Garvey movement gained steadily in momentum. "Garveyism" stimulated the first large-scale production and sales of black baby dolls in the country. UNIA executives and officials puffed on *Marcus Garvey* brand cigars; millinery shops owned by Garveyites offered "a variety of styles in chic summer hats" turned out by "expert Negro designers;" and steam laundries run by Garvey followers offered to do the family washing.[28] Indeed, one of the hit recordings of the day was a disc put out by Columbia Records entitled "Black Star Line." The reverse side was entitled "My Jamaica."[29] Marcus Garvey was the talk of the town. The writer remembers little black boys standing in front of the Garvey headquarters in Harlem and chanting:

> Marcus Garvey, black as tar
> Tried to go to Heaven on a Hershey bar.
> The Hershey bar broke, and down he fell.
> Instead of going to Heaven, he went to hell.

Chauvinism among Negro peoples in every country increased. From Costa Rica, for instance, came the news of a strike which was claimed to have been "aroused by the propaganda of Marcus Garvey in his *Negro World,* which infused labor struggles with racial antagonism."[30]

In the meanwhile Garvey's enemies in America were busy trying to cut ground from under him. In the vanguard of this movement was the Negro intelligentsia of New York City. As early as 1919 the complaints of this group had caused the District Attorney of the County of New York to question Garvey at random about his organization.[31] Perhaps Garvey could have weathered the gathering storm had it not been for the thefts that were rapidly being uncovered in his organization. More serious, however, was the bad judgment exercised in the purchase of the ships for the Black Star Line. With the United States Army literally purchasing everything that floated to bring its troops from Europe, the prices of vessels spiraled. In this abnormal market the UNIA had purchased four ships.

The S. S. *Yarmouth* was purchased in October, 1919, for $168,500. Under its Negro master, Captain Joshua Cockbourne, she made three halting and ill-starred trips to the West Indies. Cockbourne was later replaced by a white master, but the vessel continued to be the victim of inept handling, bad seamanship, and even mutiny. The *Yarmouth* was finally ordered seized by a federal judge to satisfy a $2,320.90 judgment against her. She was finally sold for $1,625.

The S.S. *Shadyside* was purchased for $35,000 in April, 1920, for use as an excursion boat on the Hudson River. During the UNIA convention in the summer of 1920, the *Shadyside* made as many as three trips a week up the Hudson River. But Harlem Negroes, even Garvey-ites, would not or could not put up the $1.05 for the fare. Caught in an ice storm on the river during the winter of that year, the *Shadyside* went to the bottom. No salvage was attempted.

The S.S. *Kanawha:* The real value of this ship was about $10,000; yet the Black Star Line willingly paid the asking price of $60,000. In addition, Garvey spent $25,000 to have this millionaire's yacht refitted for transporting passengers and cargo. On its first trip up the Hudson River a boiler on the ship exploded, killing one member of the crew. Bound for Cuba on its second voyage, the *Kanawha* made it as far as the Delaware River, where engine trouble forced the crew to hoist improvised sails in order to make port. After a disaster-ridden voyage the ship was finally abandoned for junk in the port of Antilla in Cuba.

The S.S. *General Goethals* was purchased for $100,000 in 1924 and refitted at a cost of $60,000. It flew the pennant of the Black Cross Line, which now replaced the defunct Black Star Line. This vessel was a better ship than any of the others of the old Black Star Line, yet it was doomed to meet the same tragic end as did the rest. The maiden and only voyage of this flagship was marred by mutiny and disorder among the crew, conflicts between the white officers and black passengers, and poor seamanship. She docked in Kingston, then Havana, and finally Colon, Panama, but never returned to New York.[32]

In the spring of 1921, the Vice-president and the Treasurer of the UNIA had been instructed by Garvey to deposit $25,000 with the United States Shipping Company for the purchase of a ship for the Black Star Line. From May to September of that year Garvey was traveling in the West Indies. On his return to America he learned that only $5,000 had actually been deposited on the ship. As a result of his threats to prosecute the two officials, the deposit was raised to $22,500. In November, Garvey discovered that $11,000 of this deposit was borrowed on the organization's securities from a New York bonding company.[33] This scandal brought on an investigation of the UNIA by the United States Department of Justice. On January 12, 1922, Garvey and three other officials of the UNIA were arrested and indicted for using the mails to defraud in the promotion of the Black Star Line and the Universal Negro Improvement Association. They were released on bail of $2,500 each.[34]

The United States Government did not rush its case against Garvey and his officials. Perhaps this was because the prosecution wanted to prepare a sound case. On the other hand, the lapse of fourteen months between indictment and prosecution may have been inspired by Garvey's friends within the government, for in the fall of 1920, Garvey had publicly endorsed Warren G. Harding for the presidency.[35] At any rate Garvey used the breathing spell granted him to good advantage. Naturally, he could be expected to assume the role of martyr to his hosts of fanatical followers. The response was titanic. From all parts of the world came letters of sympathy, many of which included financial contributions for Garvey's legal defense. The convention of 1922 was described as the "greatest swarm since Garvey started his movement."[36] Indeed, the new loyalty to the "leader" impelled a delegate from British Honduras to draft a new will bequeathing to the UNIA his estate valued at about $100,000.[37]

But if Garvey's friends were aroused to a pitch, so were his antagonists. Eight Negro leaders, including officials of the NAACP, labor leaders, editors, and ministers known as the Friends of Negro Freedom, attacked Garvey incessantly. Their avowed purpose was to send him to jail or have him deported. On January 15, 1923, this group, obviously chagrined at the delay in the Garvey case, sent the Attorney General a highly emotional document which began with the following statement:

> There are in our midst certain Negro criminals and potential murderers, both foreign and American born, who are moved and actuated by intense hatred against the white race. These undesirables continually proclaim that all white people are enemies to the Negro. They have become so fanatical that they have threatened and attempted the death of their opponents, actually assassinating in one instance.[38]

The letter, further, specifically charged the members of Garvey's organization with having committed, from 1920 to 1923, a number of crimes ranging from simple misdemeanors to manslaughter. But the United States Department of Justice undoubtedly perceived the punitive nature of these allegations. Its agents were, of course, on the alert for any crimes committed within the jurisdiction of the federal government, and presumably these allegations were closely examined. However, neither Garvey nor any of his associates was ever indicted on the basis of any of these charges.[39]

The case against Garvey and his associates began in May, 1923. The government contended that Garvey and his codefendants had used the mails to promote the sale of Black Star Line stock after they were aware that the financial condition of the line was hopeless. The men were held on two indictments, each of which contained counts charging the use of the mails to defraud, as well as conspiracy to use the mails to defraud. Garvey's associates were acquitted of all charges in both indictments, and Garvey himself stood trial on only one count in the first indictment. This count stated that on or about December 13, 1920, Garvey had placed in a post office in the Southern District of New York, a Black Star Line promotional circular addressed to one Benny Dancy of 31 West 131 Street, New York City.[40] Dancy testified that he had received the promotional literature. Under extensive questioning the prosecution managed to elicit from a halting and rather uncertain Mr. Dancy confirmation of its contention that it was entirely because of the promotional literature that Dancy had purchased fifty shares of stock in the Black Star Line. This was the sum and substance of the government's case against Garvey.[41]

As the trial progressed, however, Garvey acted as though he was bent on getting himself convicted, even serving as his own attorney.

When the trial ended, Garvey was found guilty, fined one thousand dollars, and sentenced to five years imprisonment at the Atlanta penitentiary. Freed under heavy bail while his conviction was being appealed, Garvey continued in his role of Provisional President of Africa. His trial was regarded by his followers as naked persecution. Sympathy and money poured in upon Garvey. According to the *New York Times:* "As surprising as any manifestation of sentiment here, just now, is that of the negroes who in considerable numbers are declaring that the man is a hero and a martyr. . . ."[42] In the last half of 1923, Garvey estimated his followers at around six million. The Universal Negro Improvement Association counted nine hundred branches throughout the world.[43] Indeed, in faraway Africa native tribesmen were translating the columns of the *Negro World* into drum code and relaying them throughout the continent. A dispatch to the *New York Times* from London stated:

> Agitation in a form resembling Bolshevism has appeared in East Africa and sentiment favorable to the nationalist movement started by Marcus Garvey is rampant in Liberia, while the troubles in French West Africa recently required military suppression.[44]

On the more practical side of the ledger for Garvey was his interest in Liberia. As early as 1920 he had begun to establish relations with the officials of that country.[45] The purpose was ostensibly to set up a colony for Negroes who wanted to leave the western hemisphere. Significantly, the site selected for the colony lay in the midst of a vast tract of land noted for its rubber-producing potentialities.[46] Plans for the development of the land, including the building of a new town, were dispatched to the President of Liberia. Apparently impressed, the Liberian government officially accepted the plans and offered the UNIA "every facility legally possible" to help carry out the project.[47] During the next four years the Liberian government treated the UNIA almost as a sovereign power. The organization was permitted to establish its "legation" in Monrovia, the capital of Liberia. In turn, the Mayor of Monrovia was given a high post in the UNIA and voted a salary of twelve thousand dollars a year. In fact, the mayor so seriously regarded his position as a potentate of the UNIA that on one occasion he demanded precedence over the president at state functions.[48]

By 1923 the UNIA was ready to implement its scheme of colonization. The defunct Black Star Line was reorganized as the Black Cross Line, and a new ship was purchased to take the first Negro pilgrims across. A delegation of UNIA officials was sent ahead to make final arrangements with the Liberian officials. Along with them went a corps of Negro engineers and technicians plus fifty thousand dollars worth of equipment to begin the project.[49] In America the UNIA began a high-powered campaign to raise a fund of two million dollars to finance the colony. A full-page advertisement was purchased in the *New York World* in June, 1924.[50] What happened in the ensuing two months is still the subject of much speculation. But, on August 5, the delegates to the annual convention of the UNIA read the newspapers in astonishment. The Liberian government without notice to the UNIA informed the Associated Press that all existing agreements between itself and the UNIA had been canceled.[51] Some of the Association's delegates and representatives already in Liberia had been jailed, and others were to be deported immediately. Materials belonging to the UNIA had been impounded by the Liberian government. In addition, the Liberian government lodged the following note with the American State Department:

The Government of Liberia, irrevocably opposed both in principle and fact to the incendiary policy of the Universal Negro Improvement Association headed by Marcus Garvey, and repudiating the improper implications of its widely advertised scheme for the immigration of American Negroes into the republic under the auspices of this association, which the Liberian Government believes does not appear to be bona fide and has in addition a tendency adversely to affect the amicable relations of the republic with the friendly states possessing territories adjacent to Liberia. . . .[52]

While Garvey was upset by this abrupt and unilateral action, he was not taken completely by surprise. For some months previously, he had been receiving reports to the effect that the Liberians were under pressure to repudiate all concessions made to the UNIA and that the Firestone Rubber Company was interested in the same tract of valuable land to which he and his followers had been given rights.[53]

The probability is that the Liberians never intended to allow Garvey to set up shop in their country. Debt-ridden, backward, and corrupt, the black republic was using the Garvey movement as a pawn in a series of protracted negotiations with the United States government and the Firestone Rubber Company. By August, 1924, the Liberian officials had no further use for Garvey. They had signed an agreement with the Firestone Rubber Company which gave to that firm a ninety-nine year lease to one million acres of land at the rate of six cents per acre yearly, paid in gold coin. This was the same tract of land which had been promised to Garvey. In addition, with the help of Mr. Firestone, the Liberians received a loan of five million dollars from a New York City bank.[54]

Some months later in confirming the grant to the Firestone Company, a Liberian official proudly pointed out: "Labor is very cheap in Liberia and strong, healthy men work for 25 cents a day." Ambitious colored people from America would be "heartily welcomed." However, neither Garvey nor any of those associated with him would be received in Liberia.[55] By the end of 1924, Garvey's meteoric career in America, or in the world for that matter, had reached its zenith. From then on his fortunes declined rapidly. His conviction in 1923 had touched off a flood of lawsuits against him as well as against the UNIA. Then in August, 1924, a Federal grand jury indicted him on the charge of income tax evasion.[56] To Garvey, however, the bitterest blows were coming from members of his own race, not from the whites. Of him Du Bois then wrote:

> Marcus Garvey is, without doubt, the most dangerous enemy of the Negro race in America and in the world. He is either a lunatic or a traitor. . . . The American Negroes have endured this wretch all too long with fine restraint and every effort at cooperation and understanding. But the end has come. Every man who apologizes for or defends Marcus Garvey from this day forth writes himself down as unworthy of the countenance of decent Americans. As for Garvey himself, this open ally of the Ku Klux Klan should be locked up or sent home.[57]

Late in 1924 Garvey's old enemies dispatched a signed petition to the Department of Justice demanding his immediate imprisonment or deportation.[58] Finally, on February 25, 1925, Garvey's appeal for a reversal of his 1923 conviction was denied, and during the same month he was committed to the Atlanta penitentiary for the term to which he had been sentenced.[59]

In November, 1927, after having served more than half of his five-year sentence, Garvey was pardoned by President Coolidge and deported to Jamaica.[60] Meanwhile, the UNIA had been smashed to bits by money-hungry officials. Lip service was still being paid to Garvey's leadership, but his power was gone. During the next ten years Garvey made several ambitious attempts to revive the UNIA, but they were all failures.[61] Broken in spirit and poverty-stricken, he died in London in 1940. Oddly enough, he never set foot on African soil.

To a great many white people in America who knew anything at all about him, Marcus Garvey was simply a clown, a combination of Negro Baptist minister and minstrel. When Garvey was arrested, a prominent New York newspaper columnist commented that to hold him was "equivalent to 'jailing a rainbow.' "[62] Far more substantially, however, Garveyism was the first genuine mass movement to take place among American Negroes. Unlike the Black Power movement that was to shake up America some two generations later, Garveyism did not really create Negro militancy — it merely channelized an activism that had previously been generated by such black irreconcilables as Trotter, Du Bois, A. Philip Randolph, and Robert S. Abbott, and which had already exploded in the race war of 1919. However, Garveyism did produce its own isolated incidents of violent black militancy. Such an incident occurred on June 20, 1920, when two hundred Garveyites burned two American flags in a bonfire on East Thirty-Fifth Street in Chicago. Two white men were killed and a Negro policeman was wounded in the uproar that followed.[63] This was very probably the first desecration of the American flag during this century and certainly the first by Negroes.

What has become known as the Negro Renaissance reached its full flowering during the high tide of the Garvey movement.[64] In the field of literature young Negro writers and poets turned to the Dark Continent for the subjects of new verses. Thus, Langston Hughes chanted in his "The Weary Blues":

> All the tom-toms of the jungle beat in my blood.
> And all the wild hot moons of the jungles shine in my soul.
> I am afraid of this civilization —
>   So hard,
>   So strong,
>   So cold.[65]

And Countee Cullen queried:

> What is Africa to me:
> Copper sun or scarlet sea,
> Jungle star or jungle track,
> Strong bronzed men, or regal black. . . .
> *One three centuries removed*
> *From the scenes his fathers loved,*
> *Spicy grove, cinnamon tree.*
> *What is Africa to me?*[66]

The serious study of the Negro's past begun in 1915 by Carter G. Woodson won several brilliant young recruits during the Garvey era. Such men as J. A. Rogers and Arthur Schomburg rummaged through libraries and collections the world over in search of material dealing with the Negro's history. The new outlook was manifested also in the realms of music and art. The importation of African art, barely a trickle before World War I, swelled to a virtual torrent during the early twenties. African sculptures in clay, wood, ebony, and ivory became prized and eagerly sought for.[67] Also Negro composers devoted a new interest to African themes and rhythms. To summarize the new trends, in May, 1924, *Opportunity*, a Negro periodical edited by Charles S. Johnson, produced an African art issue containing African-inspired poems by Claude McKay, Langston Hughes, and Lewis Alexander. The publication featured other African art numbers in 1926 and 1928. The new pride in things black and things African fathered a drive on the part of the Negro press to substitute the term "black men" for "colored men" and "Afro-American" for "American Negro." Gradually, Negroes learned to refer to their African ancestry and heavy pigmentation less self-consciously.

In the realm of politics Garveyism accelerated the shift of the Negro electorate from the Republican to the Democratic Party. Among other things the new Negro considered himself a radical. He was beginning to distrust the hidebound traditionalism of Republican political leaders and specifically the Negro element in this group. The new self-confidence and spirit of independence among the black masses in the Northern and Eastern metropolises was manifested in new allegiances between the black electorate and Democratic political machines. On the economic front, the teachings of Garvey ran parallel to those of Booker T. Washington. Both men were interested in the establishment of a sound and thriving Negro bourgeoisie. Garvey particularly hammered away at the necessity for the building of Negro factories, the organizing of cooperative markets among American Negroes, and the establishment of international trade among the world's black population. During his heyday numerous attempts were made by his followers to establish Negro enterprises. In general, however, Garvey's economic doctrine produced little of lasting benefit to the race. In passing, perhaps it should be mentioned that the followers of Garvey were among the leaders of the Jobs for Negroes Campaign which blossomed in Northern cities during the early 1930's. Some Garveyites were to be found among the early recruits of the Black Muslims.

In the long run, however, the meteoric flash of Garvey's rise awed even his bitterest enemies, and some of the more thoughtful among them eventually paid him the high tribute of emulation. As to his attempts to translate his dreams into reality, no more poignant words were spoken of Garvey than those of Henry Lincoln Johnson:

> If every Negro could have put every dime, every penny into the sea, and if he might get in exchange the knowledge that he was somebody, that he meant something in the world, he would gladly do it. . . . The Black Star Line was a loss in money but a gain in soul![68]

5 MILITANCY ON THE BLACK CAMPUS

ON FEBRUARY 4, 1924, a Howard University publication, the *Hilltop*, carried an editorial, part of which read:

> Out of the vast host of students at Howard everyone should be a potential leader. You must be preparing to save the world from the present chaotic conditions. Be a factor in the organizations for the advancement of the Negro and humankind: *A leader should come among us to make Marcus Garvey's dream a reality.*[1]

In just about a year after this editorial appeared, student activists were calling for strikes and organizing revolts on the campuses of Fisk, Howard, and Hampton Institute; and the virus had spread as far west as the campus of Lincoln University at Jefferson City, Missouri. Of course, the *Hilltop* editorial did not and could not have sparked such widespread student unrest, but it was symptomatic of the *mood* of many of the students on black campuses in the early twenties.

Easily the most literate and the most progressive segment of the race, Negro students in the black liberal arts colleges had rejected the accommodation philosophy of Booker T. Washington and had opted instead for the militant stance of the NAACP leaders. And, if Marcus Garvey's Back-to-Africa theme did not interest them to any great degree, his insistence on race pride, Negro self-esteem, and "black worthiness" struck a responsive chord among them. More than anything else, what rankled the Negro student in the twenties was the ever present paternalism of the college trustees and presidents (almost always white), the general refusal to treat Negro students as men and women rather than as children, and the constant and none-too-subtle reminders that the black student and the black college were inferior to their white counterparts.

101

By 1925 Negro liberal arts colleges had definitely reached a cross-road. Founded during the post-Civil War period, almost all of them had had denominational beginnings. As they expanded in size and importance, they came increasingly under the direction of white trustees and administrators. Such endowments as they enjoyed they had secured through the benevolence of white foundations and philanthropists. The faculties of these institutions, at least up to World War I, were predominantly white. One reason was that the Negro race had not yet produced sufficient personnel to fill a majority of the vital teaching posts. A good many of the white teachers were dedicated people with a missionary zeal. Others were simply incompetents or rejects from the white institutions. Nevertheless, during the period between 1917 and 1927 Negro institutions of higher learning enjoyed a phenomenal growth. In 1927 a national survey indicated that enrollments in thirty-one Negro colleges and universities had increased from 2,132 in 1917 to 13,680 in 1927, representing an increase of 550 percent. The annual income of Negro institutions had also gained at a rapid rate. "For 1917 it amounted to $2,283,000, while for 1926-27 the annual income was $8,560,000, an increase of 257 percent."[2]

Total capital investment in the real properties of the universities and colleges surveyed had also been considerably increased. In 1917 the value of the physical plants of these institutions was fixed at $15,720,000. In 1927 their combined value was $38,680,000. This was a net gain of 146 percent. Perhaps the most important advance made by the Negro schools had been the large increase in their productive endowments. Of institutions covered by the survey, productive endowments in 1917 amounted to $7,225,000 with an annual yield of $361,250. By 1927 the endowments had moved up to $20,713,000 with the annual yield being $1,071,300. The gain over the ten-year period was 185 percent. The report indicated that Negro institutions with independent boards of trustees had the largest average income per institution, the amount being $261,082, while colleges under control of state authority averaged $145,526. The colleges under the control of Negro church organizations had an average income of $66,977.

The growth in prestige, size, and income of the black institutions was accompanied by a mounting demand on the part of both black students and faculty that these institutions be placed under predominantly black leadership. This demand, which in its inception was but a mild expression of racial pride and growing race confidence, soon picked up elements of racism and chauvinism. Dean Kelly Miller, of Howard University, thus voiced the view of Negro faculty members:

> The Negro race is developing a number of men who are qualified by every test of efficiency and experience to man and manage their own institutions. The foreign overlord never feels that the time has come for his erstwhile wards to assume self-government. . . .[3]

Dean Miller divided Negro colleges into three types on the basis of the racial composition of their faculties. Lincoln (Pennsylvania) and Hampton were placed in the category of those under exclusive white control. Those with mixed directors and faculty included Fisk and Howard, and those wholly under Negro support and management were identified as Morehouse, Wilberforce, and Tuskegee. Miller felt that all three types had their several relative advantages and disadvantages, but he concluded that "the inevitable drift" was toward Negro autonomy. "In pedagogy, as in physics, a body will not remain in stable equilibrium so long as the center of gravity falls outside of the basis of support."[4]

As a venerable professor and administrator of Howard University, Kelly Miller knew the mind and outlook of the Negro academicians, and his words accurately reflected both the confidence and aspirations of this group. A still considerably large number of white educators, including some who had taught on Negro campuses, held the average Negro professor in low repute. Some of these critics were out and out racists while others attempted to cloak themselves in an objectivity that was plainly transparent. Typical of this latter group was G. Victor Cools, who among other distinctions was a Fellow of the Royal Economic Society. Cools had spent five years as a teacher on the campuses of Negro colleges and universities. He felt that if the man of education is by the "very nature of his training" the man who is equipped efficiently to lead, the educated black man by these standards

> either makes a poor leader or fails utterly. He fails because the people distrust him. They distrust him because he has neither the character, integrity nor manhood to lead. . . . Too often have they [the masses] been betrayed by his unscrupulous practices — practices which germinated from the absence of character.[5]

Dr. W. E. B. Du Bois, undoubtedly among the best educated, and easily the most widely recognized, of all black leaders, viewed the growing unrest on the black campuses as involving questions far more important and pervasive than the competence or incompetence of Negro faculty, or whether there were black administrators sufficiently trained and in such supply as to man the black institutions. Du Bois felt that with the end of the so-called "missionary period" of Negro education clearly at hand, Negro schools were seriously in danger of being "sold down the river" by their Northern industrialist benefactors. In order to be acceptable, black leadership and training had to be conservative or "safe," preferably under the dominance of the Southern whites. In regard to his own alma mater, Fisk University, Du Bois noted that the need for financial support to replace the diminishing church missionary aid had forced Fisk to adopt a new policy acceptable to Northern philanthropists and Southern whites. The new policy included the deliberate curtailment of the ambition of the students by humiliation and insult, the dismissal of black teachers in favor of mediocre white teachers, discouragement of creative student activities, the use of fear to govern students, and the treatment of students with suspicion by the white administration. As a result, Du Bois concluded that Fisk needed a new president, a reformed board of trustees, and a reconstitution of its faculty.[6]

The deepening crisis on Negro college campuses was vividly demonstrated by events at Fisk University the following year. Sometime during the late evening of February 4, 1925, President Fayette McKenzie of Fisk University put through a call to the Nashville Police Department requesting police reserves be sent to the Fisk campus to quell a student riot. The events which immediately followed were subject to endless disagreement and contradictions. The white press, in general, followed the lead of the Atlanta *Constitution,* which reported:

> The disorder began shortly after Dr. McKenzie and Dr. E. B. Jefferson, Negro professor at the University, had received word that it would be dangerous for them to appear on the campus. Shots began to be fired from the windows of Livingston Hall — four-story dormitory, and fifty windows were shattered in the building. . . . The students after firing for a few minutes emerged from the dormitory and paraded on the campus. At the appearance of the police, however, they retreated in Livingston Hall and extinguished the lights.[7]

The version generally attested to by the students and other observers, however, was quite different. Upset and frightened by a student demonstration that afternoon, McKenzie is reported as having "ordered eighty white Southern policemen with riot guns into the boys' dormitory where eighty-six boys were already asleep." McKenzie is said to have given the police a list of six boys whom he named as ringleaders of the demonstration. "The white police knocked down doors, shot out windows, batted the students in the face with their clubs and paraded them to the president's house and back under guard — three policemen to each student."[8] The students had asked for a confrontation with the president. He refused and had them locked up. In court, when McKenzie was asked what the charges were against the students, he answered: "It's a long story, your honor. *These men have spoken against my administration and my policies all during the year. While I had no actual proof that they were in the disturbance, I felt that they might be behind this or anything of its nature.*" The charges against the students were reduced. "Meantime," reported the *Crisis,* "the little white chaplain was running around and requiring all students either to sign a paper declaring they had no sympathy with the demonstration or go home."[9] The vast majority of the students went home.

Actually, the crisis at Fisk University had been building up for some time. It was generally symptomatic of the unrest pervading the campuses of the major Negro institutions. The Fisk student revolt was simply the first to arise. Others would soon follow. Indeed, for several years prior to 1925, the Fisk alumni had been agitating for a revamp of the Fisk administration and especially for the removal or resignation of President McKenzie. To this end, Fisk University clubs were organized throughout the nation, and the *Fisk Herald,* a student publication, was taken over by the alumni and published in New York. They were careful to deny that McKenzie's race was the main issue, but they did charge the president with stifling "the liberties and initiatives of his Negro charges."[10] Similarly, the student agitators never mentioned race in their list of grievances against the administration. They did not have to. Every undergraduate on the campus was aware of the main focus of the agitation against the president.

But if others were devious in their attacks on McKenzie, Dr. Du Bois, Fisk's most outstanding alumnus, resorted to no subterfuges. When news of the student revolt reached him, he was virtually ecstatic in his response.

I am uplifted by the student martyrs at Fisk. . . . Here is the real radical, the man who hits power in high places, white power, power backed by unlimited wealth; hits it and hits it openly and between the eyes; talks face to face and not down "at the big gate." God speed the breed! . . . *Men and women of Black America: Let no decent Negro send his child to Fisk until Fayette McKenzie goes.*[11]

On April 20, 1925, Dr. Fayette McKenzie's resignation was accepted by the trustees of Fisk University.

Less than three months after the Fisk students rebelled, the undergraduates at Howard University followed suit. At an off-the-campus meeting on May 7, 1925, 602 students voted to stage a strike.[12] The most pressing demand was abolition of the rule which stipulated that any student who accumulated twenty absences from ROTC drill and physical education classes would be dismissed from the university. The students were protesting the dismissal of five students under this rule. Actually, however, the real objective of the student body, and subsequently of the Howard alumni, was the ouster of J. Stanley Durkee, another white president of a black institution. By his callous and rather hostile attitude toward students and faculty during the last five years of his administration, Durkee had seemed to invite recrimination. Indeed, when informed of the threatened student revolt two days before it occurred, Durkee shrugged and left the campus to keep a scheduled appointment in Boston.[13]

The student strike lasted only one week, but during that time the students managed to arouse the alumni and focus the attention of the country on the general situation at Howard University. For several years Durkee had carried on a vendetta against some of the more venerable members of the faculty. On one occasion, Dr. Kelly Miller was ordered out of his classroom to report immediately to the president's office and explain an off-campus statement.

> The president berated Miller so long and so severely that finally Miller remarked that he would slap the face of any man who talked to him like that if Durkee were not protected by his official position. "Leave the room, you contemptible puppy!" yelled the President.[14]

Dr. Miller was dismissed from his position in 1925. When public pressure apparently forced Durkee to rehire him, the *Crisis* remarked, "Mr. Durkee has discovered methods of retaining Mr. Miller's services; which is in our opinion, exceedingly lucky—for Mr. Durkee."[15]

Over a period of six or seven years Durkee had made several attempts to fire George William Cook, who had long served the university in the capacity of teacher, secretary, and dean. But the most disreputable incident to involve the president was his physical entanglement with Professor T. W. Turner of the biology department. During the middle of a heated argument in his office, Durkee arose and ordered Turner out of the room. When Turner demurred, the president said: "Well, then I'll put you out." And with that he pounced on Turner, who had on his overcoat and glasses, grabbed him around the shoulders, pushed him over chairs and around the room like a mad man; and finally when it was found that the door was too small to push Turner through he gave up. Turner, who had offered only passive resistance, left the office saying that the conference would be resumed later, but in the Courts, which was the proper place for such disorderly conduct.[16]

The Howard Welfare League reported:

> The spirit of education has departed from Howard. Visiting the institution today, the investigator discovers a system of espionage. This is operated to defend an administrative corps which, having no fixed policy, is subject to frequent attacks by the instructors disposed to preserve the traditions of education. The system is financed by preferment chiefly in the form of university patronage.[17]

Commenting on the student revolts at both Fisk and Howard Universities, the *Christian Century* warned that the "American Negroes of 1925 are a very different group from those of as recent date as 1915." The *Christian Century* noted that the summoning of the white police force of Nashville to quell the Fisk student revolt meant that either the McKenzie administration or the institution of Fisk had to come to an end. In that case, the administration met the Negro demand for change.[18] The *Christian Century* predicted that events at Howard University would have the same conclusion. And so they did. Dr. J. Stanley Durkee resigned in the spring of 1926. John Andrew Gregg, a Negro churchman, was offered the presidency but declined. The board of trustees then appointed Dr. Mordecai Johnson, who became the first Negro to serve as president of Howard University.[19]

The student body of Hampton Institute went out on strike during the early weeks of October, 1927. Here again, white racism was the root cause.[20] The principal of Hampton, James E. Gregg, was attempting to enforce a rigid policy of segregation on the campus, including all meetings in the public auditoriums and all social functions at the school. There was to be no avoidable mixing of the races at any time at Hampton. This had not always been the policy at the school, but segregation was prompted, at least in part, by an incident that had occurred on the campus more than a year previously. A troupe of dancers had been invited to give a performance at Hampton. The affair was well attended by students and faculty, as well as by Negroes from the town. A small group of white people attended also. When they observed that there were no seats or sections reserved for whites only, they "stood during the performance and glared at the comfortable Negroes and the empty benches beside them."[21]

On the following day the Newport News *Daily Press* complained:

> Here in this old Virginia community, rich in history and tradition, here where the first permanent white man's settlement was made, there is an institution which teaches and practices social equality between the white and Negro races. . . . Entertainments are freely patronized by white men and women who sit side by side with Negro men and women of the institution and other Negroes residing in Hampton and vicinity.[22]

Terribly alarmed and shaken, Principal James E. Gregg hastened to reassure the *Daily Press* that Hampton meant no affront to the whites and that he and his administration definitely did not believe in "amalgamation" of races. But the *Daily Press* would not be put off so easily. It put the following questions to Dr. Gregg:

> Do not white and colored folk at Hampton meet as social equals?
>
> Do they not sometimes eat together?
>
> Are not Hampton students taught the equality of races?
>
> Was not Booker Washington entertained socially by Hampton trustees in the North and are not black Moton [Robert Russa Moton, then president of Tuskegee] and white Gregg often thus entertained together?[23]

Dr. Gregg did not publicly answer the questions put by the *Daily Press,* but from then on racism boldly strode the halls and campus of Booker T. Washington's alma mater. But in the *Crisis* Du Bois did answer the *Daily Press.* He said that Hampton was endeavoring to keep the spirit of the laws of Virginia; but when

> white folk, however, come voluntarily as our guests, we welcome them and treat them with every courtesy, although we can expect for our students no reciprocal courtesy from them. But when they demand the right to cross this color line which they themselves have drawn . . . of race distinctions inside a Negro institution, we say, No.[24]

The Hampton students complained that Gregg had become rather frigid toward everyone since the incident, that he had placed some of the trades departments of the school under white men who were from the Ku Klux Klan section of the state, and that when one of these men died, he was honored by members of the Klan. The administration assumed that the students were of such low character that the house lights were ordered to be kept on during a motion picture to keep the students from engaging in sexual activities. The *New York Times* reported that it was precisely this type of action which ignited the student uprising on the night of October 14, 1927.[25]

Student unrest and near-revolt had stalked the campus for some time, but when the strike did come, neither the predominantly white administration nor the faculty was prepared. As one student reported:

> The conciliatory steps taken by some of the white teachers have been most amusing. . . . the wife of the most prejudiced leader on the campus, whose home is never open to any but the white teachers, sponsored auto parties to take the girls to Yorktown, some thirty miles away! Other white-haired ladies wandered around with checker boards, organized sewing bees, gave teas in their rooms, pop-corn parties, and other rather silly amusements as a sop.[26]

Dr. Gregg, in the meanwhile, was adamant. He averred that he had been made aware that there were those within the administration who were student sympathizers. But he insisted that loyalty on the part of teachers to the administration was vital and those who felt that they could not give it, could get out.

By the end of the year, the troubles at Hampton had subsided. Many students had transferred to other Negro institutions and a handful of students were suspended or dismissed. Unlike the student revolts at Fisk and Howard, the students were clearly the losers. There were several reasons for this outcome. One of them, perhaps, was suggested by the allegation that parents and alumni supported the administration rather than the students.

> At Hampton, the Alumni actually published to the world a statement; declaring, first, that they gave complete approval and consent to what the Hampton authorities had done, including the wholesale suspensions, and then, finally, promising that they would investigate.[27]

Clearly, a settlement of the problem at the Hampton Institute would have to await another day.

Among the major institutions of higher education for Negroes, Lincoln University in Pennsylvania was unique. Not only was Lincoln the oldest among Negro colleges and universities, but its students, for the most part, were recruited from the northern and middle Atlantic states rather than from the deep South. But Lincoln was unique in yet another respect. For almost seventy-five years after its founding, Lincoln University could boast of no Negro on its board of trustees or no Negro professor on its faculty. Negro teaching personnel had been limited to the rank of instructor and below. For a number of years the Alumni Association had been petitioning for a break in this tradition but to no avail. On December 15, 1925, the Lincoln University Board of Trustees flatly adopted the following:

> *Resolved:* That the Board of Trustees of Lincoln University are unitedly agreed that it is for the best interest of all concerned that the policy in regard

to the constitution of the Board of Trustees which has always been maintained at Lincoln University shall be continued.[28]

Angered and frustrated by this seeming intransigence, the alumni stepped up its pressure. The Reverend Francis J. Grimké, one of Lincoln's most distinguished alumni, thus cited the board:

> What kind of men are these? Are they in their right minds? Are they men of serious, sober thought? Have they no sense of decency, of the fitness of things? Are they so hopelessly stupid and so blunted in their moral sensibilities that they cannot see that the position which they have taken, and taken, not hastily, but after months of deliberation, is a deliberate insult to every one of the students and graduates of their University and to the whole colored race?[29]

Finally, Lincoln University was able to solve its problems amicably without student upheavals of the proportions of those at Fisk, Howard, and Hampton. In 1928 Dr. E. P. Roberts, a Lincoln alumnus, became the first Negro member of the board of trustees. The anti-Negro chairman of the board was removed. He was replaced by Dr. John N. Tinny, President of Johns Hopkins University. Dr. Tinny had been known to look favorably upon the appointment of Negro board members and Negro professors.

It was, indeed, paradoxical that the first Negro institutions of higher learning which were to inhibit white racism effectively on their campuses were to be found in the deep South. These were Atlanta University and Morehouse College. Atlanta University maintained a strong faculty of dedicated teachers from both races; it gave the alumni representation on its board of trustees; it doggedly refused to close its doors to white students; and, above all, it insisted upon social equality between the races on its campus. Precisely because of these policies, the university remained in financial straits. Du Bois states that when Edward T. Ware became president of the institution,

> he was given to understand by philanthropic agencies in the North, such as the General Education Board, that if Atlanta University would surrender some of its radicalism and conform to their notions of what a Negro institution should be they would support it.[30]

But the university refused to compromise. It continued to run its business as it saw fit, in spite of the fact that, as Du Bois wrote in 1926, it was "starving to death."

In 1906 when the youthful John Hope was elected President of Morehouse College, he became one of the first Negroes to head any major black institution of higher learning. Hope contributed a good deal to the institution's tradition of independence, racial self-esteem, and leadership training. In September, 1895, Hope was a member of the audience in Atlanta to which Booker T. Washington delivered his famous address. A short time later Hope, then an instructor in a small Tennessee college, lashed out at Washington's speech:

> I regard it as cowardly and dishonest for any of our colored men to tell white people or colored people that we are not struggling for equality. If money, education, and honesty will not bring to me as much privilege, as much equality as they bring to any American citizen, then they are to me a curse, and not a blessing.[31]

Hope was a lifelong friend of Dr. Du Bois and a fairly warm acquaintance of William Monroe Trotter. As a member of the Niagara Movement, Hope made the pilgrimage with the group to John Brown's grave at Harper's Ferry in 1906. He was the only one of his academic rank in the delegation.[32] Like Atlanta University, Morehouse College would pay dearly for its independence and "radicalism." In the matter of endowment and financial gifts, it would perennially lag behind its sister schools in the North.

Good, bad, or indifferent, racist-ridden or radical, the Negro institution had to shoulder the main burden of educating American Negroes. No white institution in the South, private or state supported, would accept a Negro student, and the attitudes of the Northern white institutions toward the Negro varied from tolerance to active hostility. Negro state schools, generally not allowed to offer liberal arts degrees, were maintained on a pittance in comparison to the budgets of white schools. Negro private schools were told to accommodate or starve. The ghost of Booker T. Washington still stalked the Negro halls of ivy.

6 BLACK POLITICS AND THE WHITE PRIMARY

For American economic minorities, such as laborers and farmers, the most effective means of registering a protest with, or of gaining concessions from, the state or national government has been the use (or the threat of the use) of political power. Indeed, with the exception of the petition device included in the First Amendment to the federal Constitution, no other legal avenue of action is open to the American citizen. Now, as we have seen, America's largest racial minority, the Negro, residing largely in the South, was practically deprived of all political power by 1900. Represented, thereafter, by those whom he could neither vote for nor against, the Negro's pleas and protests fell upon deaf ears. The power of Negro protest organizations was moral rather than political and, therefore, counted for little as a factor in national politics.

As a result of the migration of Negroes to Northern cities, new political vistas were opened for Negro leaders. The tens of thousands of blacks pouring into the wards of the metropolises were looked upon as potential votes which could be bartered for anti-lynching and anti-poll tax legislation. While Garvey paid little attention to politics and made but few efforts to influence his followers in the casting of their ballots, other leaders such as Dr. Du Bois and A. Philip Randolph hoped that black migrants could be persuaded to drop their traditional allegiance to the Republican Party and become independent voters.[1] This hope, however, soon foundered on the rocks of political realities in the Northern cities.

Political leaders in the cities to which the Negro migrated in significant numbers were aware that efforts would be made to organize the political power of the newcomer for one purpose or another and, thereby, disturb existing political balances. To prevent this, the gerrymander has been used on a large scale to decimate the voting power of blacks in urban centers. The classic form of this device is to redraw the boundaries of an election district so that the bloc vote of a minority group is broken up among a number of districts dominated by the majority. Another common practice is simply to refuse to increase representation from a district which is entitled to such an increase because of a rise in population. Many a bulging black ghetto enjoyed no more representation in the local or state legislatures than did an adjacent white rotten borough.

Another drag on the rise of Negro political power in the North was the parasitic swarm of petty Negro politicians which overran every Negro ward. Almost always devoid of loyalty to the race, these men often conducted an open market in black ballots. The rewards they received seldom amounted to more than a few paltry dollars or immunity from local ordinances against gambling and vice. The wide open red-light districts so common in Negro ghettos during and after World War I were invariably the spawn of an alliance between the Negro underworld and the local political machine. Shrewdly enough, these machines seldom failed to attempt to appease the honest portion of a Negro community by contributing to Negro civic and religious benefits. Negro civil leaders and voters thus faced a difficult dilemma. On the one hand, they had to accept a corrupt political machine as the price of recognition in the community and a few benefits. On the other hand, the cost of their failure to support the machine was a complete loss of recognition and representation.

In view of his new political freedom, Negro leaders expected that the Southern Negro migrant would miss but few opportunities to cast his ballot. However, the high rate of nonvoting in the new black belts proved otherwise. For one thing, no local or national election could attract an important segment of the Negro electorate if the welfare of the race was not directly involved in the outcome. This disinterest in "pure white politics" was, primarily, a legacy from the South. Yet another factor in nonvoting among Negroes was the presence of a large number of foreign-born blacks, especially in the seaboard cities. These people were mainly immigrants from the West Indian Islands.[2] Priding themselves on their British background, the West Indians, unlike the European immigrants, did not hasten to apply for American citizenship.[3] When their numbers were added to those of the illiterate native-born Negroes in Northern cities, the proportion of Negroes unqualified to vote generally reached impressive totals.

The extent of the Negro's participation in politics in the North varied from city to city, and in almost every case it was the local Republican machine which first gained control of the Negro vote. Yet, it must be noted that the Republicans did not seek out the Negro as much as the Negro sought out the party. For, when the Negro arrived, the majority of the Northern cities were under Republican control; and the willing black voter was welcomed only to the extent to which his support was needed to bolster the party's power. The one exception to this rule was Chicago. Until 1930 it was the only large Northern city in which a powerful machine rested solidly on Negro support.

Significant political activity among Chicago Negroes dates from the Reconstruction Era. As the years passed, the small number of black people then living in the city was slowly but steadily expanded by incoming migrants from states along the Mississippi Valley. Unwanted by the Democrats, Chicago's blacks were enrolled by the Republicans and were gradually formed into a solid bloc supporting the local Republican machine. This liaison had early results for the Negroes. The first black representative from Chicago was sent to the Illinois legislature in 1876. Since 1882 residents of the black belt have consistently elected a member of their own race to this body.[4]

When the Negro population of that city reached unprecedented proportions, no attempt was made to gerrymander the famous Second Ward into which most of the blacks were crowded. No small amount of credit for this was due to the fact that the incumbency of "Big Bill" Thompson's machine depended heavily upon the solid support of Negro Republicans. As a matter of fact, Thompson owed his successful entrance into politics in 1915 to the solid support of the Negro Second Ward. Harold Gosnell reports that Thompson often received as much as 80 percent of the black belt's vote in Republican primary elections. Big Bill's popularity with the black populace was based on a sound knowledge of the Negro's personality — a knowledge which he had been building up since 1900. As the Mayor of Chicago, he kept himself surrounded with a coterie of competent advisers on Negro problems. He took a great part in Negro civic and social affairs. Indeed, he was so lavish with municipal appointments to Negroes that at one time Chicago's City Hall was dubbed "Uncle Tom's Cabin."[5]

While Negro representatives had long been a fixture in the Illinois state legislature, the election of a black man to the Chicago City Council was not accomplished until 1915. In that year the young, energetic Oscar De Priest won a three-cornered race against two white candidates for the seat from the Second Ward. This was but the beginning of De Priest's career. Thirteen years later, with the aid of the Thompson machine, he became the first Negro to be elected to Congress in this century. De Priest immediately became a national symbol to Negroes — the herald of a new era in politics for the race. In 1934, however, the poverty-ridden Negroes in Chicago retired De Priest, largely because of his lukewarm support of the New Deal. His seat was filled by a Negro Democrat, Arthur W. Mitchell, whose chief recommendation was that he had once been Booker T. Washington's office boy. Mitchell was succeeded in 1942 by a third Negro, William L. Dawson, also a Democrat. If the Chicago Negro has been so conspicuously successful in politics, it must be remembered that in no other American city had the circumstances been so conducive to success. As a rule, the Negro has had to battle for whatever political recognition he received in the big cities. The fight has always been longer and more bitter when it involved a Democratic political machine, as was the situation in New York City.

Though the political history of the Negro on Manhattan Island dates from the adoption of the federal Constitution,[6] no really serious bid for that city's black vote was made by either the Democratic or Republican Party until after 1900. Before the turn of the century the majority of all black ballots cast in the city invariably went to the Republicans. Traditional Republicanism among Negroes, however, was not wholly responsible for this fact. Led by Tammany Hall, the Democrats of New York extended their Civil War Copperhead tradition well past 1900. The party did not solicit or welcome Negro political support. Almost to the same extent as in the Southern states, therefore, the Democratic Party in New York City was a white man's party.

Since naked hatred is seldom the motivating force in the action of a political machine, one must search for other reasons for Tammany's cool attitude towards Negroes. Primary among these other reasons is the fact that the Hall before World War I seldom found it necessary to call upon Negro voters in order to win an election. The black vote was considered to be a natural adjunct of the perennial Republican minority in city elections. In addition to the fact that it did not need the Negro vote, Tammany Hall cultivated a constituency that was often violently anti-Negro. The constituency was made up of Irish, Italian, and German immigrants who became members of Tammany Hall sometimes even before they had received their citizenship papers. Uneducated for the most part and, therefore, confined to menial employment, these immigrants were haunted by a perpetual fear of job competition from hordes of Negro newcomers from the South. This fear, transformed into hatred and violence, was reflected in race riots along the docks of New York and in police brutality, as well as in judicial callousness to the rights and welfare of the city's Negro residents.[7]

With the Negro population growing rapidly after 1900, Tammany Hall began to fret a little over its future in the wards into which Negroes were streaming. In addition, Negro civic leaders, petty politicians, and underworld characters too long out in the political cold began earnestly to press for some fruitful liaison with Tammany. Bending a little to the Negro's pleas, Richard Croker, chief sachem of the Hall, finally agreed to give the race some recognition from the Democrats. Promising to place a Negro in "every department of the city government," Croker welcomed the United Colored Democracy into the Democratic phalanx to handle patronage to Negroes.[8] Negroes soon discovered, however, that these moves were but empty gestures, for in a decade of existence the United Colored Democracy placed only one Negro in an important municipal position. Negroes repaid this insincerity by deserting the party in droves. By 1915 there were less than a thousand enrolled Negro Democratic voters in New York City.

With the Republican Party, to which the majority of the city's Negroes belonged, politics was hardly more profitable. From that organization the black voter received open recognition but no more patronage than from the Democrats. After World War I, two assembly districts were populated almost entirely by Negroes; yet the bulk of the patronage dispensed in these wards went to white residents on the fringes of the districts. Even by 1919 Negro voters had reached sufficient strength to enable them to elect black representatives to the state legislature from both districts. As time passed, however, it became increasingly evident that jobs and political protection were to be obtained only from Tammany Hall.

Thus, in 1917 when John F. Hylan, former police commissioner running for mayor of the city on the Tammany ticket, indicated that he would welcome and reward Negro support, thousands of Negroes took him at his word. Newcomers and old-timers, Republicans and Democrats among the Negro electorate voted for him. During his first administration, Hylan dealt with Negroes in a manner almost identical to that of Chicago's Boss Thompson. Political favors and appointments for Negroes were usually designed to bring the Hylan administration the maximum amount of gratitude from the race. Up until Hylan's time, for instance, no Negro medical school graduate had been able to serve his internship in a New York City hospital. Hylan, upon taking office, instituted measures that resulted in the appointment of several Negro interns at Bellevue Hospital and four Negro interns to the outpatient clinic of Harlem Hospital.[9] During the first administration Hylan appointed more Negroes than any of his predecessors had ever done. Hylan, however, did not allow his Negro support to hinge on this patronage alone. Like Boss Thompson, he seldom missed an opportunity to appear in public with Negroes. He spoke at Negro civic and social gatherings in Harlem and kissed Negro babies, always with an eye on his role as Harlem's Abraham Lincoln.

But Hylan's warm attitude toward Negroes was not shared by the sachems of Tammany Hall. Patronage to Negroes came through the mayor's office rather than from the district leaders. As a result of this difficulty, two moves were made during Hylan's second administration. First, the United Colored Democracy, which had been created under Richard Croker, was revived. Secondly, Hylan made the most important Negro appointment of his incumbency; a Negro, Ferdinand Q. Morton, was appointed one of the city's civil service commissioners. Morton was subsequently placed in charge of the United Colored Democracy, which until 1935 handled all Tammany Hall patronage to Negroes. Morton naturally became the most important Negro politician in the city.

The shift of Negroes to the Democratic Party, begun under Hylan's first term, became almost a torrent during his second term. In 1923 Tammany Hall weakened a little and helped to elect the first Negro Democrat to the state assembly. But when the Harvard-educated George W. Harris, a Negro, sought and won election as a Republican to the City Board of Aldermen, Tammany Hall conducted a two-year fight to bar him from his seat in order to replace him with a Democrat. When Harris' election was declared void by a vote of 46 to 47 in the Board of Aldermen, Tammany selected John W. Smith, a Negro and a Democrat, to replace Harris.[10]

After eight years of unparalleled progress in New York City politics, Negroes were understandably chagrined when Tammany refused to endorse Hylan for a third term. The dapper and affable James J. Walker was an unknown quantity, and Negroes eyed him with suspicion. They felt that in refusing to renominate Hylan, Tammany Hall was punishing him for his favors to their race. The trend to the Democrats begun some years earlier, therefore, was abruptly halted, if not reversed completely, in the mayoralty election of 1927. Commenting on the election, the *New York Times* felt that the overwhelming vote for the Republican ticket in Harlem was "said to be due in part to the unwillingness of the City Hall to play Hylan and Thompson politics in Harlem."[11]

No really serious bid for the Negro vote was made by Tammany Hall until 1930. Then this was not due to any political consciousness on the part of the Negro electorate or because of any threat from Negro leaders. The reason was that the Hall was facing a merciless investigation of its accumulated malpractices and was realizing that every ounce of support it could muster was needed to win coming elections. Even so, because Tammany believed that Negro support could be bought comparatively cheaply, it rejected a Negro bid for a seat in the inner councils and waited. The opportunity for a deal came when the Republican-controlled state legislature created a new judicial district in Harlem with the intention of giving the community its first two Negro judges. Tammany acted quickly. It instructed Ferdinand Q. Morton to select two Negro Democratic candidates for the posts. The Hall then conducted an all-out campaign to get its nominees elected. The success of Tammany Hall in the fight was a blow to the Republicans from which they never recovered. Negroes were extremely proud of their first two judges. A new rush to the Democrats was begun. By 1935 Negro membership in the party was of sufficient strength to compel Tammany Hall to seat the first of a line of Negro sachems in its sacred inner councils.

Some observers, commenting on American political events of the past, have suggested that the astounding shift of Negroes from the Republican to the Democratic Party in the years between 1932 and 1936 was motivated primarily by the beneficence of the New Deal to millions of poverty-stricken blacks. To deny this suggestion in its entirety would be a mistake, for Negroes, as well as whites, faced with starvation were grateful for the assistance furnished under the Roose-

velt administration. Nevertheless, Negroes' abandonment of the Grand
Old Party had deeper roots.

For one thing, the election year of 1936 brought the Negro to the
end of a sixty-year period during which time the Republican Party
failed miserably to carry out any important promise made to the race.
Many excuses were offered by the Republicans for these failures.
But, generally, the blame was laid upon Negro-hating congressmen
from the South. Republican candidates addressing Negro audiences,
especially during a national campaign, insisted that the intentions of
the party were honest, but every attempt to pass legislation giving protection to Negroes was doomed to failure in the Senate because of
the filibuster of Southern members. What a good many Negroes did
not understand was that this explanation did not apply to Republican-
controlled Senates, which could have invoked cloture to pass a measure, if the Republican Party were determined to carry the bill despite
Southern Democratic opposition.

It must be noted, however, that as early as 1912 Negro leaders
began to suspect the good intentions of the Republicans. The officials
of the NAACP, for instance, profoundly distrustful of Republican
promises, campaigned actively in behalf of Woodrow Wilson. This
was the first major break with the Republicans by an important Negro
group since the turn of the century. But it was not until 1922 during
the fight over the Dyer Anti-Lynching Bill that the race as a whole
received an insight into the political strategy of Republicans on the
race question. (See pages 61-62.) The Dyer Bill received more Negro
support than had any previous measure, and with Congress under
the control of the Republicans the bill was expected to pass in spite
of opposition. However, after carrying the measure through the
House, the Republicans abandoned it in the Senate when faced with
a continued filibuster by Southern members. Negro protest organizations promptly put the blame for the failure of the measure on the
Republicans. The Negro press pointed out that the party could have
passed the bill if it had voted to limit debate in the Senate. The conclusion that the Republicans were hardly more interested in enacting
the Dyer Bill than were the Democrats seemed inescapable. After
carrying the measure through the House, the Republicans were apparently satisfied with having made the record. What happened to it
in the Senate was none of their business. When Republican control
of Congress ended in 1930, however, the record was clear to the
Negro voter that, in spite of continued Negro support, the Republicans

had failed absolutely since 1875 to deliver on any of their solemn promises to "protect the life, liberty, and property" of the race.

The disagreeable task of "alibiing" for the failure of the Republicans on the Negro question was generally left to the host of Negro Republican politicians. These men had been serving since Reconstruction as brokers or, as some of their critics dubbed them, "errand boys" for their white leaders. During the times of Frederick Douglass and Booker T. Washington, their prestige was immense in the race. Generally, they were drawn from the bourgeois class of Negroes. Some few of them received responsible government positions.

Several factors combined after World War I to change the type of Negro Republican politician. For one thing, the migration to urban areas introduced the shady and untrustworthy ward heeler. In the South, in the meantime, Negro politicans were beginning to engage in a dog-eat-dog fight for the diminishing Republican patronage to the race. The worst in Negro politics was fast becoming identified with the Negro Republican. By 1930 the prestige of this group had degenerated to the point where the Negro protest organizations fighting to make the Negro an independent voter were able to identify Negro Republicans with the hated symbol of Negro obeisance and inferiority — Uncle Tom. In a confidential report on the Negro, compiled for the Republican National Committee in 1939, Ralph J. Bunche called for a new Negro Republican leadership which would boldly represent the interests of the Negro.[12]

As noted in Chapter 1, after the demise of the Populists in 1896, there was a definite tendency on the part of the two major political parties in this country to discard the Negro whenever and wherever possible and to make national politics wholly a white man's activity. Barred by custom from the Southern wing of the Democratic Party, the Negro (because of scant members in the North) was not yet an important factor in the Northern wing. However, with the Republicans, the process of eliminating the Negro, or at least reducing his influence, was a much more difficult task, for history had linked the fortunes of the two.

Briefly stated, the Republican case against the Negro was simple and to some extent justified, at least on the basis of political morals. The preponderance of Negroes exercising any influence within the party was in the South. And since in that section of the country the blacks had been almost completely disfranchised, Negro Republican politicians represented a nonexistent electorate.[13] Leading white

Northern Republicans felt, therefore, that Negroes were not entitled to seats at national conventions merely on the basis of tradition or sufferance and that all of the needs of white party members should be served before the needs of any Negro. Black Republicans were aware of this sentiment in the party, but they were unprepared and shocked by Theodore Roosevelt's blast in 1901 to the effect that the Republican Party in the South was a Negro party made up of politicians "who make not the slightest effort to get any popular votes, and who are concerned purely in getting Federal Offices and sending to the national convention delegates whose venality makes them a menace to the whole party." [14] Roosevelt backers in the South held bolting conventions which excluded Negroes whenever possible and sent up all-white contesting delegations. But the Taft regulars controlled the national convention; and the Black and Tans, who were solidly for Taft, were seated. Roosevelt remained consistent at the Progressive Party Convention which also met in 1912. Northern Negro bolters were recognized, but Southern Negroes were turned away.

Not until 1916 did the Republican Party formally adopt the Roosevelt doctrine concerning Negro or Black and Tan representation at party conclaves. Just prior to its national convention of that year, the Republican National Committee adopted a rule stipulating that the number of delegates from the South would, thenceforth, be based upon the number of votes cast in each congressional district for a Republican candidate in the last preceding election rather than upon the population of these districts. [15] As a result of this rule, the number of Negro delegates to the Republican National Convention, which had stood at sixty-two in 1912, was reduced to thirty-two at the convention of 1916 and to twenty-seven in 1920.

In the meantime, the Republicans also reduced the number of minor diplomatic posts and other semi-important positions traditionally given to Negroes. [16] Under Taft and Roosevelt about twenty such appointments had gone to the race. However, under Hoover's drastic reduction of Negro patronage, the number fell to nine. In 1923 the Republican National Committee discarded the rule adopted in 1916 concerning the appointment of Southern delegates. As a result, the number of Negro delegates at the 1924 national convention rose to thirty-nine. In doing this, however, the Republicans were not attempting to appease Southern Negro party hacks. They were more interested in holding the line with Northern Negro migrants who were casting ballots in increasing numbers all over the nation. Nevertheless, Negroes were becoming increasingly dissatisfied with Republican policy in general and the lily-white movement in particular.[17]

The attitude of a large body of intelligent Negro voters, including disgruntled Negro Republicans, was voiced by Du Bois in the *Crisis* one month before the 1924 elections: ". . . Any black man who votes for the present Republican party out of gratitude or with any hope that it will do a single thing for the Negro that it is not forced to do, is a born fool."[18] In spite of all this, a majority of the nation's Negro electorate voted for Calvin Coolidge. They were not yet convinced that the Democrats really wanted them.

The high point for the lily-white movement of the Republicans was reached during Herbert Hoover's campaign in 1928. Born and educated in the West, Hoover had never known or had many dealings with Negroes. In entering politics, he brought with him the then standard belief in the corruptibility and venality of the Negro — especially of the Southern Negro politician. In 1927 while director of flood relief work in Mississippi, he made an appraisal of the strength of the rival Republican organizations in several Southern states. At the national convention of 1928, only the Negro politicians too powerful to be opposed were seated. Hoover backers even solicited their support. In almost all other cases, however, it was the lily-white delegation that was seated. In a further effort to appease the powerful Negroes, Hoover set up a Negro Campaign Committee, which, however, was kept at a distance from convention headquarters and told to leave the South alone.

But with the nomination won Hoover speedily reversed himself. He organized a separate campaign committee under the chairmanship of an unknown lily-white for the purpose of getting the vote of the South without the aid of the regular Black and Tan organizations. The zealousness of this committee resulted in several clashes in the South between the rival factions of the Southern Republicans. It was becoming plain to Negroes that Hoover was not soliciting their support — that he did not even want it. Negroes in the South who chose to remain with the party found themselves in a strange situation, for the Ku Klux Klan in their feverish efforts to defeat Alfred Smith gave their wholehearted support to Hoover. With this impossible situation facing them, over a dozen leading Negro Republican newspapers openly proclaimed their switch to the Democrats. Several prominent Negro leaders did likewise and pleaded with the Negro electorate in general to vote for Smith.

Handicapped by Smith's religion, the national Democrats, on the other hand, were making their first serious bid for the Negro vote. Special Negro-for-Smith Organizations were set up in over a score of states with almost half of these being in the South. Smith supporters stressed the Republican link with the Klan and constantly reminded the blacks that Republicans were definitely attempting to discard them. In the South the Smith Democrats trampled on tradition and openly solicited Negro support. The Negro was once again an issue in Southern politics, and there can be little doubt that this fact played a prominent part in the decision of many a white Southerner to vote for Hoover.

As is usually the case whenever the Negro is a factor in Southern politics, both the Republicans and the Democrats attempted to capitalize upon the poor whites' old fear and hatred of Negro domination. Besides smearing Smith with the brush of "Rum and Romanism," the Southern Hoovercrats charged the Smith Democrats with favoring social equality as well as conspiracy to turn over the Southern democracy to the blacks. Nothing seemed to pique the Democrats more, however, than the statement made by Republicans in the South that Smith employed a Negro stenographer while governor of New York State and that he planned to appoint a host of Negroes if he became president. Thus, in September, 1928, the Democratic headquarters in Washington, D.C., issued the following memorandum:

> Governor Smith does not have, and never has had, a Negro stenographer, and in the employment of Negroes by the State of New York under his administration this has been done only to fill such [positions] as they are given in the South, to wit: porters, janitors, charwomen, etc.[19]

Not to be outdone, Senator Theodore G. Bilbo of Mississippi came out with the widely publicized accusation that Hoover had at one time become friendly with and had even danced with a Negro woman. Hoover simply replied that Bilbo's charges were "most indecent and unworthy."[20]

As far as Negro Republicans were concerned, however, the most important conclusion they could draw about the entire campaign was "that the Hoover forces were trying to encourage the 'lily-white' Republican organizations in the South."[21]

Republican presidential candidates before Hoover may not have been particularly concerned about the Negro; yet they kept their real opinions to themselves, and none with the exception of Roosevelt ever made a statement which cost him a single Negro vote. Hoover, on the other hand, felt that he could win without the aid of black ballots. This was Hoover's real message in most of his statements dealing with the Negro or with the South. After one such statement in Tennessee a Negro Republican leader cried, "The Republican Party has shown us the gate. Now let all the colored people walk out of this gate."[22]

In the decade preceding 1928, Negro voters in many Northern cities were weaned from their allegiance to the Republicans in municipal and state elections. But even in the face of Hoover's ill-concealed antagonism to the Negro, the bulk of the race in the 1928 election voted the Republican ticket. However, there were some reasons for this. Hoover received about 75 percent of the black vote in Republican strongholds such as Chicago and Philadelphia. This support was an indication of the ability of the Thompson and Vare machines to hold the line, rather than of preference for Mr. Hoover. In localities where there were no strong Republican organizations, Hoover received from half to less than half of the black ballot. Of the 75,000 votes cast in the four assembly districts populated by Negroes in Manhattan, Smith received almost a thousand more votes than Hoover.[23] Smith's religion cut down his vote among Negroes almost as much as it did among whites. Because black people were predominantly Protestant, they were as susceptible as other Protestants to the anti-Catholic propaganda of the campaign.

Those among the Negro Republicans who were fearful of Hoover's intention toward the race had but a short while to wait before the worst of their fears were confirmed. On March 27, 1929, just three weeks after his inauguration, Hoover at a press conference announced his determination to break the back of Negro Black and Tan power among the Southern Republicans. He claimed that he was interested in seeing sound Republican organizations built up in all of the Southern states, but his new program was to be carried out first in Georgia, Mississippi, and South Carolina.[24] The Republican boss of Georgia was Benjamin Davis, father of the Negro official of the American Communist Party, Davis knew what was coming, for he had been removed from a responsible position in the Hoover campaign in his state. Except for those in the South, Dean Kelly Miller's rationalization of the situation was accepted by most Negroes. He observed that such Negro leadership as there was only served to influence delegates to the national Republican conventions to put men in office who would grant minor concessions to the Negro. No appreciable change in the political status of the Negro could be expected to come out of the existing pattern.[25]

In addition to his treatment of Southern Negro politicians, several other incidents occurred during President Hoover's incumbency which did not win for him any friends in the Negro race, nor any for the Republicans for that matter. Notable among these incidents was the "Parker Nomination." Judge John J. Parker, a federal circuit court judge, was nominated in 1930 to fill a vacancy in the United States Supreme Court. The nomination immediately aroused the interest of Negro organizations. Because the circuit court judge was a Southerner, Negroes were concerned lest his presence in the Court jeopardize the outcome of cases involving the civil and political status of the race. Thus, shortly after Parker's nomination became known, the NAACP began a close inspection of his past record as a judge, as well as of his background in North Carolina. The Association soon discovered that Parker, in his speech of acceptance of the Republican gubernatorial nomination in North Carolina in 1928, accused the Democrats of raising the racial issue in the campaign. He went on to say, ". . . the participation of the Negro in politics is a source of evil and danger to both races and is not desired by the wise men in either race or by the Republican Party of North Carolina."[26]

This statement was considered by Negro leaders as constituting sufficient grounds for opposing the judge's confirmation. Anti-Parker mass meetings were held in several cities with several white organizations, including the American Federation of Labor, participating. When Judge Parker denied the statement attributed to him, the NAACP had photostatic copies made of the article and sent them to the President and the senators as well as to the press. The campaign against Judge Parker was maintained up until the last day before his confirmation was voted upon. The reason for his defeat, if not primarily attributable to the opposition of Negroes, is difficult to discover.[27] The action of the United States Senate in his case marked a most dramatic and unprecedented recognition of the Negro's rising political power.

There was no great rush of Negroes from the Republican to the Democratic Party in the presidential elections of 1932. Some changes were registered; yet, in but few instances, the rate of change was the same as it had been in previous national elections since the beginning of the migration. Republican machines steadily lost Negro votes, and Democratic machines continued to gain them. The big changes for

Negroes came, as they did for whites as well, in 1936. A major factor in this shift of political alignment among Negroes was, of course, the race's esteem for President Franklin D. Roosevelt, who had shown more consideration for them than any Chief Executive since Lincoln. A second important factor was the demise of powerful Republican organizations in several Northern cities after 1932. Negro Republicans seeking additional relief funds or relief jobs in these cities had to call upon Democratic political bosses. In addition, the newly powerful Democrats generally improved upon the Republican Party policy of dispensing patronage to Negroes. No longer were a few traditional Negro positions to be shuttled back and forth within an airtight clique of Negro bigwigs. Instead, the numerous agencies sprouting in the New Deal garden provided careers for many bright young Negroes fresh from the graduate schools of the big universities. Locally, the Democrats followed the practice of spreading their largess to Negroes as widely as possible.

Overall, the twenty-year period of Northern Negro politics from 1916 to 1936 presents a picture of steadily mounting protest against Republican Party politics. In one of its facets, this protest was directed against Negro Republican politics. Generally, the Negro migrants who settled in the Northern slums were rock-bottom poor. It was only a matter of time before they would begin to question their so-called traditional alignment with a political party which nominally spoke for the middle and upper classes. In switching to the Democratic Party, the Negro masses were not only seeking their proper political level, but were also becoming more sophisticated, more class conscious, and more radical.

In the border and deep Southern states the Negro had been effectively blocked out of politics since about 1910. The provisions of the Second Mississippi Plan, plus the Grandfather Clause, had done their work mercilessly and efficiently. The politics of the South in 1910 were quite adequately reflected in the words of Senator Vardaman of Mississippi:

> It matters not what his [the Negro] advertised mental and moral qualifications may be. I am just as much opposed to Booker Washington as a voter, with all his Anglo-Saxon reenforcements, as I am to the cocoanut-headed, chocolate-colored, typical little coon . . . who blacks my shoes every morning. Neither is fit to perform the supreme function of citizenship.[28]

The white South wanted and got a "nigger-proof" political system.

By 1915, however, the dikes had sprung a leak, or rather a hole had been punched in them. By its decision in *Guinn and Beal* v. *United States* the Supreme Court had brought an end to the operation of the infamous Grandfather Clause in the Southern and border states.[29] While the white South considered its bastions against black politics to be still intact, a slightly less than casual search was begun for a replacement for the "Clause." As it happened, a Supreme Court decision that had nothing to do with Negroes or Negro voting presented a likely prospect in 1921. The Federal Corrupt Practices Act of 1910 limited by criminal penalties the sums which might be spent in congressional election campaigns. In 1918 Truman Newberry, a senatorial candidate, spent a great deal more than the statutory amount in winning the Republican nomination for the United States Senate from Henry Ford. Newberry was convicted of violating a federal statute. The United States Supreme Court in a five-to-four decision set the conviction aside on the grounds virtually that primaries were not elections and hence were immune, at least on the federal level, from statutory controls over elections.[30] The state of Texas, however, was interested only in the distinctions between a primary election and a regular election and the clear implication that primary elections were the business of the state and, hence, exempt from federal control. Texas enacted its first statewide white primary law in 1923.

Contrary to what is generally thought, however, the *first* Texas white primary law as such was not inspired by the decision in the *Newberry* case nor was the *Nixon* v. *Herndon* case the first Texas white primary case to reach the United States Supreme Court. On January 27, 1921, some four months before the *Newberry* decision was handed down, the City Democratic Committee of Houston, Texas, made and published a rule that Negroes would not be allowed to vote in the Democratic primary election to be held on February 9, 1921.[31] A few days later a group of local Negro Democrats filed for an injunction restraining the committee from enforcing the rule. After the request for the injunction was denied in the lower courts, the case finally reached the United States Supreme Court on appeal October 6, 1924, some three years later. The Court held the opinion that the election for which the injunction was being sought had long since been held and that, in any case, the rule promulgated by the Democratic Committee of Houston was for a single election only. However, in their opinion:

If the case stood here as it stood before the court of first instance, it would present a grave question of constitutional law and we should be astute to avoid hindrances in the way of taking it.[32]

The 1923 Texas law was enacted by the state legislature and applied to the entire state. Simple and to the point, it read: ". . . in no event shall a Negro be eligible to participate in a Democratic party primary election held in the State of Texas."[33] The full import of this statute cannot be grasped unless it is realized that Texas, like the entire South, was a one-party region — "The Property" of the Democratic Party. The Republican Party in most of the South existed on paper only, and it was a rare case indeed in which the party ventured to field a candidate for any important office. As there usually was no Republican candidate running in the regular election, the man who won in the Democratic primary had for all practical purposes won the office. This meant that the Democratic primary was the only meaningful election in the South. To be excluded from it, as Texas was proposing to do to Negroes, was in effect to be disfranchised. On the other hand, the Negro disfranchising devices already on the books in the South were no longer completely reliable in keeping Negroes from the polls. After 1920 the literacy rate among Negroes in the South began to rise perceptibly as more and more Negroes were able to read and write. The emergence of a professional and business class in the Negro race meant that more Negroes could and would pay the poll tax. Other Southern states were quick to adopt the Texas device.

In July of 1924 the NAACP decided to challenge the Texas law with a case coming out of El Paso. Dr. L. A. Nixon, a Negro citizen of good standing and wide repute in that city, was a regularly enrolled member of the Democratic Party and had paid his poll tax. On July 26, 1924, he attempted to vote in the Democratic primary election, at which candidates would be nominated for local and state offices, as well as for seats in the United States House of Representatives and the United States Senate. When Dr. Nixon presented himself at the Ninth Precinct in El Paso, the officials in charge refused to hand him a ballot. They cited the Texas statute of 1923.[34]

In order to enable a test case of the law to be made, however, the election officials furnished Dr. Nixon with a statement which certified that he had not been allowed to vote. Thus arose the case known as *Nixon v. Herndon.*

The case went to the United States District Court for the Western District of Texas, which upheld the election officials in their refusal to allow the plaintiff, Dr. L. A. Nixon, to vote. On appeal the case went on to the United States Supreme Court. The NAACP employed as counsel in the case a white El Paso attorney, Fred C. Knollenberg, who incidentally had been Dr. Nixon's personal attorney. The NAACP assigned Moorfield Storey to work with Knollenberg in the preparation of the brief. When argument on the case began on January 25, 1927, it was observed that the state of Texas was not officially represented. However, when counsel for the NAACP had completed arguments for the plaintiff,

the red-haired young man jumped up and asked permission to file a reply brief for the State of Texas. The young man was identified as Dan Moody, Attorney General of Texas and newly elected Governor of the State. The Supreme Court gave him 30 days in which to file such a brief and the N.A.A.C.P. then applied for time in which to file a brief replying to Texas. This was granted to Mr. Spingarn in behalf of the N.A.A.C.P.[35]

The United States Supreme Court rendered its decision early in 1927. Justice Oliver W. Holmes, speaking for the Court, found the Texas statute void as a denial of the equal protection of the law. He said:

We find it unnecessary to consider the Fifteenth Amendment, because it seems to us hard to imagine a more direct and obvious infringement of the Fourteenth. . . . States may do a good deal of classifying that it is difficult to believe rational, but there are limits, and it is too clear for extended argument that color cannot be made the basis of a statutory classification affecting the right set up in this case.[36]

In speaking of the reaction of NAACP officials to the decision, Walter White says: "In our jubilation over the victory, we naively believed that disfranchisement by means of 'white Democratic primaries' was settled. We were soon disillusioned. . . ."[37]

And so they were, because Governor Dan Moody of Texas hotly denounced the decision and declared that Texas would not permit Negroes to vote no matter what the Supreme Court said. But cooler heads in Texas prevailed. They had noticed, as the NAACP lawyers had not, that Justice Holmes had limited his opinion to *state* action; he had not said that the party itself could not bar Negroes. In special session the Texas legislature ruled that every political party in the state through its state executive committee should have the power to prescribe the qualifications of its own members and in its own way should determine who should be qualified to vote or otherwise participate in such political party. The Democratic Party hastened to declare that only white Democrats who were qualified under the Constitution and the laws of Texas would be eligible to vote in Democratic primaries. With Dr. Nixon again as the plaintiff, the NAACP lawyers prepared to begin the fight anew. This time the case would become known as *Nixon v. Condon.*

The new case was decided in 1932. This time the Court was divided five to four with the conservatives sharply dissenting from the majority decision. Speaking for the majority, Justice Benjamin Cardozo, who succeeded Holmes, declared:

> Delegates of the State's power have discharged their official functions in such a way as to discriminate invidiously between white citizens and black. . . . The Fourteenth Amendment, adopted as it was with special solicitude for the equal protection of members of the Negro race, lays a duty upon the Court to level by its judgment these barriers of color.[38]

Cardozo seemed, however, to stress state action in the case. But what if the state of Texas severed all connections by law or otherwise with the activities of political parties? In other words, could the Democratic Party of Texas function as an exclusive, private, white man's association? In his dissenting opinion, Justice C. McReynolds declared that it could so act.

Obviously taking its cue from these decisions, the state convention of the Democratic Party of Texas, acting as a *private non-statutory* group, solemnly excluded Negroes from participation in any of its activities. And so, when William Grovey demanded an absentee ballot from County Clerk Townsend of Harris County, Texas, for a forthcoming Democratic primary election, he was refused. Townsend read the exclusionary rule of the state convention to him. When Grovey decided to bring suit, NAACP lawyers took his case. This became known as *Grovey v. Townsend.*[39] In its decision handed down on April 1, 1935, the Supreme Court in a unanimous opinion rejected Grovey's plea. Recalling its invalidation of the two previous attempts to exclude Negroes from the Democratic primary, Justice Owen J. Roberts speaking for the Court said:

> We held this was a delegation of state power to the state executive committee. . . . and therefore, . . . prohibited by the Fourteenth Amendment. Here the qualifications of citizens to participate in party counsels and to vote at party primaries have been declared by the representatives of the party in convention assembled and this action upon its face is not state action.[40]

Walter White expressing the reaction of the NAACP to this decision said:

> It should not be difficult to imagine the gloom we all felt. Years of hard work and heavy expense appeared to have gone for naught. But we could not afford

to give up in despair. We had to continue the struggle, whatever the cost, to make effective what should have been settled for all time by the Fourteenth and Fifteenth Amendments. . . ."[41]

But what the Court had done in *Grovey* v. *Townsend* was virtually to emasculate the Fifteenth Amendment. For according to the decision in this case, any political party, North or South, Democratic or Republican, or even Vegetarian, could exclude Negroes or those of any other race, creed, or color from participating in its nominating process or from qualifying for office on its ticket. This would mean exclusion from membership in the political organizations that monopolize American politics and dominate American government. In short, it would mean virtual disfranchisement.

Why did the Supreme Court do this? Was it so naive, so myopic, that it could not discern that the Democratic Party of Texas and the state of Texas were identical and that what was involved here was rank, unjust discrimination? Or was racism the answer? Granted that Justice McReynolds had been Attorney General in President Wilson's "segregationist" cabinet, the other eight justices could hardly have qualified as anti-Negro. Moreover, a majority of the Court had sustained the Negro, Dr. L. A. Nixon, in the two previous white primary cases. For the answer, perhaps one should look to the temper of the times in which the case was decided. As the years go, 1935 was a poor one indeed for the Court. Its prestige stood at its lowest ebb in sixty years. It was being mercilessly assailed from all quarters for its paleolithic view toward social change as proposed in New Deal legislation. As the attacks continued to mount, the Court seemed to become even more conservative. The liberal voices became silent, and reaction began to speak unanimously. This, perhaps, was the vortex in which the Southern Negroes' right to vote was lost in 1935. It would take nine years and a new Court to regain it.

7 BLACKS, REDS, AND THE GREAT DEPRESSION

The Black-Belt Republic—Jobs-for-Negroes— The National Negro Congress

THE COMMUNIST PARTY has been notably unsuccessful in its attempts to organize and use Negro unrest in the United States for the achievement of Communist goals. As with its attempts to infiltrate the American labor movement, so with Negroes the Communists attempted to either organize their own Negro organizations or infiltrate existing Negro organizations. Both methods finally failed. Even in the midst of the economic strains of the Great Depression, the American Negroes resisted the siren call of communism and remained wedded to American ideals. Three Negro movements in particular show the methods used by the Communists to seek Negro support: the Black Belt Republic, the Jobs-for-Negroes, and the National Negro Congress.

1. THE THIRD INTERNATIONAL AND THE BLACK BELT REPUBLIC

With the advocates of world revolution directing Soviet policy during the regime of Nikolai Lenin, it was inevitable that in plotting the overthrow of American capitalism the Third World Congress of Communists International would designate a special function for the American Negro. In a letter to an American Negro Communist, Leon Trotsky himself thus made known the objectives of the Communist Party with respect to blacks in the United States:

> The training of black agitators is the most important revolutionary problem of the moment. This problem becomes more complicated in the United States of America on account of the abominable stupidity and race hatred among the privileged circles of the working class itself, which do not want to recognize negroes as brethren in labor and struggle. . . . One of the most important methods of struggle against this capitalistic corruption of minds is to waken the

human dignity and revolutionary protest among the black slaves of American capital. This work can be best carried on by devoted and politically educated negro revolutionists. Naturally the work must not assume the character of black chauvinism, but must be carried on in a spirit of solidarity among all laborers regardless of the color of their skin.[1]

When it assembled in Moscow in the autumn of 1922, the Third International prepared to construct a long-range revolutionary program for America's black masses. Several promising young American Negroes had been invited to give their views on the possibilities of converting the Negroes in America to Marxism. One of these envisioned the possibility of an early Moscow Congress of "all the revolutionary negro organizations in the world 'to realize a united front of all workers against capitalism and imperialism.' "[2] Claude McKay, in addressing the International, asserted that "the negroes of America were denied the right of free assembly and were often lynched, one purpose of the capitalists being to turn the minds of the worker from class war by inciting him to race war."[3]

The campaign to enlist Negro support is summed up in the following by Benjamin Gitlow, once an important functionary in the inner councils of the American Communist Party:

The Party created a special Negro department, built special Negro organizations, issued Negro papers and periodicals, made every inducement for Negroes to join the Party, took advantage of every opportunity to penetrate existing Negro organizations and to participate in Negro movements, for the purpose of bringing its program before the Negro masses. The Party membership was impressed with the importance of Negro work. Every new Negro member brought into the Party was looked upon as a Communist achievement, and Negro Communists were actually accorded special privileges.[4]

The first of the Negro organizations mentioned by Gitlow in the above was established in Chicago in October, 1925. This was the American Negro Labor Congress. Well advertised in Negro communities beforehand as a new Negro protest organization, the Congress was attended by unsuspecting delegates from Negro labor unions, farm and fraternal organizations, and benevolent societies, in spite of warnings by William Green, president of the American Federation of Labor, about the Communist backing of the Labor Congress.[5] At the open sessions of the Congress, special emphasis was laid upon the need for greater organization of Negro farmers and workers. Big American labor unions were called upon to admit Negroes to membership and full participation in all offices and affairs. In fact, every known mistreatment of the Negro was aired and denounced in typical Communist fashion. Nor was the relevance of the class struggle overlooked.

The Negro's historic fight for freedom was interpreted at the Congress as being but a facet of the world struggle against capitalism.[6]

Naturally, the Congress was hailed by the Communists as a huge success, the "beginning of a movement with far-reaching implications."[7] Nevertheless, its annual meetings after 1925 were very poorly attended, and by 1930 it went out of existence. One of its founders explains that the "A.N.L.C. was too narrow in its approach," and that "it was almost completely isolated from the basic masses of the Negro people. . . ."[8] He felt that while the class content of the Congress' program was essentially correct, it was not "carefully adapted to the feelings and moods of the Negro people."[9] Be this as it may, the probability is that Negro organizations, at first unsuspecting, soon discovered the real nature of this "front" movement; and though they agreed with its professed aims, they were unwilling to align themselves with revolutionists.

As a result of the dismal failure of the American Negro Labor Congress, strategists at the Sixth World Congress of the Communists International, meeting in Moscow in 1935, recast completely the objectives to be obtained by party workers among American Negroes. In the main the new program called for the establishment of a Negro or Black Belt Republic in the South Atlantic states commonly known as the Black Belt. Counting solely upon the predominance of Negroes in this area, the architects of the plan were either ignorant of, or disdainful of, the impossible obstacles confronting the creation of a Negro Soviet in America.[10] The grandiose scheme behind the plan is thus described by Gitlow:

> It was hoped through a Negro minorities movement in the United States to give leadership to a colored nationalist movement of world proportions in the countries of South and Central America, Africa, Asia and the Antipodes. The American Nationalist Negro movement, Moscow believed, would provide the leadership for such a world movement. Besides, the Communist Party could dominate the American Negro movement, because it was believed possible for a small handful of American Communists to organize and control the two million Negro workers in American industry. . . .[11]

In spite of the objections of American Communists, who were appalled by the stupidity of the plan, Moscow ordered that it immediately become the theme of Communist propaganda for Negroes. Indeed, it was to be inserted in the Communist Party platform for the 1936 presidential campaign. In addition to a widespread use of propaganda, the chief strategem which was to be followed in converting Negroes to the support of the Black Belt Republic idea was the capture of

Negro organizations.[12] However, taking their cue from Garvey himself, the great majority of Garveyites were anti-Communistic. Garvey early recognized the real motives of the Communists:

> The danger of Communism to the Negro, in countries where he forms the minority of the population, is seen in the selfish and vicious attempts of that party or group to use the Negro's vote and physical numbers in helping to smash and over-throw by revolution, a system that is injurious to them as the white underdogs, the success of which would put their majority group or race still in power, not only as communists but as white men. To me there is no difference between two roses looking alike, and smelling alike, even if some-one calls them by different names.[13]

Though the Communists knew the NAACP to be basically conservative, the tactics of infiltration and eventual capture were, nevertheless, to be pursued. Then, too, Dr. Du Bois was known to be at least a lukewarm disciple of Marxism. Du Bois explained his position on communism as follows:

> I was not and am not a communist. I do not believe in the dogma of inevitable revolution in order to right economic wrong. . . . On the other hand, I believed and still believe that Karl Marx was one of the greatest men of modern times and that he put his finger squarely upon our difficulties when he said that economic foundations, the way in which men earn their living, are the determining factors in the development of civilization, in literature, religion and the basic pattern of culture. And this conviction I had to express or spiritually die.[14]

However, the NAACP was in essence a product of the promise of American democracy, its ideological and historical antecedents going back to the abolition movement. At its founding in 1909, it set for itself the achievement for American Negroes of those rights and responsibilities generally available to other citizens of the United States. Nor had the NAACP ever departed from the methods originally embraced: gradualism rather than revolution, nonviolence rather than force, legalism rather than direct action. The organization never considered a fundamental reorganization of American society along any lines except in the matter of the Negro's place within that society. In holding fast to this position, the leadership of the NAACP was sustained by what proved to be a rather accurate reading of the mind of the American Negro.

By 1935 even the most rabid Communists had to admit that their Black Belt Republic program for Negroes was unsound. Though they had been able to establish cells in the UNIA, the Communists were never able to capture its leadership. After the demise of Garvey the UNIA no longer wielded any influence among Negroes. It is also certain that the left-wingers never gained a foothold within the NAACP. The one brief period of notoriety for the Black Belt movement came as a result of the celebrated *Herndon* v. *Lowry* case.[15] Angelo Herndon, a Negro Communist, had been convicted and sentenced by the state of Georgia under a Civil War statute for inciting a riot. The specific charge was that Herndon distributed a book which urged the establishment of a Black Belt Republic in the South. The book "also advocated strikes, boycotts, and revolutionary struggle for power against the white bourgeoisie."[16] Herndon's conviction was, of course, the signal for a renewed espousal of the Black Belt Republic among Negroes. It seems, however, that black people were more interested in Herndon's civil rights than in the general program of the American Communist Party. Thus, after the reversal of Herndon's conviction by the United States Supreme Court, the Black Belt Republic vanished into the realm of forgotten ideas.

By 1930 the American Communist Party saw the complete frustration of over a decade of effort to establish itself in the leadership of the Negro race. Gitlow states:

> Our Negro program was originally built around the demand that the Negro people in the United States be accorded full racial, social and political equality. Yet in spite of our efforts and the large sums of money spent on that sort of propaganda, we made very little headway among the Negro masses. The Negroes in the United States refused to flock into the Communist Party and gave little credence to our promises.[17]

Though this is an accurate appraisal of the effect of Communist propaganda among Negroes, Gitlow neglects to credit the American Negro with sufficient intelligence to discern that the Communist Party was not really concerned about the true interest of the Negro. The party remained bankrupt on ideas for propaganda among Negroes until the advent of the *Scottsboro* case and the great depression.

2. THE JOBS-FOR-NEGROES CAMPAIGN

In addition to its disastrous effect on the economic status of the Negro, the depression of the 1930's forced Negroes to reexamine seriously their objectives in the American social order. Until 1929 the demand for civil and political rights nursed by Negro protest groups had become so loud that no other protest could be heard. With the Wall Street crash tilting American class levels, a large portion of bourgeois Negroes dropped to a submarginal status. Because this

Negro bourgeois class constituted the backbone of Negro protest groups, there was a drastic reshuffling of the objectives of Negro protest organizations. The demands for civil and political equality definitely could not be discarded. But because starvation is such a powerful catalyst to social action, Negroes pushed their historic demands into the background and raised a claim which hitherto had been but faintly heard — the demand for economic fair play for the race.[18]

The fight for political and civil rights had long been hampered, ironically enough, by the lack of these very rights themselves. In fighting for economic fair play, however, Negroes were able to choose a weapon to which they had comparatively unrestricted access — the boycott. The Negro version of the boycott meant that not a Negro dollar was to go to any producer or retailer of goods or services who did not pursue what the local Negro community considered to be a fair policy with respect to the employment of Negroes. The most familiar slogan in the race soon became: "Negroes! Don't buy where you can't work."

The first situs of the Jobs-for-Negroes campaign was the famous South Side of Chicago. In this heavily populated, depression-ridden area, Negro citizens responded to the pleas of a weekly newspaper, the *Whip*, and got the first Negro job drive under way.[19] In spite of the fact that the campaign was spearheaded by a church group, instances of violence multiplied as the drive progressed. Pickets began using force to prevent Negroes from entering outlawed establishments. The most spectacular results were not achieved, however, until James L. Kelly, a Negro labor agitator, took charge. Skilled in the techniques of mass picketing, Kelly mobilized several hundred Negroes and marched them from store to store in Chicago's Negro ghetto. His first results came with chain and department stores. Within a year, beer, bread, whiskey, and milk companies succumbed. Naturally, the success of the Chicago drive soon captured the attention of Negroes in other areas.

In December, 1933, a pamphlet entitled "The X-Ray Picture of Detroit" was circulated among the motor city's Negroes. This tract, written by a Negro, Snow Grigsby, was an attack on the hiring policy of the city of Detroit with regard to Negroes. Aroused by Grigsby's charges, the blacks held mass meetings and eventually organized the Detroit Civil Rights Committee. This committee directed a Jobs-for-Negroes campaign in the city which resulted in placement of additional Negroes in municipal departments as well as in such utilities as the Detroit Edison Company and the Michigan Bell Telephone Company.[20] The new drive began to pick up momentum rapidly throughout the nation. In every case the objective and strategy were the same. In Cleveland, Ohio, in 1933 Negroes organized the Future Outlook League and established branches throughout the state. The Negro Victory Committee appeared in Los Angeles and fought for both Negroes and Mexicans. In Baltimore, Maryland, a Negro clair-voyant abandoned his avocation to direct a successful fight against hiring practices of that city's utility companies.

The new campaign did not even spare the nation's capital. In 1933 several Negro youths watched the white owner of a hamburger grill in the Negro district dismiss his black employees and replace them with whites. The youths immediately threw a picket line in front of the establishment. When business fell off rapidly, the grill rehired the Negroes. Because of this modest but surprising success, Negroes in Washington, D. C., organized the New Negro Alliance to conduct a full-scale Jobs-for-Negroes campaign. Unlike the drives in other cities, the New Negro Alliance operated smoothly and without violence. Pickets for the larger stores in the more densely populated areas of the Negro district came from the legal, medical, and teaching profes-sions.[21] Indeed, Negro observers commented that the picket lines re-sembled a Negro fashion parade. In addition, the Alliance had the as-sistance and blessing of several members of Howard University's faculty. Generally, the movement was as successful in Washington, D. C., as it was in other cities. But the activity of the Alliance came to an abrupt end in 1934 when injunctions were obtained by store owners restraining the Alliance from picketing and door-to-door campaigning. The Alliance conducted a four-year legal fight which ended success-fully when the United States Supreme Court in 1938 ruled against the injunction.[22]

In Harlem, the great black ghetto of New York City, the Negro's drive for jobs reached the climax of noise, blood, and success. Harlem was pivotal in Negro America; hence, it was pivotal in this campaign. From 1910 to 1930 Harlem, the largest Negro community in the Western Hemisphere, had increased in population over 800 percent. Since this rise in numbers had occurred in so short a span of time, the Negro in this community had had virtually no time to solidify him-self economically. Out of ten thousand business enterprises in Harlem, Negroes controlled about nineteen hundred.[23]

When the great depression struck the community, a large number of

Negro laborers and porters were dismissed from their jobs. Female domestics, in a frantic and pitiful competition for work in the Bronx, drove their hourly wage down to as low as ten cents per hour.[24] The net result of this situation, of course, was a spiraling increase in petty crimes and prostitution. The rate of juvenile delinquency in the community showed the effect of the depression on Negro children. Indeed, in the early nineteen thirties, it was common knowledge that the majority of Harlem's seventy-five thousand children were suffering from malnutrition. Negroes, though constituting only 5 percent of the city's population, received 23 percent of the city's relief grants.

In the midst of this situation, a veteran of Chicago's Jobs-for-Negroes drive arrived in Harlem to begin a new campaign. This towering black Negro had the pretentious name of Sufi Abdul Hamid. (His given name was Eugene Brown.) Night after night this striking man, in gaudy dress, castigated his Negro listeners on the street corners of Harlem for patronizing the white Jewish merchants in the community who did not employ an appreciable number of Negroes, especially white-collar workers. In a short time, Sufi was joined by a handful of Garvey's disciples. These professional soapbox agitators found a receptive audience on the street corners of the ghetto.[25] Their theme had been the enslavement and exploitation of the black race by white imperialists in Africa. Under Sufi they found it relatively simple to relate the Negro's misery in Harlem to the alleged world suppression of the sons of Ham.

By the fall of 1933 virtually every important street corner in the community had its agitator and its audience. In every case the cry was "More jobs for Negroes." With the harangues becoming increasingly repetitious and boring, the agitators began to borrow from the anti-Semitic propaganda of the German Nazis.[26] Unfortunately, Harlem in 1933 was fertile ground for at least a watered-down version of this propaganda. Jews had long been the main employers of Negro menials and domestic workers in the city. In some cases, undoubtedly, these workers had been paid substandard wages. Also, many of the shopkeepers in Harlem were Jewish, and there was evidence to prove that some of these were charging all that the traffic would bear.[27] While the shabby treatment of Negroes by some Jewish employers and merchants was the exception rather than the rule, Sufi and his followers pounded home to Negro audiences day after day in true Nazi style that the Jews were parasites living off the community and that they should either be controlled or run out of Harlem.

Making the most of the fact that there were but few Negroes employed in Harlem's business district, the agitators were able to attract a large following from among all classes of people. Early in 1934 Sufi and his associates organized the Negro Industrial and Clerical Alliance to conduct systematic picketing of white-owned shops. Roi Ottley thus describes their tactics:

> They swept through the community and put the heat under grocers, druggists, butchers, and owners of other small establishments, bludgeoning them into signing up with the Sufi organization — which, in fact, meant paying tribute for "protection" against violence. The "take" was several hundred dollars a week.[28]

In the latter part of 1934 the Jobs-for-Negroes drive began to encounter difficulties all over the country. White merchants in several Northern communities obtained temporary and permanent court injunctions restraining Negro organizations from picketing their establishments. Generally, the courts acted on the basis of rulings that the Negro organizations involved were not labor unions and, therefore, could not claim the same immunity from injunctions granted to labor unions by the Norris-LaGuardia Act.

Spurred by this turn of events, the white merchants of Harlem began to defend their own interests. The vulnerable spot in the jobs campaign of Harlem's Negroes was its use of anti-Semitic propaganda. Thus, in September, 1934, several Jewish newspapers joined in an attack on Sufi, the leader of the movement. Charges that Harlem was under the spell of a black Hitler began to appear. The Negro Industrial and Clerical Alliance was labeled a Nazi-front movement among Negroes. In fact, eyewitnesses were reported as having seen Sufi in direct contact with members of the Nazi Bund of New York. One of these eyewitnesses was Claude McKay, who states the following:

> It was only after the wide publicity given him as a "Harlem Hitler" that the Sufi had his first contact with American Nazis. It happened that I was at his office one day trying to get some facts for an article when two Germans or German-Americans called on him. They invited him to a meeting in Yorkville. Later he told me that he had gone with his chief aide. . . . "I was curious," he said, "to find out what the pure blond Nordicans could have to offer to the pure black Africans when their Hitler says we are no better than monkeys. But I couldn't imagine cooperating with the Nazis any more than with the Ku Klux Klan."[29]

Finally in October, 1934, several hundred merchants succeeded in bringing Sufi before a magistrate's court on a charge of disorderly conduct which specified that his organization was conducting a race war against the Jews. Sufi was acquitted, but the unfavorable publicity given the Negro Industrial and Clerical Alliance brought an end to its activities. After 1934 the Jobs-for-Negroes campaign was directed by a group of Negro leaders known as the Citizens' League for Fair Play. Under this group the drive was peacefully and more intelligently conducted and achieved far more success than it did under Sufi.

The winter of 1934-1935 was a particularly bleak one in Harlem. Unemployment and its fellow travelers, starvation, prostitution, and crime, reached an all-time high in the community. The thousands of idle Negroes lolling on street corners furnished ready audiences for the army of agitators who at this time literally were speaking in shifts. There could be little doubt in the minds of intelligent listeners that these men wanted to convert the area into a tinderbox. The explosion which all Harlem expected and for which city officials should have been prepared, but curiously were not, occurred on March 19, 1935.[30] As with most such occurrences, the incident which set off the spark was ridiculously unimportant. A young Puerto Rican boy was seized in a five-and-ten-cent store in the area for stealing a pocketknife. Store detectives hustled him to the basement, presumably, to punish him. With already raw-edged emotions, Negro patrons rushed from the store and magnified the incident to outsiders. Within one hour, rumors were flying through the community to the general effect that a Negro lad had been murdered in 125th Street (the shopping thoroughfare) for a crime he did not commit. Groups of Negroes began gathering in front of white shops everywhere in Harlem hurling invectives and shouting threats but doing little damage.

Late that afternoon, a Communist-front group of Harlem known as the Young Liberators circulated the following pamphlet:

CHILD BRUTALLY BEATEN
WOMAN ATTACKED BY BOSS AND COPS
CHILD NEAR DEATH

One hour ago a 12 year old Negro boy was
brutally beaten by the management of
Kress' Five and Ten Cent Store.
    The boy is near death, mercilessly
beaten, because they thought he had stolen a
five cents knife. A Negro woman who sprang
to the defense of the boy had her arm broken
by the thug and was then arrested.

WORKERS! NEGRO AND WHITE
Protest against this Lynch Attack of
Innocent Negro People

Demand Release of Boy and Woman
Demand immediate arrest of the management
responsible for the Lynch attack.

Don't Buy At Kress
Stop Police Brutality In Negro Harlem
JOIN THE PICKET LINE [31]

The regular Communist Party organization in Harlem printed and distributed a similar leaflet at about the same time.

The very fact that these leaflets did not appear on the streets until several hours had passed made it difficult to substantiate the hysterical charges that the riot was Communist instigated.

Repercussions of the Harlem riot were felt throughout the United States. To Negroes the disorders became known as the "black Ides of March."[32] In Northern cities, especially, increased concern was manifested for the desperate plight of Negro people. Literally dozens of committees were created to study the "Negro Problem." The net result of all this was an increase of home relief and work assistance for the race. In addition white merchants with shops in Negro communities, now more fearful than ever of race riots, acceded to the demands of local Jobs-for-Negroes drives and hired Negro personnel.

After 1936 little was heard of the Jobs-for-Negroes campaigns. With their passing went the most violent manifestations of Negro chauvinism since the demise of the Garvey organization. Negro racketeers garbed themselves in the cloaks of community or race leaders, skillfully organizing and directing these drives for their own pecuniary gains. They worked with members of the Negro lunatic fringe, professional agitators, and, in some cases, criminals. The noise they made attracted the Negro public. By magnifying their gains with white merchants, these self-styled leaders were able to convince a large section of the depression-stricken Negro public that here was a tried and tested panacea for its ills. But just a casual evaluation of these campaigns reveals that the results were trifling. Even with maximum cooperation from white merchants, which usually meant the hiring of Negroes on a "fifty-fifty" basis, in few communities could black workers be employed in sufficient numbers to affect materially the level of black unemployment. Important also was the fact that the bulk of Negro purchasing power went to the lower-priced shops in white business districts, which Negroes did not picket. When the Negro communities began to realize that the Jobs-for-Negroes campaign left their larger problems still unsolved, they turned to sounder programs.

3. NEW LEADERSHIP AND THE NATIONAL NEGRO CONGRESS

Throughout its duration the Jobs-for-Negroes movement remained uncoordinated on a national scale. One of the main reasons for this was that for the first time since Reconstruction the race was without a powerful, nationally recognized leader. During the first years of the depression, the change in the direction of the Negro protest cut the ground from under old-line black leaders, and no person had risen who could gather the reins in his hands. Of the several aspirants to the race's leadership, the most outstanding were A. Philip Randolph and Walter White.

Randolph was born in Crescent City, Florida, in 1889. In his youth he migrated to New York City and worked his way through the College of the City of New York. In spite of the agitation during World War I against radicalism, Randolph became a confirmed Socialist. He and a friend, Chandler Owen, founded and edited the only Negro Socialist periodical in America, the *Messenger*. This publication later became well known among Negroes not because of its uncompromising hatred of capitalism, but rather because of its leadership in the attack on Marcus Garvey. This was Randolph's first important mistake. His incessant and vitriolic campaign against Garvey degenerated into a controversy between West Indian and American Negroes. A West Indian Negro on the *Messenger's* staff resented Randolph's views and resigned.[33] By 1925 the *Messenger* had lost most of its interest to Negro readers. In the same year, however, Randolph received an opportunity to recover lost ground. He was chosen general organizer of the newly formed Brotherhood of Sleeping Car Porters. The *Messenger* was quickly purged of its radicalism and converted into the first Negro trade union journal. During the next twelve years Randolph gained the steady support of the Negro race for his uncompromising fight for recognition of the porters' union by the Pullman Company.

Unlike Randolph, who managed to achieve some renown among the Negro masses, Walter White had been known mainly among the rank and file of the middle-class Negroes. White was a handsome, blue-eyed mulatto, who had never had any difficulty in passing for a white person. After graduating from Atlanta University, White studied in France. In 1915 he was made Assistant Secretary of the NAACP, and in 1932 he took over the post of Executive Secretary.[35] White was probably the nation's most outstanding authority on lynching. Usually mistaken for a Caucasian, he made personal on-the-spot investigations of nearly fifty lynchings. His experiences have been recounted in his book *Rope and Faggot, a Biography of Judge Lynch*.[36]

Intelligence, a driving energy, and a proven race loyalty combined to make White one of the most valuable leaders of the race. Nevertheless, his name was known only to a fraction of the Negro masses. The main reason for this, of course, was White's connection with the NAACP. This organization remained wedded to what was increasingly being viewed as a narrow and legalistic approach to the American race question. However, in its chosen field the NAACP rendered invaluable service to the Negro. After 1920 the organization continued its fight against lynching. Also, it waged an almost single-handed battle against white primary laws and the poll tax. Under the Roosevelt administration, the Association sponsored two anti-lynching bills, both of which were "talked to death" in the United States Senate. But because of the unfortunate, yet persistent, stigmas of color-consciousness and upper-class sympathies, the NAACP was seldom able to arouse more than the passive interest of the black masses in any of its fights.

Randolph, White, and other less-known Negro figures were all in more or less the same position. They had achieved far greater renown among white and Negro liberals than they had among the Negro rank and file. Most of them had opposed the Garvey movement and none had taken part in the Jobs-for-Negroes campaigns. Adam Clayton Powell, himself an aspiring young leader, thus commented:

> Paradoxically, the national headquarters of every [Negro] national organization were located in New York City. These Negro leaders of world headline fame could walk on a hot crowded Saturday night from one end of Lenox Avenue to the other and not five people would know them.[37]

If the majority of old-line Negro leaders were blind to the shift in objectives of the Negro protest (a shift from political and social equality to economic security), there was a resourceful and indefatigable group working within the race which was quick to sense the change. This group had suffered one frustration after another in their efforts to organize the enigmatic Negro. In spite of his poverty the Negro had steadfastly insisted upon giving his political and civil rights a priority over his economic needs. When the depression reversed this order, the Communists seized the opportunity to try to sell the Negro a watered-down Americanized version of the class-struggle doctrine. In every important Negro community in the country, squads of Marxists, infiltrated the ranks of Negro unemployed. The Negro was told that lynching, segregation, and discrimination, evil enough in themselves, were merely the concomitants of the far greater evil of wage slavery, of which the Negro was always the chief victim.

The Communists further insisted that to rely solely upon political and civil rights as a solution for all of the ills of the race was a grievous mistake. Communists maintained that the depression was not merely part of an ordinary business cycle but, rather, the first stage of the imminent collapse of capitalism. Thus, the Negro should join forces with white workers who were victims also and prepare for the day when the proletariat would come into power. On these grounds the Communists opposed, and in some cases even attempted to sabotage, the Jobs-for-Negroes campaign. The party looked upon the movement as the attempt of one group of workers to take the jobs of another. The Communists urged Negroes to join the workers alliance instead and fight for the creation of more jobs on work relief.

The new drive among Negroes showed unmistakably that the party had learned from its past errors. No one tactic was relied upon to the exclusion of all others. Workers sent among Negroes were equipped with some knowledge of the race's history, psychology, music, folklore, and peculiar customs. According to Gitlow, who probably had a hand in evolving the new strategy for corralling Negro members, Communist Party members were urged to make every effort to establish personal as well as social relations with them. Negroes were brought into the party, not on the basis of their Communist leanings but by the promise that in the Communist Party they could enjoy a sociable evening together with whites on a basis of equality. Negroes who had recently joined the party were pushed into places of leadership simply because they were Negroes. They enjoyed preferred treatment in the party. This was done not out of sympathy or consideration for the Negro masses but for purely political reasons.

In the years immediately following 1932, it became commonplace for Negroes attending social, civic, political, and even religious functions to glance around and spot a smiling white face or an unfamiliar Negro apparently interested in the evening's proceedings. This was the Communist. How did he get there? He either walked in uninvited or inveigled an invitation from a friendly and/or unsuspecting member of the group in question. The Communists made it a point to send attractive white female members of the Communist Party to social functions attended or sponsored by young Negro males. Of course, the open fraternization between white girls and Negro men did not go unnoticed by white non-Communist males, but an observer for the *Commonweal* rationalized it this way:

> Communism has painted many a black man red. The annual May-day demonstrations in which plump Jewesses parade arm in arm with hollow-cheeked Negroes; the inter-racial balls during which high-heeled low-brows mix freely with low-heeled high-brows . . . are but occasional belchings of a bilious racial stomach hungering for justice.[38]

Indeed, the number of marriages between white female Communist Party members and Negroes at one time occurred at such a brisk pace that Negro women took alarm. Concerning this situation, McKay tells the following story:

> I remember visiting in 1938 the pioneer Negro member of the Party, Grace Campbell, and finding a group of women assembled at her hotel. They had come together to discuss the subject of all the Negro party leaders' being married to white women. They were a bitter lot. They argued that it was an insult to Negro womanhood that their radical leaders should take white wives, especially as the Negro woman is nationally regarded as being on a lower social and moral level than the white woman. They felt that the Negro Communist leaders were supporting the general national attitude by marrying white wives.[39]

Negro leaders, who had hitherto regarded the black masses as being immune to Red propaganda, began to warn the public about Communist activity within the race.[40] The Marxists seemed to be everywhere. At a Communist Party convention held in Chicago in 1932, five thousand of the fourteen thousand persons in attendance were Negroes.[41] When two Negroes were killed in an eviction riot in Chicago's South Side, the Communists organized what was probably the most unusual funeral procession in the city's history. For fully three-quarters of an hour several thousand Negroes and whites marched up the streets of the Black Belt carrying Communist banners and placards and singing the songs of the Red International in the style of Negro spirituals.[42] It was difficult to tell whether the Communist gains were superficial or otherwise, but the *Commonweal* warned:

> On the surface it would seem that Russian red and American black is a coming color scheme. Why not? The Negro has a grievance. Christians refuse to heed it. Communism listens sympathetically. And when men are hungry and their children are fainting for bread, a promise seems better than a threat. Most of us who are not ourselves nursing the ills of poverty have a feeling of aloofness from the misery of our colored brother.[43]

For the Communists no event was of greater propaganda value among Negroes than the *Scottsboro* case. From the very outset the party was determined to associate itself, and itself alone, with the struggle to free the Negro lads sentenced to die for the rape of two white girls on a freight train on the outskirts of Scottsboro, Alabama. When news of the case broke, innumerable organizations and groups throughout the country offered aid. As the leading Negro protest group, the NAACP proceeded to coordinate the activities of all parties interested in the case. This included the Communist International Labor Defense.[44] The NAACP quickly obtained the services of Clarence Darrow and Arthur Garfield Hayes. Angered by the attempt of Communist lawyers to make the case their own, Hayes and Darrow proposed that all lawyers contributing to the defense of the boys sign the following statement:

> We represent the defendants. We represent no organization. The lives of 8 boys are at stake. It is unimportant who enlisted our interest. We will engage in no controversy between groups. We have agreed to work together to try to save these boys and our responsibility is to them and to them only.[45]

Operating under party orders, the Communist lawyers refused to sign the pledge. This was an unmistakable indication of Communist intentions. As a result, Hayes, Darrow, the NAACP, and virtually all non-Communist groups interested in the case withdrew. They were willing to work with the Communists, but not under them.[46]

The International Labor Defense was not new to Negroes. Since its inception in 1925 as the legal branch of the American Communist Party, it had been a frequent participant in cases involving the Negro. It fought peonage, police brutality, residential segregation, and Jim-Crowism whenever an opportunity appeared for it to do so. To the International Labor Defense, therefore, the *Scottsboro* case was a godsend. Elaborate machinery was set in motion to milk the case of its last drop of propaganda value. Mass meetings and mock Scottsboro trials were held anywhere audiences could be assembled. Every means of communication was utilized to pour protests into Scottsboro, Alabama.[47] As the Communist campaign reached high gear, no city in the world remained ignorant of the fate of the unfortunate black boys. When the United States Supreme Court reversed the first of the convictions in 1932,[48] the Communists, of course, were lavish with praise for the indomitable spirit and brilliance of their legal warriors. One wonders to what extent the reversal was motivated by the obvious and flagrant injustice of the original convictions.

The Communists did gain immense prestige among Negroes as a result of their association with the *Scottsboro* case. The unsophisticated

Negro masses might be pardoned for having gone overboard in hailing the "new defenders" of the race. But many Negro leaders and intellectuals could also be heard. The Chicago *Defender*, one of the country's leading Negro weeklies, drew the attention of its readers with the headline "WHY WE CAN'T HATE REDS." Continuing, it said:

> We may not agree with the entire program of the Communist Party, but there is one item with which we do agree whole-heartedly and that is the zealousness with which it guards the right of the [Negro] Race.[49]

In the opinion of some observers Marxism was a fad, a temporary affliction besetting jaded Negro intellectuals. To some extent, this diagnosis may have been correct. But one should not underestimate the perennial causes of radicalism among any people. Poverty-stricken and frustrated, Negro intellectuals and workers alike were grasping at a promise — a Red promise, but still a promise. The following statements are the results of a symposium conducted by the NAACP in 1932 on the subject, "Communism and the Negro."

> The Communists are going our way, for which Allah be praised. Carl Murphy, *The Afro-American,* Maryland.

> . . . barriers to the more abundant growth of the Negro must be removed, but despite the theories behind Communism, we do not think it offers the way out for the Negro which shall be most beneficial and lasting in the long run. P. B. Young, Norfolk *Journal and Guide,* Virginia.

> Since America's twelve million Negro population is so largely identified with the working class, the wonder is not that the Negro is beginning, at least, to think along Communistic lines, but that he did not embrace that doctrine en-masse long ago. William M. Kelley, *Amsterdam News,* New York.

> I have known personally of some racial brethren going Red purely because of the chance to mingle freely with white women in the movement. Then they need no longer ogle secretly or with their personal safety threatened. . . . If enough of us would go Red, Okeh; when we get that way in little bunches it breathes nothing but new trouble for an already over-burdened race. Frank M. Davis, *The Atlanta World,* Georgia.[50]

The consideration shown the Negro by the federal government during the early days of the New Deal was undoubtedly the most effective antidote for the spread of communism among the Negro masses. Had President Roosevelt followed the practice of his predecessors of dispensing largess to just a few so-called Negro leaders while ignoring the black masses, the Communists would have been handed a tailor-made propaganda line for use among Negroes. Much valuable advice on the conditions and needs of Negroes throughout the country was provided the President by Mrs. Roosevelt and Henry Wallace. Indeed,

Mrs. Roosevelt was seen so often in Negro ghettos and took such an interest in Negro problems that she became known in the race as the "Great White Mother."

At the very beginning of the New Deal, the Roosevelt administration encouraged Negro organizations to form a top group among themselves which could be called upon by federal officials for expert advice on Negro affairs. Twenty-two Negro organizations responded by setting up among themselves a body which took the name of the Joint Committee on National Recovery.[51] In August, 1932, the committee was joined by the NAACP, which thereafter provided the committee's major financial support.[52] During the first three years of its existence the Joint Committee did yeoman work for Negroes with the New Deal. Under the chairmanship of George Haynes and with John P. Davis as executive secretary, it helped to obtain fairer treatment for Negro farmers in the administration of New Deal agricultural programs. The best work rendered by the committee, however, was its exposure of the anti-Negro practices of Southern employers with respect to the codes of the National Recovery Act. One of the first effects of these codes in the South had been the displacement of Negro workers. Southern employers felt that if they had to pay minimum wages of twelve to fourteen dollars a week, they would not pay them to Negroes.

In May, 1935, the Joint Committee, in cooperation with the Division of Social Sciences of Howard University, sponsored a meeting at Howard to discuss the new problems of the Negro arising out of the depression and to formulate some general program of action. At this meeting the National Negro Congress was conceived.[53] The idea of a super-Negro-protest organization had long been current among Negro leaders, and it is very probable that more than one member of the group thought in the same vein. Among those present at the meeting were Dr. Ralph Bunche, of Howard University, and John P. Davis, of the Joint Committee. Dr. Bunche remembers that the idea for such a congress grew out of a conversation at the meeting, between himself and John P. Davis.[54] After the meeting was over, Dr. Bunche invited several of the participants to his residence to discuss the project. At this second meeting emphasis was placed upon the fact "that the awakening of a response from the Negro masses had not been accomplished in the field of economic and social betterment for any large part of the Negro population."[55] All agreed that concerted and well-directed action by a congress of Negro and white organizations would be the remedy.

Sometime later, delegated persons of the group drew up a "call" on which were listed the aims of the proposed congress and the date for a first meeting. The call was sent to Negro and white organizations of every description. Since interest in the Negro problem, rather than political or economic views, was alleged to be the sole criterion for invitation to the initial meeting of the congress, the fact that bids fell into the hands of the brethren of the Communist Party was not surprising. Under these circumstances, therefore, the Marxists were given the first real opportunity to share in the recognized leadership of the Negro race.

The National Negro Congress was slated to open on February 14, 1936, at the Eighth Regiment Armory in Chicago. The sponsors had planned four general sessions. The first session was not held, because Mayor Edward J. Kelly did not appear to give official sanction and welcome to the group. Another kind of welcome was given the Congress by the "red squad" of the Chicago Police Department. They "threatened to close the Congress almost before it opened on the grounds that it was a 'radical organization meeting for the purpose of spreading a subversive doctrine.' "[56] On February 17 the first meeting of the Congress finally got underway with Charles Burton, the opening speaker, reminding the Communists present that the distribution of objectionable literature inside the armory was prohibited.

The geographic distribution of the delegates showed that the group was drawn largely from Northern urban organizations. Present were 817 delegates representing 585 organizations from twenty-eight different states. From Illinois, Indiana, New York, Michigan, Ohio, Pennsylvania, and Wisconsin came 743 delegates. Only fifty-five delegates hailed from the South. Although the delegates representing civic, religious, and educational organizations were in the majority, their lack of sharply defined social and economic views made them little more than spectators at the Congress. From the outset, the actions of the Congress were in the hands of the planning committee, which, in turn, was dominated by delegates from Northern protest and labor organizations whose obvious intention was to make the National Negro Congress a militant and radical movement. Dr. Kelly Miller, who attended the meetings, wrote the following:

> The spirit of radicalism predominated throughout the proceedings. The reds, the Socialists and Communists, were everywhere in ascendency, either in number or indomitable purpose, or in both. The conservative delegates who constituted a considerable proportion of the conference, were either out-numbered or out-maneuvered.[57]

The program adopted was essentially the same as that outlined in the call which brought the body into being. A. Philip Randolph won easily over other candidates for the presidency of the Congress. John P. Davis was elected executive secretary. The structure of the permanent organization resembled a pyramid. At the base were local councils to be established wherever possible in the nation. The locals were to be grouped within districts, fifteen in number, each of which was to be governed by a vice-president and a District Council. Top direction was placed in the hands of the president, secretary, treasurer, and the National Executive Council, which numbered seventy-five members.[58]

For financial support the National Negro Congress decided to depend upon contributions solicited by the locals rather than upon regular dues or assessments. However, each local was required to pay an annual fee of two dollars, half of which was to be retained by the local itself, and the other half was to go to the national organization. The enthusiasm which characterized this first meeting was carried by the delegates back to their respective communities. Within a few months almost thirty local councils were formed in the country. Before the year was out, however, the ardor of the organization's promoters was dampened by the apathy of the Negro masses. In addition, the Congress had to bear the constant and scathing denunciation of Negro clergymen who feared that the Congress would become a Communist-front organization.[59]

The second annual meeting of the National Negro Congress was held in Philadelphia in 1937, and by contrast to the 1936 affair it was dull indeed. The 1,149 delegates who attended listened to speeches and adopted resolutions which, in the main, followed the pattern of those of the previous Congress. The really significant activity of this meeting was on a *sub rosa* level. For while unsophisticated Negro delegates from the hinterland contented themselves with listening to resolutions and speeches on the "new-world-a-comin'," delegates from the CIO unions and the Communist Party groups fought for control of the organization. Indicative of growing Communist influence in the Congress was the fact that two of the chief speakers at the meetings were James W. Ford, of the Communist Party, and Ernest Rathway, editor of the *Daily Worker*. While the Congress still bulked large to some Negroes, those who scanned carefully the organization's financial statement for 1936 and 1937 undoubtedly perceived its limited possibilities.

Financial Report for 1936-1937[60]

Contributions

Miscellaneous contributions	$4,251.62
Quota (from locals)	224.69
Loans	779.26
Affiliation fees	98.25
Literature and supplies	154.54
General	19.50
Total Contributions	$5,527.86

Disbursements

Salaries	$1,909.64
Miscellaneous expenses (light, rent, telephone)	1,345.98
Travel	663.65
Payment on loans	311.70
General	261.04
Literature and supplies	424.08
Postage	402.77
Total Disbursements	$5,318.86
On hand as of September 1, 1937	$ 209.00

In 1936 the National Negro Congress decided to set its youth group apart from the parent organization. In 1937 the youth group achieved full autonomy. It took the name of the Southern Negro Youth Congress and operated from Richmond, Virginia, as a federation of Southern youth organizations.[61] Following the example of the larger group, the new organization held annual meetings. Local councils were set up to conduct youth forums, programs on crime reduction, health projects, and vocational guidance programs. Because of the special problem which faced the Southern Negro, the Youth Congress decided to take no militant stand on the question of Negro rights in the South.

Membership for the Youth Congress was recruited mainly from the rank and file of the poorer Southern Negroes. To some extent this was policy, since it was the purpose of the organization to build a mass basis. On the other hand, upper-class Negroes perceived that the Youth Congress, because of the infiltration of Communists in the local councils, was becoming a front group and refused to let their young ones join.[62] In 1940 Dr. Bunche in an investigation of the Youth Congress found, among other things, that the Negro boys and girls who belonged to it were "terribly confused and often frustrated," and that the Congress was taking "its cue, in the major essentials, from the 'line' laid down by the American Communist Party."[63]

There were no meetings of the National Negro Congress in 1939.

The reasons for these omissions have never been made quite clear. But if, as some observers have speculated, the ruling clique of the Congress was attempting to evade capture by the Marxists, it was simply postponing its doom. For when the chairman's gavel opened the third meeting of the Congress in 1940 in the nation's capital, the setting had been rigged for the hoisting of the Red Flag. Although it was impossible to ascertain the number of Communists or Communist sympathizers present, whatever they lacked in numbers, they soon made up in activity on the convention floor.

The keynote of the sessions was sounded by John L. Lewis. As always, Lewis was impressive as well as exciting. The large audience included officials of the federal government and diplomats of foreign powers. In his thundering voice Lewis demanded that the United States stay out of the war in Europe. Since he was aware that his hearers were predominantly Negroes, he drove home the point that America's first obligation was the building up of democracy at home, especially for such downtrodden groups as the blacks.[64]

Just prior to Lewis's speech the National Negro Congress had adopted a constitution that scrapped the nonpartisan pledge which it had endorsed in 1936 and 1937. This action was taken despite the uncompromising objections of A. Philip Randolph and his followers. Randolph had seen the handwriting on the wall. On the second day of the Congress, when he was scheduled to speak, Randolph resolved to set things straight. With word going around that fireworks were expected, over seventeen hundred people jammed the hall to hear the Pullman porters' chief. Everyone listened attentively until Randolph asserted that the Soviet Union was pursuing a policy of power politics and that what was in the interests of the Russian state was not necessarily in the interest of world peace and democracy. Then a large section of delegates, mainly white, arose noisily and left the audience.[65]

Randolph continued his attack. He emphasized that the Communists took their orders from Moscow and, hence, could never be relied upon to pursue a constructive policy on the Negro questions. He wanted a leadership

> free from intimidation, manipulation or subordination, with a character that is beyond the reach and above the power of the dollar . . . a leadership which is uncontrolled and responsible to no one but the Negro.[66]

By the conclusion of the speech, the original audience of seventeen hundred had dwindled to less than five hundred. Those who remained were mostly Randolph's friends and followers.

As the Congress neared its close, the activity of the Communists was obvious to all except the rank-and-file Negroes. Dr. Bunche, an observer at the meetings, described this latter group as being oblivious to everything except the "perfervid speeches . . . demanding anti-lynching legislation, the franchise and full democracy for the Negro."[67] To those who were familiar with Communist tactics, it became plain that here was no simple operation of boring from within or infiltration. The Communists were gambling for big stakes. At no time since they had begun their work among American Negroes did they ever have an opportunity such as they had now. The Congress was a virtual "emporium" of Negro organizations, and it was logical to assume that the capture of the leadership of the National Negro Congress meant the capture of the leadership of the Negro race.

At the last meeting Randolph, weary and defeated, laid down the gavel and arose to address a watchful audience. As he spoke, his successor moved down the aisle to a front row seat. This was Max Yergan, then a virtually unknown employee of the Young Men's Christian Association. Since this was his resignation speech, Randolph's remarks were brief but candid. He warned the delegates against any alliance with other political organizations because: "I believe that the Congress should be dependent on resources supplied by the Negro alone, . . . for where you get your money you also get your ideas and control."[68] As Randolph concluded, Yergan was nominated and elected president by acclamation.

At the close of this last meeting of the 1940 Congress, there could be little doubt that the Communists had obtained their objective. Yet the fruit for which they had labored so skillfully and successfully soon turned to ashes in their mouths. The Negro public had not been very enthusiastic over the Congress in 1936. But even this ardor cooled perceptibly after the dull and uneventful meeting of 1937. Generally, Negro and white publications were not unaware of the Marxist Trojan horse within the Congress. They had repeatedly warned Negro organizations to clamp an iron control on the Congress or lose it entirely. When it became obvious to all in 1940 that the Communists had really captured the Congress, Negro organizations by the score began to drop their affiliations; and after this time the National Negro Congress lost its importance to the Communists as well.

There can be little doubt that the greatest opportunities for Communist success among Negroes were presented in the decade ending in 1940, and the Communists made the most of them. Indeed, the

Negro was waylaid and attacked by every strategem known to modern propaganda warfare. The prizes were allegiance and leadership of the Negro race in America. The failure of the Communist bid should be evident to anyone who gives the matter a thought. What is not so clear, however, is why the Communists failed. Most people make the mistake of assuming that poverty-stricken, illiterate, and socially depressed groups are especially susceptible to radical propaganda. Certainly the existence of these conditions among a group will result in revolutionists being given an audience. Some fraternization with them will occur; opportunists and the extremely disgruntled will join them. But to win a people from one way of life, no matter how bad, to a new one is a change that has often required centuries.

The common conscience of white Americans has produced the belief that the Negro is a potential radical. The Communists reached this conclusion by another method. As we have seen, it was Trotsky himself who painted the glowing picture of Communist possibilities among American blacks. The error which Trotsky and his successors made had dogged the Communist Party's Negro program since its inception in 1920. It explains the party's failure with the Negro. The Negro is not a potential radical, and reason or logic cannot make him one.

There are several facets to the American Negro's conservatism. For one thing, the impact of religion on Negroes, especially those in the South, is much stronger than it is among whites. Also, Negroes emulate American conservatism in politics and economics whenever they can. Their aim has always been to become respectable and middle class; and to them "the dictatorship of the proletariat" is apt to sound like mumbo jumbo. They have steadfastly held on to the conviction that a redress of the ills which beset them is to be obtained within the framework of American democracy and by time-honored methods. In addition to their conservatism, Negroes have also drawn conclusions about the practical consequences of an open, mass affiliation with a revolutionary group. These have been aptly summed by James Weldon Johnson in the following:

> There is no apparent possibility that a sufficient number of Negro Americans can be won over to give the party [Communists] the desired strength; and if the entire mass were won over, the increased proscriptions against Negroes would outweigh any advantages that might be gained. Every Negro's dark face would be his party badge, and would leave him an open and often solitary prey to the pack whenever the hunt might be on. And the sign of the times is that the hunt is not yet to be abandoned.[69]

Since it is a movement which must of necessity keep most of its business secret, reliable data about the Communists has always been difficult to obtain. No one but the party chiefs knew the actual numbers of Negroes who belonged to the movement at any given time; and, of course, they cannot be relied upon for reliable information. Ex-party members and observers, however, have offered estimates of from two hundred Negro Communists in Cleveland, Ohio, to as many as five hundred in Detroit and New York, where strong left-wing labor unions existed. These estimates apply to the middle 1930's, during which time the Communists enjoyed their greatest popularity among Negroes. In the half dozen larger cities in the United States the Communists very probably never had more than a total of two or three thousand Negro members at any one time. In view of the assumed fertility of the Negro for radical propaganda and the intense efforts of the party, this total would seem a pitifully small return.

To avoid overemphasizing the failure of the Communists to recruit more black members, some important factors must be taken into consideration. First, communism is a militant religion which follows a doctrine of the elect almost to the same extent and intensity as did the seventeenth-century Calvinists. And like the Calvinists, the Communist Party does not accept a person as a member merely because of his willingness to join. Indeed, with white mistresses, money, and prestige as bait, the Communists could certainly have had more Negro workers than they did have at any time. However, potential party material is rigorously screened before acceptance, observed at length after acceptance, and mercilessly cut loose on the first indication of unfaithfulness. A large Negro membership was not a primary objective of the Marxists or the lack of it their major failure. Their chief frustration was their inability to convince the masses of blacks that revolution rather than gradualism offered the better chance for complete freedom.

On the other side, Communist activity within the race left some discernible imprints. For one thing, the militancy of the protest movement as a whole, which had already been aroused by Garvey, was further hardened by the Communists. The specter of Negro and white Reds savagely battling the police in New York's Union Square, the élan with which they leaped into every situation involving a denial of some right to a Negro, and their defiance of white Southerners in Dixie itself could not be passed over lightly by Negro leaders. The black masses did not demand that their leaders adopt the tactics of the Communists, but neither would they tolerate any longer the dictation of race strategy from armchairs. The result was a greater effort on the part of Negro leaders actually to do some leading.

Secondly, the Communists did much to gain for the Negro's fight for economic equality a priority along with the other objectives of the protest movement. As we have seen, middle-class Negro leaders did not feel the harshness of economic inequality as much as did the masses. The fight the middle class led was primarily for civil and political rights since they suffered from the lack of these along with the masses. As early as 1920 the Communists had been decrying the stepchild status of economics in the race's program. During the depression of the nineteen-thirties they skillfully picked to pieces the shallow Jobs-for-Negroes campaign. And while *their* doctrine-laden program was unpalatable to the race as a whole, their hammering on the economic front helped to make the Negro more conscious of the need of economic equality.

In the early 1930's Negro and white Communists campaigned intensively to reduce the Negroes' distrust of labor unions. Of course, as long as the AF of L monopolized the labor field, the efforts of the Communists were largely fruitless. After the advent of the CIO, however, Communist-controlled industrial unions rapidly moved Negroes into places of power and prestige. Credit for the Negroes' new attitude toward labor unions cannot be given entirely to the Communists. Nevertheless, a large percentage of the new Negro labor leaders arising after 1935 belonged to the Communist Party. In meetings and conferences with the other Negro leaders on race issues, they did much to spread the idea of the need and value of labor solidarity between black and white workers.

In the long run, competition from the Communists did much to reinvigorate Negro protest organizations. In their nineteenth-century outlook and their often clumsy and ineffective methods, Negro protest movements were no match for the zealous and skillful Communist agents. New methods, new personnel, and greater publicity had to be obtained by these groups to enable them to meet the challenge of the Communists. While Communists never actually reached their goal of capturing Negro leadership, they remained at least a serious threat until 1940, when as a result of the advent of World War II regular Negro leaders were able to assume full command of all aspects of race leadership.

After the end of World War II, Communist Party activities among Negroes were not as visible as they had been before the war. The weighty proscriptions of the federal government against the Party caused the Communist iceberg to submerge farther below the surface. Nevertheless, the Communist Party structured a new program for Negroes, if, indeed, it could be called new. At the plenary session of the National Committee of the Party held in New York City in December, 1946, a resolution was adopted in which was proclaimed the new "Marxist-Leninist" plan for the American Negro — the right of self-determination — or self-government — especially for the Negro people in the Black Belt area in the South where they are in the majority.

Basically, this line was but a revival of the Black Belt nostrum of the 1930's. Its resurrection was strongly criticized by Negro Communist Party members. Doxey Wilkerson, one of the critical Negroes, dubbed it "theoretically incorrect and therefore disastrous."[70] After 1950, however, the Black Belt Republic idea was laid to rest a second time and perhaps this time for good. At any rate, the indomitable Communists could be counted upon to continue their pursuit of the ever-elusive Negro American.

8 THE ORIGINAL MARCH ON WASHINGTON

BECAUSE THE OBJECTIVES of the National Negro Congress were strongly influenced by the Communists after 1940, direction of national Negro policy, especially during World War II, fell to the lot of a group of influential Negro leaders known informally as the Federal Council or the Black Cabinet. The term Black Cabinet had long been a part of the jargon of Negro politicians. Originating during the period of Frederick Douglass's regime in Republican Party politics, the term had been applied consistently to whatever group of Negro leaders happened to be exercising some influence with the party in power in Washington, D.C. After 1895, for instance, Booker T. Washington and his Tuskegee machine constituted the Black Cabinet. James Weldon Johnson tells of his experiences with the Black Cabinet in Washington during Theodore Roosevelt's administration:

> In Washington, I found myself a non-resident member of the "Black Cabinet." This was a group made up of colored men who held important federal positions in the capital. At the time, it included the Register of the Treasury, the Recorder of Deeds for the District, the Auditor of the Navy Department, an Assistant United States Attorney General, a Judge of the Municipal Court, and the Collector for the Port of Washington. . . . Those of the group who lived in Washington customarily met at lunch and discussed the political state of the nation, with special reference to its Negro citizens. On such matters, Booker T. Washington was chief adviser to President Roosevelt, and became the same to President Taft; but the "Black Cabinet" was not without considerable influence and power.[1]

There was no such group during Woodrow Wilson's tenure in Washington. But during the twelve years of Republican rule after 1920, Benjamin Davis and Perry Howard directed the affairs of this unofficial body.

The Black Cabinet of World War II included few Negro political figures.[2] Among its members, however, were such outstanding people as Walter White, of the NAACP; Lester Granger, of the Urban League; Channing Tobias, of the Young Men's Christian Association; Judge William H. Hastie; Mrs. Mary McLeod Bethune; A. Philip Randolph, of the union of porters; and a score of lesser lights. No formal organization held the group together. Cooperation among them was purely voluntary, and it was motivated by their interest in the welfare of the race.

With the entrance of the United States into World War II, the group drew up the following war program for American Negroes:

1. Establishment of at least one mixed army unit of blacks and whites on a volunteer basis.
2. 100 per cent elimination of anti-Negro discrimination by employers, unions, and Government.
3. Abolition of the poll tax as a means of excluding Negro voters.
4. Acceptance of Negroes in Washington, on policy-making boards as well as in advisory capacities.
5. Extension of strong punitive powers to the Committee on Fair Employment Practice.
6. Complete protection for Negro soldiers from anti-Negro civilian and military police.
7. Opportunity for Negroes to become officers in the Navy. Enlistment for posts other than messboys were opened only recently.
8. Training of far more Negro pilots for the Air Force than can now be accommodated at the single Negro field at Tuskegee, Ala.[3]

In addition, top federal officials were glad to have at their disposal a group which could apprise them of the political temper of Negroes as well as to advise them on the selection and handling of Negro personnel. The Black Cabinet came to be considered the guardian of the 82,000 Negroes employed by the federal government. At one time, the union of Negro leaders and federal officials was so close that members of the Black Cabinet were looked upon as salesmen for the New Deal.[4] One observer thus described the operations of the black pressure group:

Today's Black Brain Trusters don't beg. These new Negro leaders have shed every tradition handed down from slavery days. They operate efficiently through official government agencies, through their press with a million and a half readers, through shrewd lobbying in Congress, even through direct pressure on the White House. Specifically, the Black Brain Trust is divided into the government and non-government branches. The government branch in Washington consists of race-relations advisers in numerous departments who look out for Negro interests. But they would be fairly impotent if it weren't for the outsiders — union leaders, preachers, politicians, editors, and heads of national organizations who can turn on the political heat when ordered. The

Washington boys provide the fancy footwork; the others provide the heavy punches. As a team, they work as smoothly as Joe Louis and his managers.[5]

The Black Cabinet was not very well known among the Negro masses, but every Negro who sought a well-paying position with the federal government soon knew that it was a power to be reckoned with. It was believed, although never entirely proved, that all significant Negro appointments were first cleared through this group. Naturally, this type of power could be expected to cause some animus, especially among those who were denied positions because of what they alleged to be a rejection by the Black Brain Trust. "Porkbarrelensis Africanus"[6] was the name given the group by one critical Negro writer.

Aside from its work for the hordes of Negro employees on the federal payroll, however, it was well known that the group was largely responsible for the appointment of the lone Negro general and a few other high Negro officers in the United States Army. In addition, the cabinet directed the campaign which led to the enlistment of the first Negroes in the United States Navy, Marines, and female auxiliary organizations in the armed services. The group also secured the appointment of several Negroes as civilian advisers to top military and civil officials. With the death of President Roosevelt, the Black Cabinet went the way of other New Deal satellites. Like its status and organizational structure, much of what the group is given credit for having done was of temporary nature. In terms of long-run accomplishments, the Black Cabinet highlighted the importance and the necessity of cooperation among Negro leaders in times of crises for the race.

With the United States moving ever closer to a showdown with the Axis powers in 1940, members of the Black Cabinet were both emphatic and persistent in their demands for total and immediate abolition of segregation in the armed services. It would be inconceivable, they thought, for America to field an army whose racial practices would meet even the approval of Adolf Hitler. They were, therefore, shocked and dismayed at the press release handed out on October 9, 1940, by Stephen Early, the White House Press Secretary.

The statement declared that the traditional policy of segregation [in the armed services] would be continued and that, except for the three already established Negro regiments, all present and future Negro units in the Army would be officered by whites.[7]

The policy of the United States government toward Negro servicemen in World War II, therefore, would be the same as it was in World War I. Negroes would be on short rations once more.

When Walter White, at a White House conference, pleaded for the upgrading of Negro enlisted men in the navy, Secretary of the Navy Frank Knox responded, "We can't do a thing about it because men live in such intimacy aboard ship that we simply can't enlist Negroes above the rank of messman." [8] The navy agreed to accept Negroes for general service in 1942 but established a segregated training station for them. The department then called in Lester Granger of the National Urban League as a consultant to the secretary. The Marine Corps reluctantly began accepting Negroes in 1942 but did not allow Negro personnel to do much of the fighting. For the most part, the more than sixteen thousand Negroes accepted were confined to menial or construction work. Out of about twenty-two thousand second lieutenants in the army, fewer than one thousand were Negroes; there were about seven Negro colonels out of a total of five thousand, and one Negro brigadier general. The racial problem in the Army Air Force became so intolerable to William H. Hastie that in 1943 he resigned his position of Civilian Aide to the Secretary of War.[9] Hastie later wrote a series of blistering articles on the Army Air Force's policy of discrimination against Negroes. Widely published and widely read, these observations by Hastie very probably influenced official thinking when the postwar abolition of discrimination was undertaken in the armed services.

On the whole, the treatment of the Negro serviceman by the civilian population in the South was just as bad in World War II as it had been in World War I. Wanton brutality or unwarranted assault, harassment, insult, segregation, and discrimination were the order of the day. Literally, anyone could get better treatment in Dixie than a "nigger in uniform" — even Nazi prisoners of war. One such case that drew wide attention concerned a group of German prisoners of war who were being shipped under Negro guard to internment on the West Coast. In the diner the Negro soldiers had to wait their turn to eat in the segregated "curtained" seats at the end of the cars while the German prisoners ate without delay with the other white passengers.[10] The poet Witter Bynner described the incident:

> On a train in Texas German prisoners eat
> With white American soldiers, seat by seat
> While black American soldiers sit apart —
> The white men eating meat, the black men heart.[11]

Thoroughly outraged by the ill treatment accorded Negroes in the armed services and discrimination in the mushrooming national defense industries, Negroes steadily became more militant as the war moved into high gear. Indeed, 1943 almost blossomed into a long hot summer. More than a dozen serious racial clashes erupted from one end of the country to the other. The most serious of these occurred in Detroit and Harlem.

Harlem blew up on the hot Sunday night of August 1, 1943.[12] The trouble began as the result of a rumor that a Negro soldier had been killed in a westside Harlem hotel by a white policeman. Overcrowding, threadbare poverty, and unemployment had long marked Harlem as the nation's number one black ghetto. But the upheaval was not a race riot; rather, it was the spontaneous outburst of the community's anger against the white merchants in their midst. Confined principally to Harlem's main business thoroughfare, the rampaging mobs destroyed upwards of $225,000 in property.

The worst of that summer's racial troubles, however, were in Detroit. As happened later in Harlem, the riot began on a hot Sunday night. As usual, a rumor sparked the conflagration. By Monday morning Detroit was virtually a city gone mad.[13] Nothing to equal this had happened in an American metropolis since 1919. Negro workers returning home from the night shift and unaware of the troubles were dragged from trolley cars and mobbed in Cadillac Square. Negroes in turn began to chase down fleeing whites and stomp them. But the police, recruited mainly from among the poor white migrants from the South, were malevolently anti-black. Walter White gives this eyewitness account of one of the worst episodes of the upheaval:

> Police searchlights lighted up the building as though it were a Hollywood stage setting. Then the police began riddling the building with machine guns, revolvers, rifles, and deerguns. Tear gas was shot into the building to force the terrified tenants to evacuate it. It was a terrible sight when men, women, and children who had escaped death only by throwing themselves flat on the floors of the building emerged, some of them wounded, with hands high in the air at the orders of the heavily armed policemen. The helpless victims were beaten by officers as every obscene gutter phrase was hurled at them.[14]

Casualty totals of the riot were thirty-four dead, twenty-five of whom were Negroes. Most of these were killed by the police. Also, over six hundred persons were injured during the riot. Approximately six thousand federal and state troops eventually restored order in the city, and the citizens of Detroit surveyed the damage.

One of the chief causes of Negro unrest during the early stages of the war was the bland refusal of defense industries to hire any appreciable number of Negroes or to upgrade the pitifully few they did take on. Racial discrimination in war plants was denounced not only by the Negro but by liberal newspapers and organizations throughout the country as a practice worthy of a fascist nation. These protestations evoked some response from governmental officials. Between August, 1940, and July, 1941, pronouncements came from the President, from Congress, and from several federal agencies against the exclusion of racial and religious minorities from war work.[15] However, the complete lack of machinery to enforce these declarations of policy left the problem unsolved.

With conditions showing no promise of improvement, in the spring of 1941, Negroes decided to take the situation into their own hands. Thus, under the leadership of A. Philip Randolph, president of the Brotherhood of Sleeping Car Porters, they began mobilizing in New York City for a new protest movement called the "March on Washington."[16] The avowed purpose was to transport as many Negroes as possible to the nation's capital and to protest directly to Congress and to the President. In short order, buses were hired and special trains were chartered for a demonstration of fifty thousand people to take place in Washington on July 1, 1941. The Negro press and pulpit played its part in whipping up sentiment. Pullman porters carried the word to Negro communities throughout the country. Mayor Fiorello LaGuardia and the President's wife pleaded, without success, with Negro leaders to call off the movement. Just a few days before the critical date, Randolph and other leaders were called to Washington. They went demanding the issuance of an executive order forbidding discrimination.[17] Sitting with the President were ranking members of his cabinet and representatives of the Office of Production Management. The first draft of an executive order against discrimination was rejected by the black leaders because it did not include governmental agencies. Finally, Mr. Roosevelt wrote his famous Executive Order 8802, the first such presidential action affecting Negroes since Lincoln's Emancipation Proclamation. The "March" was called off, and Negroes quieted down to see what they had achieved.

The President's Committee on Fair Employment Practice, which became the official agency set up under Executive Order 8802, was a war agency and nothing more. Undoubtedly, the Negro masses who placed their faith in the March-on-Washington movement hoped for federal action giving them some sort of permanent protection against discrimination. The leaders of the movement were more realistic. They well understood the urgency of the situation in which they were acting. Also, they knew that it would be much easier to secure action from a sympathetic Chief Executive than to wring concessions from a Congress which included such an articulate minority as the Southern bloc. The provisions of Executive Order 8802 represented the limits of the concession to the race that President Roosevelt could then make.

In the order the President simply stated that it was the policy of the United States to encourage full participation in the national defense program by all citizens regardless of race, creed, color, or national origin, and that there was evidence that available and needed workers were being barred from defense industries on those grounds. Defense industries and labor unions were reminded that it was their duty to cease all discriminatory practices. All federal agencies concerned with vocational and training programs for war production were ordered to administer such programs without reference to race, etc., and further, all contracting agencies of the government were required to include an anti-discrimination clause in all contracts thereafter negotiated by them. The order further provided for a five-man committee to serve without compensation with the duty to receive and investigate complaints in violation of the order and to take appropriate steps to redress grievances which it found to be valid.[18] In Executive Order 9346, which was issued two years later, the Fair Employment Practice Committee received express authority to hold hearings and make findings of facts, but this it had been doing since its inception.[19]

The history of regulatory agencies in America reveals that most of these bodies have had a difficult time in creating substantive policy. This has usually been a slow process, very often depending upon a hit-or-miss formula. In carrying out their duties as they saw them, public officials have often been called down by the courts. Sometimes they have been pushed too fast by the groups they represented, and at other times they have been stopped completely by those opposing their policies.

The advent of the Fair Employment Practice Committee (FEPC) posed a new question for public administrators. The science of public administration had provided techniques for the handling of economic and social conflict situations. But could these be applied profitably to any facet of the race problem in America? The limitations in its legal mandate, as well as those imposed upon it by the social and political forces with which it had to deal, heightened the importance of discretion to the FEPC. Nowhere in Executive Order 8802 or 9346 were the practices of racial or religious discrimination proscribed on purely moral grounds. There was no hierarchy of values in these mandates. There was but one value — the successful prosecution of the war. Discrimination was outlawed only where it interfered with the war effort. The authority of the President to issue these orders stemmed from the First War Powers Act passed by Congress on December 18, 1941. He had no other constitutional or delegated authority from Congress to outlaw such discrimination. This limitation on its scope placed all nonessential industries outside the jurisdiction of the FEPC. In this connection, the Committee was faced with the problem of defining what was an essential industry. The Committee later solved this problem by adopting a list of essential industries used by the War Manpower Commission. Ultimately, however, the FEPC compiled a list of its own.

Executive Orders 8802 and 9346 did not contain a definition of discrimination, nor did the FEPC ever draw up such a definition for its own use. However, the Committee compiled a list of criteria by which discrimination could be identified. This list, presumably, was what the field examiners used in their handling of cases. While its executive mandates did not prohibit such, the FEPC did not *initiate* any action. Every case it handled had to be based upon a signed complaint from someone. This was obviously a means of limiting the number of cases coming before the agency. Another effort to limit its scope of action was the Committee's distinction between discrimination and segregation in employment. The former was held to have involved unequal treatment in employment opportunities and conditions, and the latter was defined as imposing a separation of workers with equal treatment for all. On several occasions before Congress, the chairman of the FEPC insisted that it was the policy of this agency not to take action in any cases involving mere segregation of employees.

The greatest weakness of the FEPC was its total lack of power to enforce its orders. The powers to subpoena witnesses and records, to compel testimony, and to enforce directives through the courts or the attorney general are considered to be essential equipment for a regulatory agency. But, like all other bodies which originated from the war powers of the Chief Executive, the FEPC had to refer non-compliance cases to the President for his disposition. He could order governmental seizure and operation of the plant involved. With its manifold limitations and extremely limited budget (eighty thousand dollars for its first fiscal year), there can be little doubt that the Fair Employment Practice Committee was conceived by President Roosevelt to be nothing more than a wartime conciliatory committee whose main purpose was political — the appeasement of Negroes.[20]

Many people have believed that social segregation (by which is meant all forms of discrimination) is so deep seated in the habits and customs of the people that any attempt to eliminate it by federal fiat would lead to civil war. "You can't cure prejudice with legislation!" is a type of argument which was used widely against the Fair Employment Practice Committee, especially in the South. This argument was evolved in 1875 for use against the Force Bill of that year. It has been most recently resurrected in arguments against civil rights legislation. It is an argument which many writers have shown to be a confusion of terms, because no distinction is made between discrimination and prejudice. They hold that whereas no sensible government would attempt to eradicate racial intolerance by passing laws against it, both federal and state governments have successfully attacked discrimination in trade practices and discrimination against labor union activity, as well as that against religious groups. However, Southern opinions on the race problem had long ago reached an almost unreasonable stage. Legalistic and sociological arguments against the FEPC and similar measures were transparent. Southern opposition was based on the historic belief in the doctrine of Negro inferiority. Thus, Southerners would not tolerate any interference by the federal government in the race question because, they held, social equality or even dominance by an inferior race could result.

This situation imposed a difficult, but unavoidable, choice of values upon the FEPC. The South was part of the social context in which it had to operate. The Committee had either to adapt its policies to the demands of that region, which would have meant doing nothing, or to buck the opposition it was sure to arouse by holding hearings and issuing cease and desist orders when its findings so warranted. Enforcement would be left to President Roosevelt.

9 THE POLITICS OF FEPC

BY THE SPRING OF 1942, it was apparent that the Fair Employment Practice Committee was going to attempt to live up to the purpose of its appointment. In arriving at this decision, a serious rift developed among members of the Committee. The FEPC announced that it would open hearings in Birmingham, Alabama, on June 18 on complaints against several shipbuilding companies and labor unions operating on the Atlantic and Gulf coasts. Pressure was immediately put upon the President and the Committee to call off the hearings.[1] All this caused no change in the plans of the Committee, but three weeks before the date of the hearings Mark Ethridge, a Southerner, resigned the chairmanship, though remaining as a member of the Committee. The reason was revealed on the very day of the hearings. With racial tensions in Birmingham at the kindling point as a result of the FEPC open hearings,[2] Mark Ethridge arose in the hearings room of the Committee on June 18 and declared: "No power in the world — not even in all the mechanized armies of the earth, Allied and Axis — could force the Southern white people to the abandonment of the principle of social segregation."[3] Earl B. Dickerson, a Negro member of the Committee, leaped to his feet to answer the former chairman:

> I am unalterably opposed to segregation, whether in the South or North. Concession should not be made to the South, which after all is still a part of the geographical boundaries of the United States. There should be no "pussy-footing" on segregation by members of the Committee.[4]

Following this tiff, the FEPC proceeded with its hearings in relative tranquility. Afterwards the Committee went back to Washington to receive the plaudits of the President.

In the meantime, however, the foes of the FEPC had busied themselves to prevent a repetition of the events of June 18 in Birmingham. The success of their efforts came like a bombshell to the FEPC and its supporters. On June 30 President Roosevelt, without prior notice even to the Committee, announced that the FEPC would thenceforth function under the War Manpower Commission and receive its orders from Paul V. McNutt, the commission's chairman. The President had, conveniently, forgotten all the promises that he had made to increase the budget and field offices of the Committee. Given the job of quietly putting the FEPC to sleep, McNutt canceled hearings on discrimination against citizens of Mexican descent which the FEPC had scheduled for El Paso, Texas, in September. Three months were frittered away on the questionable task of defining the FEPC's precise status and functions within the War Manpower Commission. And, finally, what amounted to a shell-game arrangement between the War Manpower Commission and the Bureau of the Budget held up the FEPC's budget for four months — August through November, 1942. But the biggest blow to the FEPC was to come in January 11, 1943. On that date McNutt told the press that he had ordered the FEPC to postpone indefinitely its scheduled hearings on complaints against twenty-three railroads, most of which were in the South. As a result of this action, a nationwide protest descended upon McNutt as well as upon the President.[5]

The *Commonweal* pointed out on January 29:

As a result of last fall's election, the importance of this bloc in the carrying out of the Administration's policies has naturally increased. So long as both houses of Congress were almost overwhelmingly Democratic, it was possible to oppose Southern Congressmen on this one question, making it up to them by favors in other directions. But under the present situation this is no longer the case. The margin in both Senate and House is too slim. Evidently the Administration has felt that it must sell its Negro policy down the river.[6]

But amid all the furor caused by his action, McNutt quietly accepted the resignations of four of the FEPC's five members as well as those of almost the entire legal staff. The FEPC was now defunct in all but name. This was the price it paid for attempting to carry out its mandate in the South.

In the following months the pressure of Negro and other minorities forced Mr. Roosevelt to consider revitalizing the FEPC. To this end several conferences were held between the President and the leaders of minority groups. On May 27, 1943, the White House announced the issuance of Executive Order 9346, which increased the FEPC to a chairman and six members and extended the scope of the agency to include government bureaus. Four days later the new chairman, Father Haas, of the Catholic University, made announcements which aroused speculation about what the FEPC's policy toward the South would now be. Scheduled hearings on complaints against the Capital Transit Company in Washington, D.C., were postponed indefinitely. This company had threatened a complete stoppage of its transportation system in the capital if directed by the FEPC to hire Negroes as motormen and conductors on its trolley cars and buses. In addition, Father Haas stated that the approval of the new committee had been placed upon the segregation of Negroes in the yards of the Alabama Dry Dock Company. The justification claimed for the action was that the FEPC had been requested to approve this setup by several federal agencies interested in speeding up the construction of ships. In bestowing its blessing, the new committee demonstrated that it was not following the line laid down by Dickerson in his answer to Ethridge in Birmingham the year before.

Any questions about the nature of the FEPC's new policy toward the South must have vanished with the *Dallas News* case. In May, 1944, the regional director for the FEPC in Dallas, Texas, noticed an advertisement in the *Dallas Morning News* which read: "Wanted — Colored man to work at night as paper handler, essential industry."[7] Such an advertisement was a violation of Executive Order 9346, and consequently the regional director in Dallas ordered the newspaper to cease carrying this ad. However, when the chairman of the FEPC learned of the directive issued to the *Dallas Morning News*, he hastened to overrule his regional director and immediately dispatched an apology to the paper. The reason later given for this action was that the FEPC had been drawing up a new list of essential industries from which newspapers were to be excluded. Quite possibly, the FEPC had intended to restrict its activities further before this case arose. The impression must remain, nevertheless, that more than any other factor the location of this newspaper in a Southern city precipitated such a reversal by the chairman.

One must be careful, however, not to heap general discredit on the Committee's policy in the South after May, 1943. Southern opposition both in and out of Congress had been consolidated to a considerable degree. But, as its *First Report* indicated, the FEPC had by no means abandoned activity in the South.[8] In avoiding the more difficult situations, the Committee was observing the rule that self-preservation is as valid for a public agency as it is for an individual.

During its first three and a half years of existence, the FEPC had no occasion to appear before a congressional body. The Committee had been included within the Office of Production Management, the War Production Board, and the War Manpower Commission successively; and its budget during this period was supplied from the war funds of the President. Hence, there was no necessity for the Committee to come before the Appropriations Committees of the House of Representatives and the Senate. There were few remarks on the floors of Congress relative to the FEPC outside of the occasional pot-shots taken by Senator Bilbo and Representative Rankin.

But this long holiday from congressional scrutiny ended abruptly in December, 1943. During that month the action of the FEPC in the *Southern Railway* case (see pages 178-182) aroused Southern industry as it had seldom been aroused before. Southern congressmen were beseeched to put an end to the Committee's activities in the South. This led to the seizure of the FEPC's records by the Smith Committee of the House of Representatives, which was then investigating executive agencies. An investigation of the activities of the FEPC followed. On January 11, 1944, officials of the FEPC began to make a series of appearances before the Smith Committee to answer charges lodged principally by the Southern railroads and the Philadelphia Transit Company to the effect that the FEPC had exceeded its authority in issuing cease and desist orders to them. The hearings which followed were conducted in an atmosphere of hostility to the FEPC. The complaints were heard with patience and sympathy even when the attacks on the FEPC became vicious. There was but one man on the Smith Committee who could even remotely be considered friendly by the FEPC officials — this was Representative Jerry Voorhis of California. The Smith Committee was headed by Representative Howard W. Smith, of Virginia, whose reputation as a labor baiter and New Deal foe was well known. Obviously, the investigation was an attack against President Roosevelt as well as against the FEPC by anti-administration Democrats in the House. The same type of treatment accorded the FEPC by the Smith Committee was subsequently meted out to the War Manpower Commission and the Office of Price Administration.[9]

The FEPC had received status as an independent agency within the executive office of the President with the issuance of Executive Order 9346 in May, 1943. While the Committee's budget was supplied from the funds of the President for the fiscal year ending June, 1944, from that time on, all appropriations had to come from Congress.

Thus, in May and June, 1944, the FEPC had to appear before House and Senate subcommittees on appropriations. The hearings which followed were the prelude to a month-long congressional battle almost ending in a second disaster for the Committee. In hearings held by both the House and Senate groups, Malcolm Ross, the FEPC's new chairman, had to stand relentless questioning for the action of his agency in the *Southern Railway* case. At one point in the Senate subcommittee's hearings, Senator Russell insisted that the FEPC was "attempting to pillory the South," and that it rallied to its support people all over the country who looked down on the South "as being a group of barbarians."[10]

What the congressmen were especially interested in learning from Malcolm Ross was just how his Committee defined discrimination. It was apparent that the congressmen were insisting upon a distinction between segregation and discrimination. The FEPC might legitimately act against discrimination in employment, but any interference with segregation was taboo. Such interference was construed as an attack upon the customs and traditions of the South and an attempt to impose by legal fiat the practice of social equality among a people who did not want it. Ross answered that the FEPC was not interested in segregation "*per se,*" but that since mere segregation might result in discriminatory practices, the Committee felt that they had a duty to see whether that actually was the case.[11] For instance, in the *Point Breeze* case, a Western Electric plant located at Point Breeze, Maryland, established what it considered to be equal facilities for black and white employees. Upon examination of these facilities, however, the FEPC declared that the installation of duplicate facilities could not help but lead to discriminatory practice. Distinguishing between discrimination and segregation was one thing, but holding to the distinction was another matter. Ross's answer did not satisfy the Southern congressmen. Thus, when the National War Agencies Appropriations Bill came before the House and Senate for passage, the Southern bloc in each body voted almost to a man in favor of an amendment to strike out appropriations for the FEPC. In the House the amendment lost by eighteen votes; in the Senate the margin was four.

To the FEPC and its friends this narrow escape for the Committee was the handwriting on the wall. By 1945 the Southerners might well get the necessary votes to carry through their intentions. The only thing that might save the FEPC was legislation giving the Committee statutory basis. Accordingly, several bills were introduced in both the House and the Senate. During the fall and winter of 1944, hearings were held on all of these proposed measures. By April, 1945, the House Committee on Education and Labor reported out a bill sponsored by Representative Mary Norton, of New Jersey.

However, the obstructionist tactics of the FEPC's foes in Congress began to appear. No rule could be obtained to bring the Norton Bill on the House floor for discussion. The House Rules Committee was almost evenly divided between the enemies and supporters of the FEPC. Thus, whenever the request for a rule for the Norton Bill was the business before this body, the Southerners would absent themselves, thereby preventing a quorum. The supporters of the Norton Bill then began efforts to obtain the necessary 218 signatures on a House petition to force the bill out of the Rules Committee. In the meantime, Southern industrialists, led by the Southern States Industrial Council, circularized the Senate for a filibuster in case the bill should come before that body. Their plea was answered by a group of Senators headed by Allen J. Ellender, who vowed to filibuster if necessary to kill any version of the FEPC.

On May 24 the Chavez Bill, a Senate version of the Norton measure, was reported out by the Senate Committee on Education and Labor. But with the threat of filibusters from Senators Bilbo and Ellender, the possibilities of this measure ever becoming law were as slim as that of the Norton measure in the House. By the end of May all hopes of obtaining a permanent FEPC were waning.

On June 1 the House Committee on Appropriations did the expected. It reported out the National War Agencies Appropriations Bill for 1946 with no mention of the $599,000 requested by the FEPC. The nationwide protest which resulted against this action was sufficient even to move the President. Thus, on June 6 Mr. Truman dispatched a note to Representative Clarence Cannon, Chairman, House Appropriations Committee, reminding him of the vital work which the FEPC had accomplished since the beginning of the war and insisting that the agency be continued. Next day the War Agencies Appropriations Bill came up for general discussion on the floor of the House. Representative Vito Marcantonio immediately demanded to know the exact reason why the FEPC had been excluded from the bill. Cannon's first answer was that since legislation was pending to establish a permanent FEPC, his committee had not thought it necessary to include any appropriation for it.

This did not satisfy Marcantonio, and upon further questioning,

Cannon pointed out that this bill included several war agencies which had no statutory basis and that the rules of the House permitted a member to knock out the appropriation for any of these agencies on a single point of order. To facilitate passage of his bill, he had, therefore, requested a rule from the Rules Committee waiving points of order, but he was told by certain men on the committee that no such rule would be granted if certain items were included in the legislation. Cannon insisted that this made it incumbent upon his committee to exclude the appropriation for the FEPC. Later, but on the same day, the Rules Committee issued two rules on the War Agencies Appropriations Bill: one waiving points of order, the other prohibiting all amendments to restore funds to the measure. Thus, with the FEPC effectively barred, the National War Agencies Appropriations Bill was passed by the House and sent to the Senate for approval.

In the Senate the Appropriations Committee voted to restore the appropriation for the FEPC, but the actual restoration faced two obstacles. First, any Senate amendment adding funds to an appropriation bill is out of order unless two-thirds of the members vote to suspend a rule prohibiting such amendments. Secondly, FEPC enemies vowed to filibuster to prevent any restoration of funds for the agency. However, after several attempts to compromise and two days of filibustering, the Senate finally agreed upon a six-month appropriation of $250,000 for the FEPC.

Now began the third phase of the battle. The House refused to attend the conference on the War Agencies Appropriations Bill as passed by the Senate. The measure was tabled, and the House Appropriations Committee wrote a new measure from which the FEPC was again excluded. This time, however, Cannon was unable to obtain a rule protecting his bill from points of order. Thus, when the new bill came up for passage on the House floor, Marcantonio struck out ten war agencies on successive points of order in obvious retaliation for the exclusion of the FEPC. In this emasculated condition, the new bill was sent to the Senate, which refused to consider it.

The deadline for passage of the War Agencies Appropriations Bill was June 30, but the stalemate between the House and Senate continued for two weeks thereafter. Finally, on July 13 the diehards in the House agreed to $250,000 for the FEPC. These funds were sufficient for only six months of operation by the agency. By August, 1945, the FEPC was rapidly closing its field offices in preparation for complete liquidation by the end of the year.

After 1945, proponents of the FEPC carried on a campaign through-out the nation to have the FEPC made permanent by congressional enactment. But as the conclusion of World War II also ended the urgency of war production, the champions of FEPC thereby lost their major argument. FEPC bills were introduced in both houses of Congress, but with the employment of minorities no longer a patriotic duty or a necessity for national defense, these measures were smothered in committees.

To the majority of Negroes, however, the FEPC had been an agency deserving effective and intelligent support. This support, which was at all times generously given, was kept aroused and spirited by the Negro press and pulpit. In addition, such Negro organizations as the NAACP, the Brotherhood of Sleeping Car Porters, the National Negro Congress, and others dedicated themselves to fight for the perpetuation of the agency. But the godfather of the FEPC was the March-on-Washington movement. This was at first intended to be only a temporary organization. But the early weakness of the FEPC, coupled with the antagonism which it quickly aroused in the South, caused the leaders of the March-on-Washington movement to organize permanently. After 1941 the March-on-Washington movement was the group which sounded the tocsin whenever the FEPC needed aid, and under the sponsorship of the movement, thousands of people belonging to all races gathered annually in Madison Square Garden in New York City to rally for the FEPC.

As a result of this connection, the movement was at one time able to exert considerable influence on the policy of the FEPC. The extent of this influence is nowhere better demonstrated than in the events leading up to and following the *Southern Railway* case. This case, involving discrimination against Negro firemen and porters by Southern railroads, was brought to public attention by the Brotherhood of Sleeping Car Porters, led by A. Philip Randolph, who was also chairman of the March-on-Washington movement. It was undoubtedly due to his influence that Milton P. Webster, vice-president of the Brotherhood and also a member of the March-on-Washington movement, was appointed to the first FEPC. Randolph was determined to have the railroads cited by the FEPC for their discriminatory practices. By the middle of 1943, Negro organizations and newspapers were all clamoring for action against the Southern carriers. The discriminatory practices in question had grown out of changing circumstances in the railroad industry. During the period between the Civil

War and World War I, the jobs of firemen on steam locomotives had been unwanted by whites and thus open to Negroes. However, after 1920 the introduction of diesel locomotives and the steadily deteriorating economic conditions in the South made the fireman's job more acceptable to whites. Unions composed of white firemen were recognized by the employers as the official representatives of all employees and were able to work out agreements with the railroads which militated against Negro employees. Many of these agreements were approved by the National Railroad Adjustment Board between 1930 and 1940.

Nevertheless, these agreements were apparently not displacing the Negro rapidly enough, nor were the white unions satisfied that they had sufficient protection against the influx of Negroes expected as a result of the impending war. Hence, on February 18, 1941, seven railroad labor unions (white) and fourteen Southern railroads signed an agreement which effectively clamped down on any possibility of the Negro regaining his former strength in the industry. This document, the Southeastern Carriers' Conference Agreement, restricted the proportion of Negro firemen and helpers that could be hired to less than 50 percent of the total number of employees in each class. The agreement also required that positions caused by new runs and vacancies be filled by those who met certain restrictions which effectively screened out Negroes and allowed the displacement of Negro firemen by white firemen, regardless of seniority.[12]

Negro employees quickly became aware of what was happening to them under this agreement, and in a short time they lodged over fifty complaints with the new FEPC. In addition, the International Association of Railway Employees (for Negroes) appealed to the head of the Selective Service System and to President Roosevelt stating that the discriminatory policies of the Southern railroads and unions were responsible for the unfair application of the Draft Law to Negroes, since railway employment had been declared a draft deferrable occupation.

The first Fair Employment Practice Committee hearings on these complaints, which became known as the *Southern Railway* case, took place on June 18, 1942, in Birmingham, Alabama, along with hearings on other cases. However, the case proved to be too large to handle at that time, and the FEPC decided to designate a special time and place to hold the hearings. This postponement gave the railroads the time they needed to gauge the power and the importance of the new agency. The railroad lobby in Washington got busy. Congressmen were requested to use their influence with the President to have the hearings called off or postponed indefinitely. But the railroads did not reckon with the power of Negro political pressure. The result was a prolonged tug-of-war which lasted for two years. *Time* magazine, calling the *Southern Railway* case the hottest problem in domestic politics, held that "in political terms, if FEPC moves forward, it is damned by the Southern Democrats; if it stands still, it receives the scorn of the Negro population — and may lose the all-important Negro vote"[13] for the Democratic Party.

Thus, on two occasions hearings were scheduled for the case, but for one reason or another were temporarily canceled each time. The third postponement, made by McNutt of the War Manpower Commission, under whom the FEPC had been functioning since July 30, 1942, was intolerable to Randolph and his supporters. Delegation after delegation descended upon Washington demanding that the hearings in the *Southern Railway* case be rescheduled. In fact, so many of these groups called to see McNutt that on January 19, 1943, he instructed his receptionist that he would be "out" if any more delegations called. But Randolph finally won his fight and the hearings were held in September, 1943.

When the hearings were finally opened in Washington, D.C., on September 15, 1943, not fourteen but twenty-three railroads were cited to appear.[14] Complaints had been filed against other carriers operating in the Northern and Western sections of the country. For four days a subcommittee of the FEPC headed by Milton P. Webster, Randolph's colleague, listened to the testimony of witnesses, mostly Negroes, but also including some Jews and Mexicans. None of the unions appeared, but some of the railroads were represented by counsel. No witnesses were cross-examined nor was testimony offered in defense of the roads. However, a joint statement signed by all twenty-three carriers in reply to citations from the FEPC was placed in the record. This statement read as follows:

> For many years the railroads have afforded employment opportunities to Negroes which, to our knowledge, have not been equaled by those of any other large industry. In the normal course of business, as those problems are worked out by patience and good understanding, these opportunities should improve. To attempt to enforce utopian equality now would, in our opinion, have precisely the opposite effect. It would result in discontent and friction among employees or conditions worse than friction. Nor are railroad employees the only ones to be considered. Any attempt on the part of the railroads to insist that their patrons of every class and pursuit, and wherever located,

should do business with Negroes in all positions on the railroad, could not fail to produce destructive friction and perhaps worse. Neither the employees nor the patrons of the railroads could be expected to change overnight their long-standing views regarding racial problems, and any attempt to force them to do so by governmental decree could not fail to do harm rather than good.[15]

Hearings were terminated in the case on September 18.

About two months later, on November 18, the FEPC announced that it had found the railroads and unions guilty of an eight-count violation of Executive Orders 8802 and 9346. Most of the complaints against the Southeastern Carriers' Conference Agreement were held to be valid. Six general directives were issued to the roads and unions. The Agreement was ordered to be renegotiated, modified, or set aside; the unions were directed to drop all provisions from their constitutions which had the effect of excluding employees because of their race, religion, or national origin; and all future agreements between the roads and the unions were to be negotiated in the light of Executive Orders 8802 and 9346.[16] All parties were given thirty days in which to notify the FEPC of steps taken to comply with the directives. The seven Northern and Western roads immediately notified the Committee of their willingness to negotiate the entire matter. Three of the unions involved sent notices of their refusal to comply, and the other four simply disregarded the directives they received.

There was but scant hope of compliance by the fourteen Southern carriers. Sensing this, Negro leaders and newspapers began a campaign to turn public opinion against the roads. Hence, on December 3, 1942, a full-page advertisement was run in the *Washington Post* and in a slightly condensed form in the *New York Times,* the *Chicago Tribune,* and other papers throughout the country under the following headline:

By This *Great Decision*
AMERICA'S HONOR IS VINDICATED
AND RADIO TOKYO IS ANSWERED[17]

In this advertisement the entire *Southern Railway* case was reviewed including the findings and directives issued by the FEPC, and the Southern railroads and unions were mercilessly flayed for their admitted discrimination against the Negro. The article was signed by Milton P. Webster (the FEPC member under whom the hearings were held), A. Philip Randolph, and three other Negro leaders.

As a result of this advertisement, the attention of the entire country was focused on the case, and the railroads now hastened to defend themselves in the press. Negro newspapers joined in the fight and began urging President Roosevelt to seize the roads if they refused compliance. Finally, on December 13 the fourteen Southern railroads sent a joint answer to the FEPC rejecting all orders from the body. The roads claimed that since the Southeastern Carriers' Conference Agreement was negotiated according to procedures set up by the Railway Labor Act, it had the force of law and could not, therefore, be annulled by a mere directive of the FEPC. The railroads contended that the FEPC did not have the legal authority to issue such directives. A copy of this statement along with other materials in defense of their position was sent by the roads to every member of Congress.

By December 29 the FEPC, satisfied that an impasse had been reached, sent the entire case to the President for his disposal. About a week later, on January 3, Roosevelt announced his appointment of a special committee headed by Walter P. Stacy, Chief Justice of the Supreme Court of North Carolina, to investigate the matter. But, as it developed, this was a quiet means of smothering the whole affair. No decision ever came from that body, and very little was heard of the *Southern Railway* case after it was turned over to that group.

As a result of the case, the full extent of the weaknesses and limitations of the FEPC was broadcast to American industry. The challenge from the Southern railroads showed that cease and desist orders from the Committee could be disregarded almost with impunity. The lesson was quickly learned. On December 27, exactly two weeks after the railroads refused to comply, when the Philadelphia Transit Company rejected directives from the FEPC, they copied almost word for word from the statement of the railroads. Similar action soon followed from other parties cited by the agency, such as the Seafarers International Union and the International Brotherhood of Boiler Makers.

Some Negro, Jewish, and Catholic protest groups, in their desire to simplify the reason for the defeat of the FEPC in this case and its subsequent weakness, led their followers to believe that the Southern bloc in Congress was solely responsible. The Southerners, on the other hand, were quite willing to accept the blame since they thereby gained prestige in Southern communities as the defender of white supremacy. However, the demise of the FEPC in 1945 and the failure of Congress to revive it thereafter must be attributed to the unreadiness of the American people as a whole for such legislation. If this fact was seldom, if ever, recognized by the agency's defenders, it was never forgotten by the members of Congress. Careful lest they alienate their Negro constituencies, congressmen from the North, East, and West usually went on record as favoring the agency. When buttonholed, they usually agreed to vote affirmatively whenever the FEPC bill came to a vote. Actually, however, few congressmen ever expected or wished that such a measure would reach the floor of the House. But in the event that this did happen, the old Republican strategy of dealing with so-called "Negro legislation" could be relied upon. Namely, the bill would be allowed to pass in the House and then be sent to a more or less sure death in the Senate at the hands of the Southern stalwarts.

The foes of fair employment bills were successful in attacking such legislation on the grounds that it catered to the special interest of the Negro. The American public as a whole never fully realized that the FEPC benefited not only the Negro but most of the racial and religious minorities as well. Yet, part of the blame for this misconception must be attributed to the leaders of the organization which originally sponsored the agency. The March on Washington began as a Negro movement, but within a short time it enjoyed the support of white labor, civic, and religious groups. Much of this support was lost, however, when A. Philip Randolph, mindful of the way in which Communists had sabotaged his leadership of the National Negro Congress, began to cast a wary eye on white supporters. Randolph finally insisted that the March-on-Washington organization be kept a 100 percent Negro movement. The result was that the much-needed financial contributions from the white groups began to fall off. As contributions from Negroes did not take up the slack, the organization rapidly lost stability and prestige. By 1946 it existed on paper only with its national headquarters in a Harlem bookstore.

10 THE FIRST ASSAULT ON PLESSY v. FERGUSON

By THE END of World War II the NAACP, while refusing to broaden its area of combat, had managed, on the other hand, to discard its middle-class tag. Membership in the organization, which had remained well under forty thousand for its first thirty years, skyrocketed to over a half million. The most outstanding single factor accounting for this rise was the work performed by this organization for Negroes during World War II. Throughout the war the Association was literally swamped with letters from Negro soldiers and sailors or their families complaining of segregation, discrimination, or ill-treatment in the armed services.

In drives to increase its membership and influence among Negroes, the NAACP was not content to rely solely upon the victories it had won in the field of civil and political rights before the courts. It decided, at last, to take its message and pleas to the grass roots of this Negro nation within a nation. The long-standing practice of representatives of the Association in membership campaigns had been to concentrate upon the business and professional classes of Negro communities. The poorer Negroes, even though some of them could afford to do so, were not too often asked to join. In many of the tightly controlled Negro communities in the South, local NAACP branches enjoyed a prestige comparable to that of college and professional fraternities. People seeking membership had to be of the right color or to have reached a certain accepted level of education or monetary income. However, these none too democratic qualifications for membership in the Association were discarded in one quick move by the national headquarters. Quantity rather than quality of members became the new watchword. Field organizers from headquarters instructed branch officials to solicit members in every area and from all levels of Negro communities. The qualifications for membership in the Association were reduced to the signing of an application plus the payment of a one-dollar fee.

The bulk of the NAACP members were drawn from rural and semirural areas since it was in these sections that the Negro was most likely to suffer mistreatment from the hands of white men. In addition, the monthly or semimonthly meetings and rallies of the typical local branch of the Association offered one more relief from the perpetual boredom which so often beset the lives of rural folk.

Among Negroes in the larger cities, however, the NAACP branch was very often rated as just another Negro clique. This had not always been the case. But as time passed, the urban blacks had less need to band together for mutual protection. In addition, the urban Negroes had profited immensely from the new liberal movements arising during the 1930's. The CIO unions, which were in the forefront of these movements, organized workers irrespective of their race or creed. Many of these unions also established auxiliary organizations whose duty it was to combat race hatred in industrial plants, as well as in local communities as a whole.

On other fronts the liberal movement helped to bring about a more enlightened and less patronizing attitude toward the Negro. Long oblivious to the so-called Negro question, white newspapers, civic, and religious groups began to suspect that such a question really existed. For the Negro the net result of this new attitude was a greatly increased interest everywhere in his political and social welfare. Where he once fought alone for his rights, he now had the assistance of a new white man. There was hardly a liberal or radical movement in any Northern city without its Negro contingent. The loser in this trend was the 100 percent Negro organization.

No charge had been more often hurled at the larger Negro organizations than the one to the effect that their policies had been controlled by white directors or by outside philanthropists who contributed to them financially. As a leading Negro group, the NAACP, of course, was a chief target of this criticism, which the Association was never able to combat effectively. By 1946, however, the Association was quick to point out that because of the half-million, dues-paying membership its board of directors did not need to solicit funds from philanthropists or foundations.

The Board of Directors of the NAACP consisted of forty-eight members, one-third of whom were elected annually. While this arrangement seemed fair enough on the surface, the method of nominating these directors was criticized both inside and outside of the organization for placing too much power in the hands of the board itself. Under the constitution of the Association, nominations to the board of directors were made by a nominating committee which consisted of four members of the board of directors and three delegates elected at the Association's annual conventions. While the constitution provided for the making of nominations by petition of at least thirty members, this device was seldom used. The prestige and influence of the board members plus their majority on the Association's nominating committee gave the board the real power in nominations and, consequentially, in elections. By this "safe" method of selecting its ruling hierarchy, the Association had been able to exclude radical Negroes from policy-making positions. The rank and file of the Association was predominantly composed of lower-class Negroes, but the direction of its affairs remained in the hands of the Negro conservatives. In the post-World War II period, the chief critics of the organization were Negroes. Intellectual or radical for the most part, these latter-day critics had often been more interested in subverting the large membership of the Association than in bringing about fundamental improvements in its structure and policies. Typical of this line is the following shrewd, compound generalization offered the Negro reading public by George S. Schuyler, a leading Negro writer once employed by the Association:

> What is wrong with the NAACP is its defensive psychology. Those who founded the organization, and whose philosophy still dominates and guides it, thought primarily in terms of defense and were zealous to do something *for* the Negro rather than teach the Negro to do something for *himself.* They regarded the NAACP as a policeman and lawyer rather than architect and builder. It could stir the group to hysterical complaint and yammering supplication, and so increase the hypersensitivity which hampers the initiation of a program for general advancement, and waste the Negro's time and energies in campaigns for such superficial and ridiculous "reforms" as capitalizing the "N" in Negro, raging against inoffensive motion pictures like *Song of the South,* denouncing Hollywood's Negro actors for trying to make a living, and kindred idiocies. But it has never been able to conceive or inaugurate any broad and fundamental program for Negro advancement.[1]

Although Mr. Schuyler neglected to define his "kindred idiocies," other reforms he mentioned, such as capitalizing the "N" in Negro, were pushed by the NAACP largely because of the interest of Negro people themselves. If this reform was idiotic to Mr. Schuyler or inconsequential to the Negro reading public, nevertheless it meant the end of a long-standing affront to the race.

By "broad and fundamental program" for Negroes, Mr. Schuyler was simply reviving the ancient and moth-eaten doctrine of Booker T. Washington: Southern Negroes should be urged to organize tight cooperatives among themselves for the marketing of farm products; the Northern Negro should become more of an entrepreneur individually where possible, but preferably on a cooperative basis. Sound in *theory*, this concept has seldom, if ever, been possible to put into practice among any sizable group of Negroes. Recognition of this fact was partly responsible for the NAACP's refusal to sponsor such a program. The difficulties of alleviating the plight of the Negro sharecropper were formidable enough for the national government when it was equipped with the farm programs of the New Deal. A mere educational campaign by a Negro protest organization would be less than futile in view of the towering rate of illiteracy among the Southern Negroes, plus the ever-present hostility of the Southern whites.

As early as 1934 the aging Dr. Du Bois, who for over a quarter of a century had pounded furiously and relentlessly upon the seemingly unassailable walls of American caste distinction, had begun to doubt the wisdom of Negro protest strategy. These misgivings were to some extent motivated by Dr. Du Bois' partial conversion to socialism.[2] But more importantly, he had slowly but definitely come to accept the basic tenet of Garveyism that the black race in America, as in every other land, must accept segregation and proceed to build up its fortunes unaided by the white race.

In the winter of 1934 Du Bois thus summed up his new philosophy in the *Crisis:*

> It is the class-conscious working man uniting together who will eventually emancipate labor throughout the world. It is the race-conscious black man cooperating together in his own institutions and movements who will eventually emancipate the colored race, and the great step ahead today is for the American Negro to accomplish his economic emancipation through voluntary determined cooperative effort.[3]

When other leaders of the Association took exceptions to these opinions as compromising the organization's position in the eyes of the public, Du Bois retorted that "the N.A.A.C.P. has conducted a quarter-century campaign against segregation, the net result (of which) has been a little less than nothing" and that the Association had "not made the slightest impress on the determination of the overwhelming mass of white Americans not to treat Negroes as men."[4]

Du Bois' opinions appearing in the *Crisis*, which he edited, were becoming intolerable to the directors of the NAACP. Negro and white leaders who looked to integration rather than segregation as the solution of the race problem began to demand a public answer to Du Bois. Led by Walter White, the Association took to the pages of the *Crisis* in March, 1934. Readers were informed that Du Bois spoke for himself and not for his colleagues in the NAACP and that the organization would continue its fight against segregation in any form and at all times. But Du Bois only became more incensed. Selecting White as his whipping boy, Du Bois reminded the blue-eyed executive secretary that he was, for all practical purposes, a white man and, therefore, did not know what it really meant to be black. With this advantage, White, as well as other Negroes of his color, according to Du Bois, naturally could be expected to oppose enclosing the race within the walls of segregation.

Obviously referring to the leaders of the NAACP, Du Bois heatedly asserted:

> Some people seem to think that the fight against segregation consists merely of one damned protest after another. That the technique is to protest and wail and protest again, and to keep this thing up until the gates of public opinion and the walls of segregation fall down.[5]

Enraged, disgusted, and weary, Du Bois, in the summer of 1934, broke off his connection with the NAACP.[6] In a parting shot at the Association, he wrote:

> Today this organization, which has been great and effective for nearly a quarter of a century, finds itself in a time of crisis and change, without a program, without effective organization, without executive officers, who have either the ability or disposition to guide the National Association for the Advancement of Colored People in the right direction.[7]

Thus ended the short and turbulent conflict. Du Bois, brilliant, sincere, and ever a slave to his convictions, wrote *finis* to his long career with the NAACP.

With the resignation of James Weldon Johnson as executive secretary of the NAACP and that of Du Bois as editor of the *Crisis*, the first great period in the career of the NAACP had come to an end. It had been something of a halcyon period, one in which experiment, expediency, and crisis confrontation had been the order of the day. After the inauguration of Walter White as executive secretary in 1934, the Association embarked upon the second and quite possibly the greatest phase of its history. White had been with the Association since 1918 and had served a hard apprenticeship both in the national office and in the field. He was ready to reshape the policies and programs of the organization, to stabilize its major activities, and, above all, to recruit fresh, young, and vigorous professional talent — especially Negroes.

Under White's directorship the main focus of the NAACP would be upon the *full* implementation of the Negroes' civil and political rights — the genuine enforcement of the Thirteenth, Fourteenth, and Fifteenth Amendments for the first time since their enactment some seventy years before. To this end White's first important appointment was that of the brilliant Charles H. Houston as the first full-time director of the Association's legal department.[8] Houston had graduated Phi Beta Kappa from Amherst College and had been the first Negro to become editor of the *Harvard Law Review*. To assist Houston, the legal department secured William H. Hastie, the brilliant young cousin of Houston, who had also made Phi Beta Kappa at Amherst and editor of the *Harvard Law Review*. And, finally, the staff acquired the services of the young Thurgood Marshall. Marshall had studied law at Howard Law School under the tutelage of Charles Houston. As the NAACP's legal staff, these three men would ultimately constitute one of the most formidable and expert team of lawyers on constitutional law in American history. Before they disbanded, as a team they would win better than 95 percent of the cases they argued in the federal courts. Indeed, it was these men who, while on the faculty of Howard University's Law School, laid the foundations of the law course known as "Civil Rights."

In terms of the chances for success, the new legal battery of the NAACP could not have made its appearance at a more propitious time. In 1937, following President Roosevelt's abortive attempt at "packing" the Supreme Court, the old justices began to die or to retire. Six of them were over seventy years of age. During the next four years Roosevelt was able to appoint a virtually new Court: James Byrnes, of South Carolina; Hugo Black, of Alabama; Stanley Reed, of Kentucky; Professor Felix Frankfurter, of Harvard Law School; William O. Douglas, who had served on the Securities Exchange Commission; and Governor Frank Murphy, of Michigan. The new Court quickly abandoned the constitutional position maintained by its predecessor. It adopted a new and broadened view of the commerce, taxing, and general welfare clauses of the Constitution. The principles of those famous dissenters, Justices Holmes and Brandeis, became cornerstones for the new majority. The NAACP lawyers calculated that the new Court with its new and liberal justices would bring a fresh view and new consideration to cases arising under the much disputed Fourteenth Amendment. They hoped that in the process they could better plead the Negro's cause and secure some of the changes they considered to be long overdue. With this in mind the NAACP legal staff took the case of Lloyd Gaines,[9] a graduate of Lincoln University in Missouri who was suing for admission to the all-white University of Missouri Law School. Gaines had been refused admission solely on the ground that he was a Negro, but the state agreed to pay his tuition in the law school of any adjacent state which would accept him, pending such time as Missouri should itself build a Negro law school. Kansas, Nebraska, Iowa, and Illinois admitted nonresident Negroes. Gaines had refused the out-of-state aid and had demanded admittance to the University of Missouri Law School.

In the decision handed down on December 12, 1938, the new Supreme Court sustained the hopes of the NAACP lawyers. In what was essentially a new reading of the equal-protection-of-the-laws clause, the Court stated:

> The basic consideration here is not as to what sort of opportunities other States provide, or whether they are as good as those in Missouri, but as to what opportunities Missouri itself furnishes to white students and denies to negroes solely upon the ground of color. . . . [Manifestly,] the obligation of the State to give the protection of equal laws can be performed only where its laws operate, that is, within its own jurisdiction.[10]

The Court ruled that Gaines was "entitled to be admitted to the law school of the State University in the absence of other and proper provision for his legal training within the State."[11] Gaines never entered the University of Missouri Law School. Sometime after the decision, he simply vanished from sight and his disappearance has been shrouded with mystery ever since. The state of Missouri, however, quickly built a Negro law school; and other Southern states, clearly reading the handwriting on the wall, prepared to follow suit.

In 1940 the NAACP decided to take the case of *Melvin O. Alston* against the *School Board of the City of Norfolk, Virginia.*[12] Alston had initiated action to eliminate the gross differential between salaries paid to white teachers and those paid to Negro teachers. Teachers of both races were required to meet the same standards of education and experience. The case was heard in the United States Circuit Court of Appeals before three justices, one of whom was John J. Parker. In

1930 the NAACP opposition had been partly responsible for the United States Senate's failure to confirm Parker as an associate justice of the Supreme Court.[13] Nevertheless, at the conclusion of the argument Judge Parker congratulated Hastie and Marshall on the brilliance of their presentation.[14] Parker both wrote and read the decision which wiped out an annual differential of $129,000 between the salaries of white and Negro teachers in Norfolk, Virginia. During the fifteen-year period following 1940, the legal staff of the NAACP prevailed in more than fifty such cases in various Southern and border states. This action helped to add more than three million dollars annually to the paychecks of Negro teachers.[15]

In 1944 William Hastie and Thurgood Marshall of the NAACP legal staff won their greatest victory in behalf of the political rights of the Negro race. This was the decision in the *Smith* v. *Allwright* case.[16] Up until 1941 the Supreme Court in a series of rulings beginning with *Newberry* v. *U.S.* in 1921 had declared primary elections, even those involving federal offices, to be immune from congressional regulations. It was principally upon the basis of those rulings that Texas and other Southern states barred Negroes from participating in state Democratic Party primary elections. However, in 1941, the new Supreme Court, in the case known as *United States* v. *Classic*,[17] reversed previous rulings and proclaimed the primary elections to be elections within the meaning of the Constitution and hence subject to federal regulation. Armed anew with this decision, Hastie and Marshall began plotting the destruction of the Southern white primary laws. What they aimed at specifically was a reversal of the decision in *Grovey* v. *Townsend*.

In 1940 Lonnie Smith sought to vote in a Democratic primary election in Texas and was barred because he was a Negro. Represented by Hastie and Marshall, Smith appealed the adverse rulings in the lower courts and carried his case on through to the Supreme Court. The decision in the case was rendered on April 3, 1944. In nullifying the Texas white primary practices, the Court said that "when convinced of former error" it had never "felt constrained to follow precedent," and that throughout its history it had "freely exercised its power to reexamine the basis of its constitutional decisions." It was invoking the "well-established principle of the Fifteenth Amendment, forbidding the abridgement by a State of a citizen's right to vote."[18] *Grovey* v. *Townsend* was overruled.

The white primary was dead. In spite of all the frantic efforts of South Carolina, Georgia, and Texas to resurrect it, it remained dead. The *Smith* v. *Allwright* decision restored the ballot to the Southern Negro after a half century of virtual disfranchisement. In 1947 three years after the decision, the number of registered Negro voters in the South had risen from less than 100,000 to 645,000. By 1952 it had reached one million. More than this, Negroes were being elected to state and local offices for the first time since Reconstruction. The new political power of the Negro in the South would profoundly alter the political balance in that area; and in so doing, it would help to ring down the curtain on red-gallused demagogues and the wool-hat "po' whites."

Toward the end of the 1940's, Thurgood Marshall had become head of the NAACP legal department. Charles H. Houston was dead, and William H. Hastie had become Dean of Howard Law School. Marshall had become so well known as a result of the cases he had won that he was nicknamed "Mr. Civil Rights."[19] He expanded the NAACP legal committee to take in more gifted lawyers and established liaison with law school professors throughout the country who were willing to serve as consultants in the preparation of the Association's cases.

From 1948 to 1950 Marshall and his staff were engaged in arguing and appealing three major suits at virtually the same time. All of the cases involved Negroes seeking admission to graduate and professional schools in the South. The first of these was the case of Miss Ada Sipuel. Because the state of Oklahoma did not provide a law school for Negroes, Miss Sipuel on April 6, 1946, applied for admission to the Law School of the University of Oklahoma. When she made her appearance on the campus of the university, to the amazement of herself and her attorneys she was greeted by a large number of students, all white, of course, who welcomed her and gave a luncheon in her honor.[20] Miss Sipuel was refused admission to the university, nevertheless.

After two years of fruitless contention in the Oklahoma courts, Thurgood Marshall finally argued the case before the Supreme Court in January, 1948. Walter White, who was in the courtroom during the arguments, reported that cross-examination by the justices of the Oklahoma counsel was at times "savage." A mere four days after arguments were completed, the Court rendered its decision:

> The State must provide such education for her [Miss Sipuel] in conformity with the equal protection clause of the Fourteenth Amendment and provide it as soon as it does for applicants of any other group.[21]

In going through the motions of complying with the Supreme Court's mandate, the Oklahoma Board of Regents roped off a space in the State Capitol as a "law school" for Miss Sipuel and "others similarly situated." Three teachers were assigned to this makeshift school. Incensed at this treatment of Miss Sipuel, more than one thousand white students at the university demonstrated against the board of regents. At the conclusion of the demonstration, the students solemnly burned a copy of the Fourteenth Amendment. The ashes were placed in an envelope and mailed to President Harry Truman.[22]

Marshall hastened back to the Supreme Court seeking a directive to the university to cease its obvious evasions and to admit Miss Sipuel. But, for one of the few times in his long career before the Court, Marshall lost. The Court merely reaffirmed its original order, thus allowing Oklahoma's "basement Negro law school" to stand. Miss Sipuel never did attend this "school." Ultimately Oklahoma admitted her and other Negroes who applied to the regular law school.

Hard on the heels of the *Sipuel* case, the NAACP legal staff was again before the Supreme Court. George W. McLaurin applied to the University of Oklahoma for admission to a course not offered at the Negro institution, Langston University. When a three-judge federal court ordered his admission, Oklahoma University took Mc-Laurin in on a segregated basis. In the classroom McLaurin was assigned to a seat behind a rail carrying a sign which read "Reserved for Colored." In the cafeteria he was assigned a special table, and he was assigned a special place in the reading room of the library. Refusing to accept this "special" treatment, McLaurin appealed to the U.S. Supreme Court. His case was argued by Robert L. Carter, who was assistant to Marshall. Chief Justice Fred Vinson disapproved the restriction in a unanimous decision of the Court.[23]

As early as 1945 Hemon Marion Sweatt had applied for admission to the University of Texas Law School. Sweatt was a Negro mail carrier. Refused admittance, Sweatt, on May 16, 1946, commenced legal proceedings against the University of Texas. His case was handled by Thurgood Marshall. In December, 1946, the trial court ruled against Sweatt, showing that university officials had adopted an order calling for the opening of a law school for Negroes in February, 1947. Sweatt appealed. While the appeal was pending, Texas set up a Negro law school in a basement in a building in Houston. The school had no independent faculty or library. The teaching was to be carried on by four members of the University of Texas Law

School faculty who were to maintain their offices at the University of Texas while teaching at both institutions. Few of the ten thousand volumes ordered for the library had arrived, and the school lacked accreditation. Sweatt appealed on through to the U.S. Supreme Court.

Meanwhile, the case became a state-wide issue in Texas. Some two thousand white students from the University of Texas jammed into an auditorium to shout their support of Hemon Sweatt in his fight for admission to the university. Going even further, the students established a University of Texas Chapter of the NAACP — the only all-white unit of the NAACP. Walter White states, "We were assured that as soon as Mr. Sweatt's fight was won he and other Negro students would join the college chapter and thereby cure its involuntary all-whiteness."[24] The renowned Professor J. Frank Dobie, then Chairman of the Department of English, was one of the very few faculty members who spoke out in support of Sweatt. Dobie was widely applauded for his stand. Shortly afterwards, however, the board of trustees of the university found a reason for not renewing Dobie's contract.[25]

While the case was pending in the Supreme Court, Texas opened a new Negro law school at the all-Negro Texas State University. By June of 1950 the new school boasted of a faculty of five full-time professors, a library of approximately 16,500 volumes, a practice court, a legal aid society, and one alumnus who had become a member of the Texas Bar. But the U.S. Supreme Court would not accept even this obvious improvement over the first Negro law school. Chief Justice Vinson, speaking for the majority of the Court, said:

> The law school to which Texas is willing to admit petitioner excludes from its student body members of the racial groups which number 85% of the population of the State and include most of the lawyers, witnesses, jurors, judges and other officials with whom the petitioner will inevitably be dealing when he becomes a member of the Texas Bar. With such a substantial and significant segment of society excluded, we cannot conclude that the education offered petitioner is substantially equal to that which he would receive if admitted to the University of Texas Law School.[26]

The lawsuits won by the legal staff of the NAACP during the twelve-year period from 1938 to 1950 virtually opened the gates of the white Southern state universities to Negroes. Under the *Gaines* case they could not require Negroes to seek training outside of the state; as a result of the *Sipuel* case Negroes had to be provided training substantially equal to that provided whites and at the same time as it was provided whites; and, finally, in the *Sweatt* case the Court in fact, though not in words, denied that education could at the same time be separate and equal. With the makeshift Negro professional and graduate schools clearly unacceptable either to Negroes or to the U.S. Supreme Court, a special meeting of the Southern Governors' Conference was held in 1948 resulting in the founding of the Southern Regional Education Board.[27] This new agency was given the task of establishing regional graduate and professional schools open to all students with tuition to be paid by the student's home state. In the long run, however, the Southern states found it less bother and less expensive to admit to their already established schools the few Negroes who would apply and who could meet the qualifications. The Southern Regional Education Board at that time was no more than a fact-finding agency for higher education in the South.

For a few years after 1945 the NAACP, as well as other Negro protest organizations, thought that they had what would prove to be a valuable new ally in their long and tireless fight for social, civil, and political justice. This ally was the United Nations. The Charter of the United Nations, of course, dedicated the organization to the pursuit of all commonly accepted rights and privileges for the world's minorities. Of special value to the American Negro was the continual play of the international spotlight upon the condition of the American Negro because of America's pivotal position in world affairs. Also, there were few, if any, countries in the world which would allow themselves to be criticized by Americans without pointing to the Negro question as the mote in American eyes.

The embarrassment which this development has caused American diplomatic officials at home and abroad was lucidly described by Acting Secretary of State Dean Acheson in May, 1946:

> . . . the existence of discrimination against minority groups in this country has an adverse effect upon our relations with other countries. We are reminded over and over by some foreign newspapers and spokesmen, that our treatment of various minorities leaves much to be desired. While sometimes these pronouncements are exaggerated and unjustified, they all too frequently point with accuracy to some form of discrimination because of race, creed, color, or national origin. Frequently we find it next to impossible to formulate a satisfactory answer to our critics in other countries; the gap between the things we stand for in principle and the facts of a particular situation may be too wide to be bridged. An atmosphere of suspicion and resentment in a country over the way a minority is being treated in the United States is a formidable obstacle to the development of mutual understanding and trust between the two countries. We will have better international relations when these reasons for suspicion and resentment have been moved.[28]

Shortly after the U.N. Charter was published, Negro leaders began studying the document to determine whether the term "minorities" could be construed to include groups as historically a part of a nation as the American Negro. They felt that the race would benefit considerably if its status were recognized to be within the meaning of the Charter. The first attempt to test the opinion of U.N. officials on this matter was made by the National Negro Congress on June 6, 1946, when the leaders presented to the U.N. a rather hastily written document entitled "A Petition to the United Nations on Behalf of Thirteen Million Oppressed Negro Citizens of America." The petition was addressed to Secretary-General Trygve Lie for presentation before the General Assembly and to the Commission on Human Rights of the Economic and Social Council. The petition was accompanied by a document which outlined the grievances of the American Negro. Nothing was heard of the petition after it was submitted to the U.N. in 1946.

Several months after the action of the National Negro Congress, the NAACP set a group of scholars to work on a petition of its own under the direction of Dr. Du Bois. By the fall of 1947 this petition had been completed. Consisting of six chapters and totaling 155 pages, the document was entitled "An Appeal to the World, a Statement on the Denial of Human Rights to Minorities in the Case of Citizens of Negro Descent in the United States of America and an Appeal to the United Nations for Redress." It was presented to the U.N. on October 23, 1947.

In his introduction to the paper, Dr. Du Bois charged that the discrimination practiced in the United States could not continue without infringing upon the rights of the peoples of the world, and especially upon the ideals and the work of the United Nations. Pointing out that American Negroes had a population larger than many of the member countries of the U.N., Dr. Du Bois pleaded that the petition from the NAACP be heard.

Four of the five remaining chapters were devoted to brief analyses of the legal and social status of the American Negro since 1787. The titles and authors of these chapters are as follows:

II. "The Denial of Legal Rights of American Negroes 1787-1914," Earl B. Dickerson, attorney and former member of the FEPC.

III. "The Legal Status of Americans of Negro Descent Since World War I," Milton Konvitz, Associate Professor at Cornell University.

IV. "The Present Legal and Social Status of the American Negro," William R. Ming, Associate Professor at the University of Chicago Legal Institute.

V. "Patterns of Social Discrimination Against Negroes," Leslie S. Perry, Social Worker and Staff Member of the NAACP, Washington, D.C. Branch.

In the sixth and last section of the petition, Dr. Rayford Logan, of Howard University, gave what appeared to be the legal basis for U.N. action on the American Negro question. The structure of Dr. Logan's argument was founded upon Chapter VII, Article 39, of the U.N. Charter, which read in part:

> The Security Council shall determine the existence of any threat to the peace, breach of the peace, or act of aggression and shall make recommendations, or decide what measures shall be taken in accordance with Articles 41 and 42, to maintain or restore international peace and security.

This declaration, however, is modified by Article 2, Paragraph 7, which forbids the U.N. from interfering in matters "essentially within the domestic jurisdiction of any state."

Calling for a liberal interpretation of Article 2, Paragraph 7, Dr. Logan cited the argument of a Belgian delegate to the U.N. who reasoned that a denial of human rights in any part of the world would lead to a state of tension and probably war. To prevent such dangers, Dr. Logan urged that spokesmen for minorities be given the right to present to the General Assembly petitions on behalf of minorities to insure that the Security Council would immediately consider such threats to international stability. As a precedent for consideration of the document, Dr. Logan cited U.N. action on the petition filed by India which charged mistreatment of the Indian minority in the Union of South Africa. Dr. Logan admitted, however, that the two petitions did not rest upon identical legal grounds since the Indian document charged that the Union of South Africa had broken a treaty with India. Considering the petition as a whole, it may be said that the NAACP requested:

1. That it be recognized as the spokesman for the Negro minority in the United States.
2. That on the basis of the evidence offered in the petition, the plight of Negroes in the United States be considered a threat to international peace; and,
3. That Article II, Paragraph 7 of the Charter notwithstanding, the U.N. should consider the petition.

The formal presentation of the petition caused a stir at U.N. headquarters. Officials at first refused to accept the document for discussion but later relented.[29] The American delegates flatly rejected copies offered to them for their perusal, and the chief of the British delegation quickly dispatched a note to the NAACP stating that he would not be able to help them bring their petition before the General Assembly. Among the smaller nations in the U.N., the petition aroused great interest. Dozens of additional copies were requested, and several offers of assistance were sent to the officials of the NAACP.

In view of the cold war then being waged between Soviet Russia and the United States, the USSR was undoubtedly the happiest of all to receive the petition. The denial of democracy to Negroes in America had long been a favorite topic of Soviet delegates when speaking before meetings of the U.N., and the petition was considered additional documentary proof of Russian charges. The Russians did not wait long before making capital of the NAACP paper. On December 3 at the meetings of the U.N. Commission on Human Rights in Geneva, Switzerland, the Soviet delegation moved for a full investigation of the treatment of Negroes in the United States on the basis of the NAACP petition.[30] The motion was lost by a vote of four to one. Observers weighed the USSR's solicitude for the condition of American Negroes against Soviet action two weeks later, at which time the Russian delegate to the Commission on Human Rights denounced a proposed special Court of Human Rights as an absurd idea.

With the exception of one or two dissident voices in the South, the American white press largely abstained from editorial comment on the NAACP petition to the United Nations. This silence was possibly evoked by the fact that the *Report of the President's Committee on Civil Rights,* which was published one week later, extensively substantiated the petition. In a wave of editorials the Negro press almost unanimously supported the action of the NAACP. Among those who dissented, the chief voice was that of George S. Schuyler. To Schuyler, the petition was simply a Communist plot to embarrass the United States before the world.[31] The charge that the NAACP desired to embarrass the United States before the world was probably true, for those in the Association who decided to submit the petition to the U.N. must have carefully calculated the probable reverberations. However, one would be far amiss to judge that this action was Communist inspired. In fact, the NAACP was known to be one of the most conservative groups in the United States. On the other hand, the officials of the NAACP realized that as long as the present setup of the U.N. existed, any actual consideration of the American Negro problem by that body was highly improbable. Stated in its simplest terms, the real purpose of the Association, in this instance, was to shame the American government into taking positive action on the problem of civil and political rights for its Negro minority. Indeed, results along this line came less than a month after the submission of the petition. United States Attorney General Thomas Clark, speaking at a meeting of Boston lawyers, declared that it was humiliating to him that any group of American citizens could not find redress in the courts of the United States. As a result, the Attorney General stated that he was enlarging the Civil Rights Section of the Department of Justice to protect the life and liberty of the citizen whenever the states should fail to act.[32]

The crucial need for the expansion promised by Attorney General Clark was forcefully reemphasized in the *Report of the President's Committee on Civil Rights*. The Committee itself had been created by Executive Order of President Truman on December 5, 1946. The chairman was Charles E. Wilson, president of the General Electric Company, and fourteen other men and women prominent in American life were committee members. Of course, the scope of the organization included more than investigation of the Justice Department of the United States. As the guide for its work, this Committee on Civil Rights selected the national heritage of the promise of freedom and equality for all men — "the American way," and it proposed to look into the nationwide failure to live up to this ideal and to recommend remedial action.

When published, the findings of the Committee on Civil Rights brought gasps of indignation from many Americans: "I never knew that things were this bad." Some were being truthful; perhaps others were not. However, the vast body of the citizens familiar with the inconsistencies in American democracy should not have been greatly surprised. Historic injustices to the Negro such as lynching, police brutality, peonage, the denial of civil and political rights, and discrimination in employment and in the use of public and private facilities had long been part of the mores of many sections of the United States. Those living in more liberal localities were provided almost daily by the American press with accounts and descriptions of these conditions. Wisely, however, the Committee did not devote its entire report to the case of the American Negro. All forms of racial and religious intolerance were reviewed. Nor did the Committee spare public and private persons for their near-hysterical response to the so-called Communist menace within America. The Committee recounted the legitimate grievances of the American Indian and Mexican American; it denounced the then recent injustices toward the Nisei or American of Japanese descent in California and on the foreign scene; and it mentioned the special problem of citizenship of the thirty-five thousand inhabitants of Guam and American Samoa.

The Committee thought that the very complexity of the civil rights problem called for a great deal of experimental, remedial action which might be better undertaken by the states than by the national government, thus concurring with Justice Holmes's dictum that the states were forty-eight laboratories for social and economic experimentation. The group felt, nevertheless, that national leadership in the field of civil rights was imperative if America was to check the mounting social waste and loss of international prestige caused by the disease of intolerance. As the bases for the comprehensive program of civil rights which it conceived, the Committee on Civil Rights suggested the tapping of eleven different sources of federal power within the Constitution. Three of these sources were admittedly controversial, but the others had either been approved by the United States Supreme Court or deemed to be clearly valid.

Any new federal civil rights law enacted, in the view of the Committee, would be ineffective if entrusted to the Department of Justice with its then present setup. Therefore, the first of the Committee's thirty-four recommendations was:

1. The reorganization of the Civil Rights Section of the Department of Justice to provide for:

   The establishment of regional offices;

   A substantial increase in its appropriation and staff. . . .

   An increase in investigative action in the absence of complaints;

   The greater use of civil sanctions;

   Its elevation to the status of a full division in the Department of Justice.[33]

Other recommendations included the enactment of Federal laws against lynching, police brutality, peonage, and the poll tax. The Committee did not overlook the value of "a long term campaign of public education to inform the people of the civil rights to which they were entitled and which they owe to one another." This task, it thought, could best be performed by a permanent commission on civil rights to be established within the Executive Office of the President.[34]

This document and the *First Report of President Truman's Commission on Higher Education for American Democracy,* in which segregation in American schools was denounced as wasteful and undemocratic, were hailed by Negroes as major gains in their long, uphill struggle for equality. It must be remembered, however, that these reports were but the fruits of executive interest in a serious problem, and also that the executive's power to act on the basis of these reports was almost nonexistent. For positive action on the recommendations of the two committees, the Negro had to tilt with Congress, and for this he had to improve his political armor.[35]

11 THE NEW URBAN LEAGUE

By THE MID-1920's the National Urban League, under the leadership of Eugene Kinkle Jones, executive secretary, was still on the defensive about its policy, or lack of one, with respect to the Negro and organized labor. Hence, in 1925 Jones secured a grant from the American Foundation for Public Service to underwrite a thoroughgoing study and public exposure of the extent to which organized labor was creating a class of black peons in a flourishing industrial society. He commissioned the League's new Department of Research and Investigation, headed by Charles S. Johnson, to make the study, taking "as much time as necessary to make it unassailable." The study got under way in 1926.[1] When Johnson resigned two years later to join the Fisk University faculty, where he eventually became president, Ira De Augustine Reid succeeded him as research director and continued the study, weaving into it the data garnered and verified by Johnson.

Published in 1930 as a report on Negro membership in American labor unions, the findings of Johnson and Reid contradicted the claims of the smooth-talking, old-line labor union czars. Some of them made light of the report, but the findings of the League study were never seriously disputed. They could be summed up in a sentence:

> More than 500,000 Negroes had worked in war industries [World War I], most of them in organizable jobs, but in the mid-twenties only 84,000 were carrying union cards. The vast majority had been kept out of the unions and hence constituted the bulk of those dismissed after the war.[2]

When the Great Depression struck in the early 1930's, the National Urban League counted forty-two affiliates with a combined national and local staff of 185 persons. The budget for 1930 stood at $582,000 with some $506,000 of this being the combined budgets of the forty-two locals or affiliates.³ As officers of other private organizations did, Jones went to Washington on leave as assistant to the Secretary of Commerce to help hard-pressed Negro businesses to survive. Within three years, however, Jones returned to the League, convinced that no Negro official at the Washington level could be very effective in helping to end the shoddy treatment meted out to the black population. He was convinced that what was needed was more action by Negro leadership at the state and local levels.

Accordingly, with T. Arnold Hill, longtime director of industrial relations who had served as interim executive secretary during Jones's absence, Jones launched the Emergency Advisory Councils (EAC) to fill the need. These *ad hoc* councils were set up in one hundred cities across the country. The National League officers provided to the local councils current information about the various phases of the New Deal's emergency work-relief programs, warnings about the kinds of dishonest administration practiced against Negro needy in various parts of the country, and guidelines and organizational charts to apply against possible (in some areas, probable) malfeasance on the part of local administrators. The councils were also instrumental in helping to increase the number of civil service appointments of black applicants. Anne Tanneyhill of the National League office notified each EAC and every cooperating Negro newspaper about civil service examinations to be held and their date and place of examination. She suggested textbooks that would be helpful, as well as other sources of assistance for civil service aspirants. In several states where a record was kept over a period of months, the number of Negro appointees increased gratifyingly as a result.

Quite possibly as a result of the ferment among students at Negro colleges, the League in 1929 turned its attention to Negro college campuses. It gave assistance and support to the efforts of several Negro college fraternities and sororities to direct and energize the interest of Negro school youth in continuing training as long as possible in preparation for "tomorrow's jobs," those which would be available after the depression ended.⁴ Vocational Opportunity Campaigns were organized on a nationwide scale — again by Miss Tanneyhill — in which close to a half-million Negro high school and college youths were exposed in one year to information, advice, and inspiration on "training today for tomorrow's job." The campaigns were refined and broadened, as the years went on, to extend down into the junior high school grades and upward onto college campuses; in the latter case, the vocational campaigns were "career" seminars conducted in cooperation with college officials. In this way the National Urban League gradually changed its function to that of a community organization instead of a direct service operation. Local Leagues, for the most part, ceased to operate employment offices; instead, they directed applicants to the public employment services and kept check to make sure that the service was providing what the applicants sought.

Other social agencies were pressured by the League to provide programs of service to the Negro, integrated and on the same basis as those provided to white clients. No League was expected to assume responsibility for services offered by public agencies; instead, the officers were expected to keep tabs on equality of services given and the manner of their offering. In taking such steps as these, many League leaders felt that they were "moving away" from their special publics, and in so doing that they would lose touch with their basic constituencies. They were reminded, however, that the League was not a Negro organization but one of a multiracial nature, though dedicated to improvement of the level and scope of opportunities of the Negro population.

With the coming of the New Deal, the National Urban League for the first time in its twenty-year history began to exert its power consistently and effectively on the national level in behalf of the race. As a social agency the League's attention was quickly drawn to the discriminatory treatment of Negroes in the national and state welfare projects. The League was the first to focus national attention on what Lester Granger called "unforgivable collusion" between federal agents for the Department of Agriculture and Southern white plantation owners. Henry Wallace was accused of ignoring affidavits sent to his office by Urban League investigators. This collusion consisted of the sending of reimbursement checks for Negro tenant farmers' participation to the landlords instead of to the tenants. A landlord then had the tenant endorse the check and took "his share." The pittance that was left for the Negro "cropper" virtually amounted to extortion.

The League also fought against what it termed a "flagrantly discriminatory" provision of the Federal Housing Administration's manual of instruction for underwriters. The provision stipulated that a Negro seeking a loan for the purpose of moving into or building in an all-white neighborhood would be considered as destroying the "cultural homogeneity" of the neighborhood, and therefore he could not obtain a loan. President Roosevelt's defense of the provision was expressed to Dr. Channing Tobias and Dr. Mary McLeod Bethune, two of the most distinguished national figures of that period who had sought a conference with the President at the request of the National Urban League.[5] The President declared that the purpose of FHA was not to solve social problems but to keep the real estate industry out of bankruptcy. The provision stayed in FHA's set of instructions until ten years later, when Mr. Truman eliminated it.

While the League, like other Negro organizations, favored the Wagner Labor Relations Bill, it feared that the bill's passage, unamended, would leave Negro workers (in the case of closed-shop agreements) at the mercy of the skilled-trades unions because of well-documented practices of exclusion of, or discrimination against, Negro workers. When pressed to accept an amendment barring discriminatory unions from the protection of the bill, Senator Robert Wagner blandly replied that such an amendment would certainly defeat the bill, since labor itself would oppose such an amendment.

The bill passed unamended, and its signature, in the words of Lester Granger, "cost three generations of black workers their earned leap from unskilled to semi-skilled to skilled jobs."[6]

The new unions put together by the Congress of Industrial Organizations, however, were another matter, and the views and policies of the Leagues changed accordingly. Armed with the blessing of the New Deal, CIO unions moved into industry after industry, organizing workers regardless of race, creed, color, or sex. Thousands of hitherto unorganized blacks enjoyed the benefits of union protection for the first time and were indoctrinated for the first time in trade-union practices. Proud of their new status, Negro industrial workers rapidly rose in the labor movement. Strikebreaking by Negroes, organized or unorganized, rapidly went out of style. Since employment in organized industries is first routed through the local union, Negroes seeking work in organized plants no longer had any need of going to employment agencies or Urban League local branches for work. As a result, the Urban League branches in industrial centers lost a large part of their function as middlemen for Negro labor.

At the beginning of the CIO's campaign, neither the national nor local officials of the Urban League supported the drive among Negroes. Mindful of the AFL's traditional refusal to include Negroes in its locals, the League could not be sure of the motive behind the CIO's interest in Negro workers. Consequently, it cautioned Negroes against a headlong and unthinking rush into the CIO locals.[7] But when it became plain that the new unions were treating their Negro members with the same consideration as their white members, the coolness of the League rapidly disappeared. The first to change their attitude toward the CIO were the national officials of the League. The new line was laid down by Lester Granger:

A more modern social intelligence has been shown by the C.I.O. leadership than that shown by the old time A.F. of L. leaders. Steel, Auto, Mine, and Garment Workers' Unions have shown great concern not only for the defense of civil rights, but also for protecting the welfare of the unemployed and for organizing the unorganized. Since Negroes furnish so large a proportion of the unorganized, the unemployed, and those whose civil rights are violated, they are quick to see in the C.I.O. an instrument of deep importance to their race — a new champion to defend the rights of the underdog.[8]

In time, the local branches of the League in the industrial centers of the country discarded anti-union attitudes and went over to wholehearted support of the CIO. The Chicago branch, long notorious for supplying Negro strikebreakers to Chicago industries, became a leader in the CIO drive to unionize black workers in the city. In St. Louis, League officials aided considerably in bringing Negroes into meat and steel unions of the CIO. This branch also organized a Negro labor congress for the purpose of training black workers in the strategy and tactics of labor unions. The New York branch, the largest of all the League branches, interested itself in the CIO's efforts to bring Negro women into the laundry and garment workers unions of the city. At the beginning of World War II, anti-unionism was not part of the policies or practices of any Urban League local branch in the country.

In the fall of 1941 Lester Granger was appointed Executive Secretary of the National League. Eugene Kinkle Jones had retired because of prolonged illness. Frightened and without experience in the highly involved job of fund raising, Granger was even uncertain about the reception his appointment would get from the local executives upon whom he would depend for any measure of success. Because of Jones's illness, Granger was even barred from free consultation with the former executive secretary.[9] Then, less than two months after the change in executive secretaries, the nation went to war with Japan. The Urban League board met with Granger the day after Pearl Harbor and took stock of the League's condition and resources.

As of 1940 the League had forty-five affiliates; the budget for the national headquarters had shrunk to about $60,000, with $450,000 for the local Leagues.[10]

To make matters worse, some of the most competent old-line staffers at the national office had departed. T. Arnold Hill, director of industrial relations, was gone; Elmer Carter had accepted a New York State appointment. Ira Reid had gone some years earlier to a professorship at Atlanta University; and Jesse O. Thomas, second in seniority only to Jones, had resigned for a position with the American Red Cross. Granger was left with a small, dedicated skeleton crew. This staff was expected to serve local League groups in forty-five cities in twenty-five states. A crippling deficit greeted the new executive secretary. He found that a minimum of a hundred thousand dollars was needed even to do the jobs to which the League was already committed. Granger commented: "the Board's reaction was one of shock. But members rallied quickly, and through personal gifts and pledges they insured a merry Christmas for the staff." Fund-raising activities by board members went into high gear, and by the end of the next month — January, 1942 — the deficit had been eliminated. By the end of 1942 "the League was puffing forward again. Its speed hardly discernible at times but movement was undeniable." [11]

During the first few years of Granger's leadership, the League made departures into several new areas. For example, the Rosenwald Foundation — through the interest of the foundation trustee, Charles S. Johnson, then president of Fisk University — made a substantial grant to finance the employment not only of a permanent director of industrial relations, but also of a staff of three assistants with the needed secretarial assistance. Julius A. Thomas was drafted for the director's job from the Louisville Urban League where he had become a state fixture. This two-year activity greatly widened and deepened industrial contacts throughout the nation and opened up hundreds of employer contacts to be used by local Leagues.

Thomas proved to be an excellent salesman, knowledgeable in the field of labor affairs, and quick to master the viewpoints, blind spots, and administrative structures of corporate management. He developed a nationwide acquaintanceship with key individuals in business and industry that was to stand the League in good stead for years to come. Until Thomas's accession to responsibility, the National Urban League had had only brief, casual contacts with leadership in this field of management; now there was no welfare agency in the country that could match the depth and scope of the League's for contacts with leaders of business and industry.

In June of 1942, a little more than six months after Granger assumed office as executive secretary, a small interracial group of League supporters set in motion an idea which ultimately blossomed into an institution — the National Urban League Guild. As an organization of volunteers, the Guild, composed of both men and women, is dedicated to the support and promotion of the aims and objectives set by the National Urban League. Within a few years of the establishment of the first Guild, every local League affiliate had a local chapter of the Guild to work hand-in-hand with it in its local area.[12]

The primary functions of the Guilds have been to serve as a liaison with racial and other groups in the local community, and to assist in raising funds for community projects related to the goals of the Urban League. Easily among the most popular of the Guild's projects are the Beaux Arts Balls, staged annually in leading cities throughout the country. Patronized and supported mainly by middle-class Negroes, the Beaux Arts Balls attract an ever-increasing number of wealthy white sponsors, many of whose names appear in the local or national social register. In the aggregate the annual Beaux Arts Balls have netted hundreds of thousands of dollars for both the national and local Leagues. The gain in terms of publicity and promotion is probably even greater.

With the war's close, the National Urban League had strengthened its budget and staff resources to the point that program planning could be initiated without awaiting favorable foundation action. The return of Winthrop Rockefeller from army service to resume his place on the board had strengthened its leadership connections with business and industry. A Commerce and Industry Council and a Labor Advisory Council were formed to establish formal contacts with the corporations and labor unions which had increasingly entered into support of the League's programs as well as its budget. Ranking officers represented their corporations (or unions) at regular meetings in which League programs, policy, and problems were reported. Accordingly, the 1950's showed a remarkable improvement of relationships between the League and the very influential management and labor forces in the country.

Among other League projects to be energized after World War II was the promotion of Career Conferences on dozens of black college campuses.[13] The Vocational Opportunity Campaigns had by now attained "big time" status. Executives, educators, scientists, publishers, and professional men and women in practically every area of academic interest appeared on college campuses to take part in career conferences, while local leaders met with junior and senior high school students in their own communities. "Plan and prepare" became a familiar phrase in extracurricular discussions on a hundred college campuses across the country, for the program had been refashioned on a basis that would take especial note of the racial difficulties experienced by darkskinned youth but would be equally valuable to all students, no matter what their race. "In the course of time, more than 100,000 young people were re-evaluating their potentials from new perspectives centered on sound education and better jobs." [14]

Early during the war Granger was appointed special adviser to Secretary of the Navy James Forrestal. His services were needed in dealing with the serious racial problems, poor morale, and even mutiny by Negro personnel in the Jim-Crow navy. Granger did his work diligently, efficiently, and effectively. As a result of his investigations and recommendations, Secretary Forrestal issued two executive orders, one in February, 1946, and the other in 1947, establishing as navy policy complete elimination of racial segregation or discrimination of any other sort. For his service Granger received in 1946 the Secretary's Distinguished Civilian Service Medal and a year later, the President's Medal of Merit. In 1948, as a member of President Truman's Committee on Equality of Opportunity in the Armed Forces, Granger helped to bring about similar changes in the other branches of service, though the army's final acquiescence, in the absence of any presidential urging, was not completed until the Eisenhower administration took a more active role.

By the mid-1950's, under the resourceful and imaginative leadership of Lester Granger, the National Urban League movement had achieved and surpassed, by a considerable margin, all of the goals it had set for itself in 1941. The staff had grown to three times its end-of-depression numbers. Its budget had increased from a rock-bottom figure of less than forty thousand dollars to a basic budget approaching a half million dollars. Its local affiliates — which had been trimmed to thirty-seven in number because of program inactivity or lack of cooperation with the national organization — had now passed the sixty mark, and organizational work was being carried on in several cities.

The board had greatly strengthened itself in the scope of influence and activity of its members. Financial campaigns carried on in industry and labor by representatives of those fields produced a solid basis of financial support that enabled the organization to take advantage of opportunities and to survive difficulties. Public figures of prominence and influence, recruited to head public fund-raising campaigns, had done far more than merely lend their names.

The League had achieved recognition as a community organization — the only one to apply this professional technique directly to the complicated field of race relations and Negro advancement, and possibly the largest such professional agency operating on the national scene. Its officers had made their mark on the social welfare map. Lester Granger had been an effective force in the National Conference of Social Work (now the National Conference on Social Welfare) as acting president, and later president, and had headed the International Conference on Social Work for four years. More than any other man he had "built the modern Urban League."

But perhaps the best evaluation of a half century of Urban League work was made by Nat Hentoff:

> Basically, the Urban League is a non-political, interracial social work and community planning agency that emphasizes — and often initiates — the expansion of equality in opportunity for Negroes in all phases of the national economy in our cities. It is also involved in numerous community campaigns to improve Negro housing and to insure that Negroes receive — and know about — the health and welfare services they need. As corollary goals the League works to provide career guidance for youngsters and to strengthen family life.
>
> These are thorny, complex problems and require more than just energy and dedication alone to solve. They require professionals, and the Urban League is a thoroughly trained team of professionals experienced in the field of social service. More than any other groups, they have helped dissolve the once prevalent concept of a social worker as being a mechanical system-ridden collector of case histories.
>
> The Urban League staff volunteer workers do much more than assemble facts. They utilize those facts to *change existing inequalities.*[16]

12 THE NEW MILITANTS

AFTER THE DEMISE of the Garvey movement in the early 1930's, the hordes of its members and fellow travelers discarded its banners and gaudy trappings and took up more mundane pursuits. But the black nationalism preached by Garvey had its true believers, and some among them began casting about for a new vehicle for their faith. Their search ended fruitfully in the early 1930's in the Negro ghetto of Detroit when an itinerant peddler named Wallace Fard proclaimed a new creed — Black Muslimism. As the prophet of the new religion, Fard taught that the African was brought to the New World against his will by the white man and that all black Americans were really members of Islam with Allah as their God. For the time being, the Caucasian ruled the world, but the black man would return to power in the not-too-distant future.[1]

The first meetings of the new religion were held in the homes of its handful of believers, but soon its members outgrew the arrangement and rented a hall. This hall was consecrated as the first Temple of Islam. Within three years the movement had caught on among the black population of Detroit. Three main institutions of the religion had been developed: the Fruit of Islam, a quasi-military legion of young black men; a University of Islam which was a combined elementary and secondary school; and the Muslim Girls Training Class. Early in its development Fard retired from the active leadership of the movement and left it in the capable hands of a group of young stalwarts.

Chief among these was Elijah Poole, later to be known as Elijah Muhammad, who was the Georgia-born son of a Baptist minister. Poole and his family, a wife and two children, moved from Georgia to Detroit in 1923. He made the acquaintance of Fard in 1931. While in training as one of the disciples, Poole was known as Elijah Karriem. When he became Supreme Minister of the movement, his name was changed to Elijah Muhammad. In 1932 Fard and Elijah Muhammad went to Chicago and established Temple Number Two. Wallace Fard disappeared mysteriously in 1934. Shortly thereafter, a power struggle erupted among the ministers. Elijah Muhammad apparently was forced to flee to Chicago and thence to Washington, D. C., where he established another temple. In the early forties Muhammad was convicted of draft evasion and sentenced to five years in prison. After serving two and one-half years of his sentence, Muhammad was paroled. He returned to Chicago to take up active leadership in the movement.[2]

Under Elijah Muhammad's leadership, the movement enjoyed its most rapid period of growth. Under Fard's guidance there had never been more than eight thousand members nor more than a handful of temples. Largely through Muhammad's tireless efforts, membership grew to more than 100,000, and the number of temples to fifty, scattered throughout the country.

> Muhammad's strategy has been to put the cult on parade — on the streets, in the press, in the temples, *wherever there are people*. And he has done this with impressive success. For local action, he has had an able corps of ministers in the field; but there were not many at first, and their fight was uphill. The press gave him his first major assist, for it made him "controversial"; as a columnist in one of the most important Negro papers in the country, he became a conversation piece for hundreds of thousands of Negroes across America.[3]

Perhaps the best known and most widely recognized of all Black Muslim leaders was Malcolm X. Malcolm X was born Malcolm Little in Omaha, Nebraska, in 1925.[4] He was one of eleven children and his father, who was a Baptist minister, was an ex-Garveyite and very definitely a "race man." It was probably because of the Reverend Mr. Little's militancy and aggressiveness that his house was burned by the Ku Klux Klan in 1931 and that he himself met a violent death a short time later. After the father's death Malcolm's family suffered severe privation and ultimately disintegrated. Young Malcolm drifted eastward to New York City and entered into some of the marginal activities of the Harlem underworld.

> By the age of 18 Malcolm was versatile "Big Red." He hired from four to six men variously plying dope, numbers, bootleg whiskey and diverse forms of hustling. Malcolm personally squired well-heeled white thrill-seekers to Harlem sin dens, and Negroes to white sin downtown. "My best customers were preachers and social leaders, police and all kinds of big shots in the business of controlling other people's lives."[5]

Under such circumstances Malcolm, while still a young man, established a considerable police record.

In the maximum security prison in Concord, Massachusetts, in 1947 Malcolm's life took a new direction. One of Malcolm's brothers, Philbert, was in the same jail. As a recent convert to Black Muslimism, he began Malcolm's conversion to the new faith. Thus, Malcolm began writing Muhammad every day during the rest of this term in prison; he joined the prison debating team and began to read extensively to improve his meager education. The impact of the Black Muslim teaching upon this wayward young man can hardly be exaggerated. Thus in Malcolm X's own words:

> They say a man should never be condemned or tried twice for the same crime once he has paid the penalty. Yet, when a man goes to prison and pays his debt to society, when he comes out he is still looked upon as a criminal. . . . Well, Mr. Muhammad has succeeded there where Western Christianity has failed. When a man becomes a Muslim, it doesn't make any difference what he was [doing] before as long as he has stopped doing this. He is looked upon with honor and respect and is not judged for what he was doing yesterday. And this, I think, explains why we have so many men who were in prison following Mr. Muhammad today.[6]

Out of prison in 1952, Malcolm X went to Detroit to live in the strict Muslim home of his brother Wilfred, another convert to the faith. Malcolm soon won acceptance as a student under Muhammad himself and in a short time became the Supreme Leader's favorite pupil. After becoming a full minister himself, Malcolm was dispatched to spread the faith in Boston and Philadelphia; and in April, 1954, he was installed as a minister of Temple Number Seven in Harlem. Tall, powerfully built, and light-skinned, Malcolm X was an attractive figure. To a very considerable degree he was charismatic. But, in addition, he was an indefatigable organizer and recruiter. Whereas Muhammad spoke principally to the black masses, Malcolm was sought by radio, television, colleges, and universities as spokesman for the amazing new movement among America's black proletariat. By the time of his death in 1964, Malcolm X had gained recognition as the number one Black Muslim in the country.

By and large, the rank and file of the Black Muslim movement, at least in the early years, were almost identical in kind to those who in the early 1920's responded to the exhortations of Marcus Garvey. They were recent migrants from the states of the deep South. In the main they were illiterate, rural-oriented, unskilled, and poverty-stricken. They had moved North to escape Southern white brutality, lynching, peonage, and second-class citizenship. And if the North did not entirely turn out to be the promised land they thought it would be, it, at least, was not a land entirely without some promise.

The Black Muslims recruited these newcomers by the thousands. They were taught pride of race and color, self-esteem, and black brotherhood. The ills of the black race were laid at the feet of the "white devil." And as Malcolm X stated in a TV documentary:

> I charge the white man with being the greatest liar on earth. . . . I charge the white man with being the greatest robber on earth. I charge the white man with being the greatest deceiver on earth. I charge the white man with being the greatest troublemaker on earth. . . .[7]

As he further stated:

> When you say "Negro" you're trapped right there. Makes no difference who you are nor how many degrees you have from Harvard; if you're a Negro, you're trapped. If you're black, the doors close.[8]

The black race would have to avoid and shun unnecessary contacts with whites, isolate and protect its women, and look to the development of an undefiled black culture.

C. Eric Lincoln, the foremost authority on the Black Muslims, lists five major characteristics of the movement.[9] First, the membership is made up primarily of younger people. Those between the ages of seventeen and thirty-five constitute up to 80 percent of the rank and file. In the newer temples the average age is under thirty. As an activist movement its major appeal is directed toward youth. The older members are predominantly ex-Garveyites who consider the movement to be a natural successor to the Universal Negro Improvement Association.

Second, as an avowed Islamic movement the focus is placed upon male membership rather than female predominance, as in Christian churches. While women are honored and idealized, they do not share in the basic activities of the organization.

Third, the membership is principally drawn from the lower socio-economic strata of American Negroes. When these people were recruited in the early 1930's, they were predominantly welfare recipients residing in the most hopeless and abject sections of Detroit's black ghetto. By 1937, however, these people were described as follows:

> At the present time there is no known case of unemployment among these people. Practically all of them are working in the automobile and other factories. They no longer live in the slum section . . . but rent homes in some of the best economic areas in which Negroes have settled. . . .[10]

However, Lincoln notes that Muslims do not generally live in the better residential areas available to Negroes because Muslims have continued to emphasize their affiliation with the working class.

Fourth, a significant characteristic of the Garvey movement was the fact that its leadership was made up almost exclusively of immigrant West Indians, while American Negroes constituted the preponderance of the dues-paying rank and file. Black Muslimism, on the contrary, was American through and through. West Indian Negroes were not recruited nor especially welcomed. On the other hand, the West Indian Negro, hailing from a different culture, had no particular affinity for indigenous black American organizations.

Fifth, the movement tends to be anti-Christian in emphasis. Unlike their parents who were essentially "fundamentalist" in their views toward religion, the Black Muslim youth had been exposed to the rampant secularism of the ghetto. Recruited as non-Christians, they later became anti-Christian.

As a movement the Black Muslims are neither pacifists nor aggressors. They are zealous in their obedience to the law; and they will not participate in civil disobedience, passive resistance, or "marches" for this or that cause. But as one observer put it: "They do believe in keeping the scores even, and they have warned all America that an 'eye for an eye and a tooth for a tooth' is the only effective way to settle racial differences." Indeed, every Black Muslim is expected to fight if he is attacked and to give his very life, if need be, for the cause.[11] The *esprit de corps* of the movement is best exemplified by its cadres of young males conditioned mentally and psychologically along the lines of some of the toughest modern military special forces. They are known as the Fruit of Islam. Though the duties of the Fruit of Islam generally fall under the two categories of security and discipline, Lincoln noted an emerging new role. He stated:

It now acts also as a police force and judiciary — or, more exactly, a constabulary and court martial — to root out and punish any hint of heterodoxy or any slackening of obedience among the Muslims themselves.[12]

The Muslims believe that the Negro's low status and weakness in American society is due to his lack of economic power. Thus, Muslims urge the establishment of black businesses and economic ventures. They advocate:

Pool your resources, physically as well as financially.
Stop wanton criticism of everything that is black-owned and black-operated.
Observe the operations of the white man. He is successful.

He makes no excuses for his failures. He works hard — in a collective manner. You do the same.[13]

The Muslims, incidentally, follow their own advice. They establish numerous small businesses, shops, and itinerant ventures of many varieties. Chicago has become a showcase of their enterprise. In that city Muslims operate department stores, restaurants, grocery stores, and a number of service establishments. This pattern has been followed to a lesser degree in other cities. In every case, however, the Muslim establishment is clean, efficient, and intelligently managed.

In the long run, however, the most significant characteristic of the Black Muslims is not their religious belief or their advocacy of a separate and economically independent Black State in America. Both the Communists and the Garveyites had long before urged black separation. The Black Muslims demonstrate that a mass movement among American Negroes can be built upon *militant racism* and an unalloyed hatred of the white man, and that the bland Negro handyman or porter can be transformed into an ascetic, self-confident, and potentially dangerous, true believer, ready and willing to respond to the bidding of his superiors. The Black Muslims display a new potential of the American Negro — one that white America will not relish but one with which it will have to reckon as the future unfolds.

More than a dozen years prior to the advent of Reverend Martin Luther King, Jr.'s Southern Christian Leadership Conference and the Student Nonviolent Coordinating Committee, nonviolence as an instrument of social protest had been adopted and effectively employed by an American interracial protest organization. This group was the Congress of Racial Equality. In February, 1942, James Farmer, then Race Relations Secretary of the Quaker-Pacifist Fellowship of Reconciliation, laid down the guidelines for the new organization to be known simply as CORE. The new group would pursue "positive and effective alternatives to violence as a technique for resolving conflict." It would seek to translate "love of God and man, on one hand, and hatred of injustice on the other, into specific action." [14] Farmer projected the movement's direction toward a study of the Gandhian movement. He said the new technique would be spoken of as "nonviolent direct action." [15]

Farmer was not critical of the roles of the NAACP and the National Urban League in the Negro's struggle. Indeed, he felt that they had "proved their value from specialized angles" and should be encouraged and supported. But in his judgment they had also demonstrated their "inadequacy in dealing effectively with the total aspects of a problem as comprehensive" as that of the American race problem. Thus he saw "the need for a virile and comprehensive program such as our study and experimentation in non-violence should logically lead into." Farmer thought in terms of a five- or even a ten-year plan "after which, it is to be hoped, relentless non-cooperation, economic boycott, civil disobedience"[16] would be used wherever and whenever necessary. From its very inception CORE was an interracial movement, and not until 1960 were there more Negroes than whites in the membership.

One day in October, 1942, a small interracial group of CORE members entered Stoner's Restaurant in Chicago's Loop for lunch. The proprietor met them as they came through the swinging door and stated that he did not serve Negroes and hence could not seat them. When asked why he followed this policy, Stoner replied that since the restaurant was his, he could follow any policy he chose. This was CORE's first important test of its program and its first direct confrontation with the problem. The organization went into action. For more than six months, CORE members visited Stoner's in an attempt to break the segregation policy. Stoner made the usual claim that he would lose all of his white trade if he served Negroes. He said that 90 percent of his trade came from white women and that they would not want to eat beside Negroes. One time when a CORE group seated in the restaurant thought they had broken the policy, they were

> served meat with egg shells scattered on it, or a plate of food salted so heavily that it could not be eaten, a sandwich composed of tomato and lettuce cores picked out of the garbage in the kitchen. . . .[17]

Finally, in June, 1943, CORE planned to stage a sit-in in Stoner's. Some sixty-five persons, sixteen of whom were Negroes, participated in the demonstration. They were all pledged to nonviolence. The whites agreed to remain seated until the Negroes were served. The first group (interracial) to enter the restaurant were, to their surprise, served after only a half-hour's wait. With some obvious irritation, a second group was not seated immediately after entering. Meanwhile, the police who had been summoned to the restaurant could find no cause to arrest anyone and left. Reluctantly, the management ordered the second group seated and served.

Then a very unexpected spontaneous demonstration took place — a wild applause broke out. Practically everyone in the restaurant took part in this sustained acclamation. It was a fitting climax to a well executed non-violent demonstration for racial justice.[18]

During the 1950's CORE began to abandon its lone-wolf activities and joined in cooperative actions with other protest organizations. In 1958 the organization brought about the end of discrimination against Negroes by one of the largest commercial bakeries in St. Louis. By 1960 CORE was apparently swinging into line with the new militancy of Martin Luther King, Jr. and the new Student Nonviolent Coordinating Committee. This was definitely indicated in James Farmer's promotion of the famous "Freedom Ride" through Alabama and Mississippi in 1961. With national attention drawn to its activities for the first time in its career, CORE had become a major civil rights organization. It had "joined the club."

13 THE BLACK VOTE AND NATIONAL POLITICS

THE SHIFT OF NEGRO voters from the Republican to the Democratic Party became noticeable in 1920 and continued through the national elections of 1936. Of course, the Grand Old Party was aware of this trend, but its twelve years of power from 1920 to 1932 made the party somewhat disdainful of Negro support. Indeed, as we have seen, Herbert Hoover did not even want it. After their disastrous defeat in 1936, however, the Republicans' attitude toward the black electorate underwent a radical change. With political observers freely predicting oblivion for them, the Republicans began searching for every possible iota of support for their 1940 campaign. As former friends of the party, Negro voters were to be wooed as never before.

The chief strategy of the Republicans for winning back the Negro vote as the 1940 national elections approached was that of minimizing the advances made by the race since 1932. Republican campaign speakers reminded Negroes that even under the New Deal, which some Negroes loved so much, the race was yet a long way from political and economic equality. The Roosevelt administration was sharply criticized for having failed to eliminate discrimination in federal agencies; for allowing the new defense industries to turn Negroes away from their gates; and for having failed to hold the Southern bloc in Congress in line on the anti-lynching and anti-poll tax measures. No incident which could be used against President Roosevelt escaped Republican attention.

At the Republican Convention of 1940, a total of eighty-five Negro delegates attended. With Perry Howard back on the national committee, observers noted that the lily-white movement had all but been forgotten. A special bureau of Negro publicity was created with

Emmett J. Scott, once secretary to Booker T. Washington, in charge. For work among Negroes the country was divided into an Eastern and Western division with each under the joint direction of a Negro male and a Negro female who were prominent members in the party. The Negro plank of the party's platform, which had hitherto been limited to pronouncements on civil and political rights for Negroes, now promised them a "square deal in the economic and political life of the nation."[1]

The Republican presidential candidate, Wendell L. Willkie, enjoyed a good reputation among Negroes. Long before the campaign Willkie had taken an active interest in the race. He spoke frequently at Negro meetings and conferred on many occasions with Negro leaders. At a press conference during the Republican Convention, Willkie thus opened his heart to Negro reporters:

> I want your support. I need it. But irrespective of whether Negroes go down the line for me or not, they can expect every consideration. They will get their fair representation on policy-making bodies. They will get the same consideration as other citizens.[2]

Under normal conditions, it is very probable that Willkie would have reversed the Negro trend to the Democratic Party.

For holding the Negro votes in line, the Democrats, during this campaign, were more or less content to rely upon Negro attachment to the New Deal. This attachment was strengthened by the race's great esteem for Mrs. Roosevelt and Henry Wallace. These two leaders, of course, made many visits and speeches among Negroes during the campaign. More important was the fact that millions of the Negro underprivileged in the South as well as in the North in 1940 were still receiving some form of relief assistance from the federal government. True, the administration had not done much to eliminate discrimination in federal bureaus and defense industries, but the number of Negroes affected thereby was still small; and their complaints could do little to detract from President Roosevelt's popularity. Under any circumstances, the Democrats could and did point to the fact that over eighty thousand Negroes had received employment with the federal government since 1933, and that over one hundred of these had received top positions.

While President Roosevelt's victory over Wendell Willkie was far less impressive than that which he scored over Alfred M. Landon, Negroes, nevertheless, cast more votes for the Democrats than ever before in history. The fact that he was seeking a third term undoubtedly cost President Roosevelt much white support, but this issue was apparently unimportant to Negro voters. Statistics on the black vote in ten selected cities show that President Roosevelt fell behind his 1936 total in only two instances. This loss was more than overcome by gains of from 1 to 7 percent in the eight other cities studied.

With the entry of the United States into World War II, Negroes, like other groups in the country, steeled themselves for a long and bitter struggle against the Axis powers. The blacks, as always, had their special problems; yet, they were also concerned with issues that confronted the American people as a whole. They were for a conclusive victory in the war, a realistic foreign policy designed to assure a lasting peace, and a postwar program for full production and employment. Led by their protest organizations, Negroes fought also on a broad domestic front. The race wanted an improvement in the treatment of black men and women in the armed services, the establishment of a permanent Fair Employment Practice Committee, and the enactment of federal anti-poll tax and anti lynching legislation.

The spirited campaigns conducted by Negro groups made it certain that these issues would play a prominent part in the 1944 elections. Since they were in power, the Democrats had not only to meet the incessant attacks of the Republicans for failing to clear up the Negro problem, but the administration had also to concern itself with Axis powers' efforts to make propaganda out of the Negro question. In January, 1942, for example:

> A Negro was brutally lynched in a small town in Missouri. Within forty-eight hours, German and Japanese short-wave radios were broadcasting the ugly details. The sordid details were relayed to the Dutch East Indies and India to break down resistance morale [against the Japanese] just before the fall of Java.[3]

Here was clear evidence, the Axis claimed, of how democracies treated the colored races. The attempt of the Roosevelt administration to punish the perpetrators of the crime foundered upon the rocks of states' rights.

In 1944 the national elections were marked by an unprecedented interest in the Negro voter. On the one hand, there were the anxious Republicans who had been out of power for twelve years; on the other, there were Democrats anxious over their chances to elect President Roosevelt for a fourth term. The Negro vote could be decisive. Thus, innumerable predictions were made and straw polls were conducted on the probable black vote. In a study made by Paul N. Lazarsfeld, of Columbia University, it was shown that newspaper interest in the Negro vote was far greater in 1944 than in 1940. For instance, "In the ten days after the 1940 Democratic National Convention, which followed the Republican Convention of 1940, one paper devoted nine inches to two items about Negroes. The other six carried no Negro political news." In 1944, however, for the same period, "five of the seven newspapers carried twenty-two items filling more than sixty-six column inches."[4]

As in 1940, the Republicans conducted a vigorous campaign to regain the Negro vote. In their platform they promised a congressional investigation of discrimination in the armed services, a permanent FEPC, and the adoption of a constitutional amendment outlawing the poll tax. Republican campaign speakers made political capital out of the just grievances of many Negro soldiers. They sought to link the President and even Mrs. Roosevelt with Senator Bilbo, Representative Rankin, and other advocates of white supremacy. They revived and circulated the charges that vice-presidential candidate Harry S. Truman carried a card of membership in the Ku Klux Klan. All this was good ammunition, but it could not, among Negroes, offset the refusal of the Republicans to renominate Wendell Willkie as the party's candidate for President. Governor Thomas E. Dewey was not considered a special friend by Negroes. His plea for a permanent, national FEPC sounded empty when it was recalled that in 1943, he had blocked a proposed FEPC for New York State. Likewise, his advocacy of state rights was not applauded by Negroes who realized that this was the doctrine which blocked federal intervention in their problem.

In favor of the Democrats was the fact that although the FEPC was not permanent, it was still in existence and doing beneficial work for Negroes and other minorities. In addition, the Roosevelt administration had intervened before in the Philadelphia Transit Company strike and the Detroit riot in behalf of Negroes. Female branches of the armed services had been opened to Negro women, and the edge had been taken off segregation in the transportation facilities of army posts. These deeds, however, were somewhat offset by the substitution of Senator Truman for Henry Wallace as the President's running mate. This was a bitter blow to Negroes who were hoping that Wallace would succeed Roosevelt as President.[5] Because of this action by the Democrats, two of the nation's largest Negro weekly news-papers, with a combined circulation of a half-million copies, switched to Dewey.

In order to hold their Negro support in line during this campaign, the Democrats did not rely solely upon the popularity of President Roosevelt and the work of the Democratic National Committee. The principal drive was conducted by the CIO's Political Action Com-mittee. Regular trade union channels were used to contact the half-million Negro members of the CIO unions. Negro communities were canvassed by thousands of volunteers in an intense effort to get the black folks to register and vote. No opportunity was missed to send a speaker to a Negro meeting or church. The PAC bought space in Negro newspapers and distributed among Negroes nearly five million pieces of literature. In addition, the race was reminded of the work which the PAC had done in eliminating from Congress such Negro baiters as Joe Starnes, Cotton Ed Smith, and Martin Dies. The success of this drive was manifested in post-election statistics.[6] It was apparent that Roosevelt lost some ground among the conservative black folk in the midwestern towns, but in the teeming metropolises the Roosevelt plurality in Negro votes was increased for the third successive time.

To those familiar with the thinking of Negroes in the years between 1932 and 1944, the black vote, in the main, was a vote for Roosevelt rather than for the Democratic Party. Without the President, the diatribes and insults from some members of the Southern bloc in Congress would have long since caused the Negro to beat a retreat to the ranks of the Republican Party. So, when the tragic news of Roosevelt's death broke during the afternoon of April 12, 1945, no group in America was more heartsick, lonely, and confused than up-wards of fifteen million blacks. To the deeply religious black folk Roosevelt had been next to God. Under any circumstances, it can be said that during Roosevelt's presidency, Negroes, for the first time since their liberation, placed more faith in the leadership of a white man than they did in that of any man of their own race.

The upheaval in Negro affairs was inevitable. With the easy de-pendence on F. D. R. ended, the Negro voter had now to sharpen his tradesman's acumen and enter the open market of politics. And, an open market it was, for with a Roosevelt no longer present to tip the scales the two major political parties, as far as the Negro was concerned, were almost identical twins. Under President Truman, great liberals such as Mrs. Roosevelt, Henry Wallace, and Harold Ickes — all friends of the Negro — left the Washington scene. The Black Cabinet of unofficial Negro advisers lost its power almost immediately. Top-ranking Negro appointees of Roosevelt were surreptitiously discarded or given posts far removed from the vortex of national power. To the hard-bitten Negro politician, the Democratic Party was taking on an ominous hue — lily-white. In control of both houses of Congress as of 1946, the Republicans began to suffer from lapse of memory. What about the proposed constitutional amendment to outlaw the poll tax? Was not Republican strength in both houses of Congress sufficient for them to enact a permanent FEPC law even if it were necessary to invoke cloture to bridle the Southern bloc? But these were merely academic questions. There were few Negroes at that time gullible enough to put stock in the easy promises of a desperate political party.

When Harry Truman became President of the United States upon Roosevelt's death in April, 1945, Negroes knew little about him as a person and a political figure. Truman had first come to Washington in 1935 as a senator from Missouri. His association with the Pendergast machine was well known, and in Washington he was dubbed the "Gentleman from Pendergast." Truman's political career seemed at an end in 1939 when his patron, Tom Pendergast, was sent to federal prison for income tax evasion. However, Truman surprised his friends as well as his enemies when he won reelection to the Senate on his own in 1940 by attracting the votes of laborers, farmers, and Negroes in a blistering campaign.

All doubts harbored by Negroes as to what kind of attitude Truman would have on racial matters were rapidly dispelled by Truman himself within little more than a year after he had become President. On December 5, 1946, Truman appointed a committee to investigate and report on the status of civil rights in America. Truman's Committee on Civil Rights was made up of fifteen prominent people, representative of business, labor, church, education, politics, and minorities. Its report was published in October, 1947, under the title, *To Secure These Rights*. In a message to Congress on February 2, 1948, Truman asked that the recommendations of the committee be enacted into law. He also urged the abolition of segregation and discrimination in the use of all transportation facilities in the nation.

At Truman's insistence, and over the objections of some of his closest advisers, virtually the entire report of the Committee on Civil Rights was included in the Democratic Platform of 1948. Truman, of course, realized that by so doing he was courting serious troubles from the Southern wing of the party. Demagogues from Dixie denounced his civil rights stand as a capitulation to the Northern liberals and Negroes, and an advocacy of miscegenation and intermarriage.

As Truman and his young chief lieutenant, Hubert Humphrey, had anticipated, "all hell broke loose" on the floor of the Democratic National Convention when the platform was presented for a vote. The time was July 14, 1948, and the place was Convention Hall, Philadelphia. Humphrey was mayor of Minneapolis and vice-chairman of the Americans for Democratic Action. He was also the leader of the "Northern Bloc" at the convention. The *New York Times* describes his activity during the debate on the platform:

> . . . as its principal spokesman [Humphrey] said that the country was 172 years behind the times in meeting the issue of equality. Mayor Humphrey won loud cheers and a scattering of boos for his praise of President Truman's "courage in issuing a new emancipation proclamation" and his assertion that "it is time for the Democratic party to get out of the shadow of states' rights and walk forthrightly in the bright sunshine of human rights." [7]

At the end of the fifty-eight-minute debate and with defeat staring them in the face, the twenty-two-man Mississippi delegation arose and headed for the door. That group was followed by thirteen members of the delegation from Alabama.

> [This] was for them tantamount to secession from the Democratic Party. . . . They walked through a vast, rolling wave of boos from the galleries and from among many of the "regular" delegations. There were some cheers also. But these were very nearly lost in the din, as the delegation strode forward.[8]

Three days later, on July 17, the Southerners met in Birmingham, waved the old Confederate flag, and formed the so-called States Rights Democratic Party. Governor Strom Thurmond, of South Carolina, was nominated for President and Governor Fielding Wright, of Mississippi, for Vice-president. In the election the Dixiecrats carried South Carolina, Alabama, Georgia, and Mississippi. But they failed to achieve their main objective — an all-Southern rebellion which would throw the election into the House of Representatives.

If the Negro vote was definitely moving toward Truman prior to 1948, and there were indications that it was, the drama enacted on the floor of the Democratic National Convention on July 14 virtually put it in his pocket. Then as if to seal the bargain, the President on

July 26, less than two weeks later, issued his famous executive order desegregating the armed services, as well as a companion order calling for the abolition of discriminatory practices in all federal departments and agencies. These two actions brought overwhelming praise to the President from Negro leaders and the Negro press. The desegregation of the armed services was particularly pleasing to the Negro veterans of World War II. They had not yet forgotten the raw deal they had received in the Jim-Crow armed services during the late war.

As the election day neared, all of the better-known polls predicted that Truman would lose. The Gallup Poll underestimated Truman's vote by 5 percent, and the Roper Poll by 12 percent. However, in the final tally Truman received a total of 24,105,695 votes to 21,969,170 for Dewey. The Progressives and the Dixiecrats polled 1,000,000 votes each. Truman carried all thirteen of the nation's largest cities, and it was in these strategic areas that the solid Negro vote made the difference. The Negro majority vote for Truman, well over 80 percent, was up to that time the largest black vote for any presidential candidate.

For purposes of political bargaining, the greatest asset which the Negro had (and still has) was the potential balance of power he held in national, state, and municipal elections. In 1948 this power was derived from the Negro population in seventeen states. Nine of these (New York, California, Pennsylvania, Indiana, Michigan, New Jersey, Illinois, Ohio, and Missouri) had a total of 223 votes in the Electoral College as against 266 necessary to elect a President. Significantly, these states had the largest concentration of Negro citizens of voting age outside of the South. After 1940, of course, the number of Negroes in the indicated seventeen states had increased, but these increases had not been merely relative to that of the whites. Absolute increases had been brought about by what seemed to be a second great migration of Negroes from the South since the start of World War II.

In order for his vote to be decisive where he held the balance of power, it was necessary for the Negro to vote in blocs comprising from 60 to 75 percent of his voting strength. If such blocs had been organized and thrown against Roosevelt in 1944, Dewey would have been elected. The question arises as to how often and in what states the black ballot had determined for what candidate the states' electoral votes were cast. The answer to this question can be determined, in part, by examination of actual election returns.

Before 1932 Illinois was the only state in which Negroes voted in blocs large enough to affect the outcome [of elections]. It was from Chicago, one recalls, that the first Negro was sent to Congress in this century. In 1936 the Roosevelt plurality in states with large populations was so great that the Negro vote was a negligible factor.[9]

With the 1940 and 1944 national elections closer to normal, the Negro vote carried Roosevelt in at least a half-dozen states. It is, of course, "impossible to ascertain the exact number of Negro votes cast in any state or municipality. Statistics [are] usually compiled from returns of districts or wards with heavy Negro concentrations."[10]

In speaking of the Negro's political strength in the North, Walter White of the NAACP stated:

It is not difficult to see what the Negro voters could do to the coming elections if issues of sufficient racial interest should cause a large percentage of them to cast their ballots as a unit, to vote as Negroes instead of as citizens.[11]

White was not the first to point out the importance of the strategic place the Negro holds in American politics. This practice was a part of the political stock-in-trade of Negro leaders and politicians even when the Negro had little or no political power in Northern states. In 1912 Dr. Du Bois of the NAACP attempted to bargain, first with the Progressives, then with the Democrats, on the basis of an unorganized and unknown number of Negro votes in the North and East. While Negro political power had increased tremendously, it was largely fluid. Even Roosevelt could not congeal the larger part of it in more than six states at any one time. In fact, as early as 1940, Negroes were returning to the Republican Party in important numbers. Barring a crisis in the country's race problem, it was never possible to organize the Negro vote on a purely racial basis. In politics as in other walks of life the Negro has continually pressed for integration rather than isolation. Special legislation for civil, political, and social rights remains of great importance to the race. But since Roosevelt's time the Negro has learned to appreciate his stake in issues not connected with the Negro question. The race supported Roosevelt, not in payment for any special favor, but because, as part of the one-third of a nation with which the New Deal was specifically concerned, the Negro was interested in social and economic legislation as was the white voter. The Negro's political preference in national elections was governed by domestic and foreign problems as well as his own special problems.

This dissipation of political power, of course, accounted for the smallness of gains which Negroes as a group made in national politics. For instance, it was estimated that there were about as many Negroes voting in the United States in 1948 as there were whites in the seven Southern states of Arkansas, Alabama, South Carolina, Florida, Louisiana, Georgia, and Mississippi combined. Yet, benefits which the Negro group received from politics could not be compared with those received by the Southern whites. A striking example of the inequality in power of the two groups was the fact that the seven Southern states had fifty-two members of the House of Representatives and fourteen members in the Senate. But the Negro, though holding a balance of power in seventeen states, had but two members in the House of Representatives and no Senators. In the matters of representation in Congress, special legislation, and federal patronage, the Negro also fell far behind such economic minorities as agriculture and labor. These groups had long since proven their ability to organize themselves and to conduct sustained drives for their objectives. Negroes, on the other hand, had never organized themselves nationally. Drives for special legislation had been conducted by splinter groups largely without the effective political support of the race as a whole.

No group better realized the actual weakness and ineffectiveness of Negro political power on the national level than the congressmen who represented districts populated partially or wholly by Negroes. After all, it is the business of the politician to evaluate carefully the strength of the groups and interests he represents. Fence-mending, for instance, in Negro districts was seldom done except during presidential election years. On the other hand, the Negro constituent did not visit or write to his congressman as often as did the white voter. Requests or petitions from individual Negroes or Negro organizations were received cordially enough. But often the matter was pressed no further because the Negro constituent, like many of his white brothers, was generally too lackadaisical to follow up on his congressman's actions. Indeed, there are but few instances on record where Negro voters actually "punished" a congressman for having been unresponsive to their demands. In a large measure this situation was responsible for the apathy which congressmen from the North displayed when FEPC, anti-poll tax, and anti-lynching legislation were under consideration in the federal legislature.

The Negro electorate, as a whole, exercised little or no influence with the national committee of the two major political parties. Perry

Howard, an old-line Negro politician from Mississippi, was placed on the Republican committee during the party's national convention in 1940 largely because of Willkie's policies toward Negroes. However, the Democrats always had a lily-white committee. For advice on Negro questions, it was the practice of both parties to consult congressmen from Negro districts, Negro politicians, and civic and political leaders. Negro intellectuals or leaders of protest organizations were rarely asked for their advice since their demands for the race were likely to be greater than the party in question was willing to promise. In 1939 the Republican National Committee commissioned Dr. Ralph Bunche, of Howard University, to draw up a report on the needs of the Negro for use in shaping policy on the Negro question. However, if Republican platform promises are to be accepted as evidence, Bunche's conclusive and well-written document was wasted effort.

At national conventions Negro political bigwigs were appeased with temporary sinecures consisting usually of the chairmanships of special Negro bureaus or sectional divisions. But the dispensation of regular federal patronage among Negro constituencies was hardly ever in proportion to their size or strength. The procedure followed by the congressman from the Negro district consisted usually of filling traditional Negro positions, of awarding to Negroes a few relatively unimportant jobs, and then spreading the bulk of the patronage which he controlled among big white supporters and contacts. During the Roosevelt era, which to Negroes (if to no one else) was abnormal, this pattern was broken. Under President Truman, however, the old order for Negroes was rapidly restored.

Because of the virtual impossibility of controlling or of delivering the Negro vote in national elections, the paucity of federal patronage, and the lack of recognition by the major political parties, ambitious and able Negro politicians preferred to concentrate their activities on the state and municipal levels of politics. This is not to say that the Negro vote could have been delivered by any individual or group in any *election*. Indeed, the old brokerage method of dealing with Negro votes had fallen upon hard times. But because of the smaller area of operation and the factional conflicts which frequently marked state and municipal politics, the Negro vote was often the object of keen competition. These situations provided the Negro political leader with opportunities which were seldom matched on the national scale.

In stark contrast to the federal legislature, Negroes were amply represented in law-making bodies of the states in which they were concentrated in important numbers. State election districts were smaller than congressional districts, so a ghettoized Negro population was often assured of at least one state representative. Below is a list of states and the number of Negroes who in 1944 were sitting in their respective legislatures.

California	1	Wisconsin	1	Colorado	2
Kentucky	1	Illinois	6	New Jersey	1
Indiana	4	New York	3	Ohio	2
Vermont	1	Kansas	1	Pennsylvania	4
		West Virginia	1		

Apart from the legislatures, however, Negroes were never nominated to run for high state posts. Neither were they ever appointed to the state offices which correspond in importance to those of the United States President's cabinet. In general, most states followed a well-established pattern in the appointment of Negro officials. Negroes were usually placed upon boards or commissions which brought them into a minimum contact with whites and a maximum contact with Negroes. In many cases, the Negro official was assigned to Negro cases only. Thus, an assistant attorney general usually found himself handling Negro offenders exclusively. Other agencies in which a Negro was likely to be appointed included health, education, unemployment compensation, housing, and parole. A break with this practice, however, was the appointment of Negro judges in such states as New York, Ohio, Illinois, Pennsylvania, and California.

In the securing of legislation for the protection of his civil and political rights, the Northern Negro was far more successful with the state governments than he was with the national government. There were in 1948 eighteen states with civil rights statutes on their books. As a whole, these laws were roughly similar to the Federal Civil Rights Act which the United States Supreme Court invalidated in 1883. Discrimination and segregation were generally prohibited on railroads, streetcars, hotels, restaurants, theaters, and other places of public accommodations and amusements. The statutes differed, however, in the type of remedy to be employed in seeking redress. Thus, seven states provided for a criminal prosecution only; one made a provision for a civil action only; seven allowed both a criminal action and either a suit for penalty or a civil action for damages. The remaining states permitted both types of redress but stipulated that success in an action of either kind barred all other proceedings. In the main, none of these states rigorously enforced these statutes; nevertheless, there were innumerable instances in which Negroes were awarded damages under them.

In addition to civil rights laws, the states of Indiana, Massachusetts, New York, and New Jersey created Fair Employment Practice agencies, largely as a result of the nationwide agitation for a permanent federal FEPC, which took place during World War II. The Massachusetts law was passed in 1946, and the other three were placed on the books in 1945. All four of these agencies were modeled after the one which was urged upon Congress in several bills but never adopted by that body. The Indiana agency, however, was the weakest of the four. Its commissioner was given a mandate to aid in the elimination of discrimination in employment, to make studies, and receive complaints. But the bureau had no power whatever to punish offenders. The agencies of the other three states had jurisdiction over employers of six or more persons, employment agencies, and labor unions. Much importance was placed upon arbitration and education, but in each case offenders were liable to punishment of one-year imprisonment or fine of five hundred dollars.

In 1950 there were at least eleven cities in America with a Negro population of 100,000 or over. These concentrations formed the backbone of whatever Negro political power there was, and even at its grass roots it was largely ineffective. In every one of these areas there were glaring clear-cut problems of housing, health, education, and employment calling not only for expert planning but for the formulation of intelligent Negro political programs. The Negro voter, of course, knew what he wanted and what he should get for his vote, but he did not always understand why he did not get it. The resulting frustration drove the more impatient Negroes in New York City to resort to riots and public disturbances as a means of attracting the attention of civic officials to their problems.

Actually, there never had been a dearth of intelligently planned programs in any of the important Negro communities, but the sponsors of these programs were usually protest groups which, if we remember, had never been too popular with the Negro masses. Moreover, the existence of an effective liaison between a political party and any Negro protest group would have been something to wonder at. This left the direction of Negro political affairs to party-appointed leaders, many of whom were uneducated and unscrupulous. Power became dear when there was but little of it. Among political leaders of a Negro community, there was often a petty but bitter and prolonged haggling with the local machine for place and power. In such situations the general welfare of the Negro community as a whole was inevitably submerged.

From 1935 onward from one to four Negro leaders were seated at one time in the inner councils of New York's Tammany Hall. In the Hall these men were the political representatives of the quarter of a million votes that Harlem Negroes regularly cast in elections. Yet in few sections of the country excluding the South was there less evidence of the fruits of political power. Harlem was the nation's number one ghetto. There had always been many projects and programs, but these almost never got the active support of the cynical and indifferent Negro politician on the local scene. Indeed, the net gains made by the Negroes in the twenty years of voting in New York City added up to nothing more than a few scraps of patronage distributed through obedient Negro leaders by the incumbent political machine. Hardly more could be said for the Negro electorate in other metropolises. So much for Negro politics north of the Mason and Dixon Line.

Up to 1944 the concern of Southern Negroes was not how they would use their votes, but how to get their constitutional rights to vote respected at all. This problem became all the more important in view of the fact that the bulk of the Negro population of the country lived in seven to ten Southern states. At no time since the 1890's had more than a fraction of this group participated actively in politics. Nevertheless, the situation was far from static. Important changes were working above and underneath the visible surface, and a dynamic situation full of possibilities was maturing. For one thing, the indefensible treatment of Negroes was no longer the purely local problem that Southern whites preferred it to remain. Few aspects of American democracy were more closely examined and more often commented upon by foreign observers than those presented in the South. Mounting embarrassment to Northern as well as to Southern whites was bound to have its effect upon this ugly problem. Indeed, one of the more heartening signs in the South was the steady increase in the numbers and influence of the liberal element. The strength of this group increased as industrialization and unionization of labor proceeded in this section.

More important was the fact that all possible means for the legal disfranchisement of the Negro using the loopholes of the federal Constitution had become pretty well exhausted. After 1915 the United States Supreme Court killed one contrivance after another which was designed to keep the Negro away from the Southern polls. Of course, the poll tax and literacy tests remained. However, the rise in the earning capacity of the Negro since the war, plus a widespread use by Negroes of the educational benefits of the G.I. Bill of Rights, tended to make these two devices less and less effective. The greatest cause for the resurgence of political activity among Southern Negroes was the *Smith* v. *Allwright* decision of the United States Supreme Court (see pages 192-193). The exclusion of Negroes from participation in the primary elections in the South had been far more profound than had been generally realized. Its effect upon the political thinking of Southern whites was almost as important. Some Southern states accepted the Court's pronouncement with an unprecedented calmness. Others, however, either attempted to patch up the white primary device or looked for still other means of legally barring Negroes from the polls.

The new opportunity to vote in some Southern states quickly resulted in local gains for the Negro. In an election in Savannah, Georgia, two factions of the Democratic Party fought a closely contested campaign. One faction, the Citizens' League for Fair Play, campaigned actively among the newly enfranchised Negroes, promising that if it won the election, Negro policemen would be appointed for the first time in the city's history. When the League won, promise was kept. In 1947, Negro voters in Richmond, Virgir just missed electing Oliver W. Hill, a Negro lawyer, to the Virgin House of Delegates. Hill lost to his white rival by a mere 190 vote: In June, 1948, however, Hill was successful in his campaign to win seat in the Richmond City Council. He thus became the first Negr to win such an office since the days of Reconstruction. His victory wa based largely on the solid support of the Negro Fifty-ninth Distric Surprisingly enough, Hill also received considerable white suppoi The *New York Times* stated the following: "At least 2,000 of the vot for Mr. Hill were credited to white voters. In the Fortieth Precinct, a wholly white section, he ran ahead of seventeen white candidates." [12]

In the majority of Southern states, however, voting was still a hazardous business for Negroes. Intimidation and violence as agents for Negro disfranchisement were not completely discarded. In addition, the more imaginative white Southerners were continually thinking up new ways of making voting distasteful or embarrassing to Negroes. Thus, in the Democratic primary elections in Mississippi in August, 1947, Negroes were required to swear opposition to FEPC, anti-poll tax, and anti-lynching legislation before being allowed to vote. Nevertheless, the future of the Southern Negro seemed brighter than at any time since the Reconstruction Era. Most observers agreed that the political *status quo* in the South could not and would not be maintained. It was entirely conceivable, therefore, that the next generation would witness an increase by three or four million in the number of Negroes voting in the United States.

14 WE SHALL OVERCOME

THE HISTORIC 1954 DECISION of the United States Supreme Court in *Brown* v. *the Board of Education of Topeka* marked the successful conclusion of a campaign begun by the NAACP legal department some twenty-five years previously. Perhaps no staff of lawyers in the nation's history had ever been more dedicated to the achievement of a single cause, or so equipped with the necessary expertise and information to achieve that cause. In 1930 the NAACP received a grant of one hundred thousand dollars from the Garland Fund. These funds enabled the Association to restructure and redirect its entire method of operation. Previously, limited resources and the great number of cases had limited the action of the Association to meeting crises as they arose. Under the direction of Judge Nathan R. Margold, the Association made the most complete and authoritative study of the legal status of the Negro ever undertaken up to that time. The study covered court cases on unequal apportionment of school funds, property holders' covenants, disfranchisement, civil liberties defense, job discrimination, Jim-Crow travel, and denial of equal protection of the laws generally.[1] The Association soon thereafter acquired the services of Charles H. Houston, William H. Hastie, and Thurgood Marshall. These men began bringing suits or assisting other lawyers in cases involving Negroes in federal and state courts. During the next twenty years the Association's legal staff, through its persistent attack, managed to whittle down to its bare bones the "separate but equal" interpretation of the Fourteenth Amendment. Indeed, by the time the Supreme Court reviewed the issue in 1954, it had little to do but inter the remains. In the cases given below, segregation in institutions of higher learning had been virtually abolished by 1953.

1936: Donald Murray, a Negro, enrolled at the University of Maryland Law School under court order. In *Pearson* v. *Murray* the Maryland Court of Appeals held that the state must afford equal opportunities in its own institutions.

1938: The University of West Virginia graduate and professional school voluntarily admitted Negroes. In *Gaines* v. *Canada* the United States Supreme Court decreed that the state was bound to furnish equal facilities within its borders. It ordered Lloyd Gaines admitted to the University of Missouri Law School since no Negro law school existed. Gaines never enrolled.

1948: The University of Delaware announced it would admit Negroes to any courses not offered at Delaware State College for Negroes. (The University desegregated under court order in 1950.) The University of Arkansas voluntarily admitted Negroes to its professional schools.

The United States Supreme Court in February, 1948, ordered Ada Lois Sipuel admitted to the University of Oklahoma Law School, which she did not attend until 1949. The University admitted its first Negro, G. W. McLaurin, in October, 1948.

1949: The University of Kentucky opened its graduate schools to Negroes under court order.

1950: A United States district court ordered Louisiana State University Law School open to a Negro, Roy Wilson.

A state court opened the University of Missouri to Negroes. The University of Virginia Law School admitted its first Negro under court order.

The United States Supreme Court in *Sweatt* v. *Painter* ordered Hemon Sweatt admitted to the University of Texas Law School after ruling that the separate law school at Texas State University was inferior in such intangible criteria as standing in the community, tradition, and prestige.

In *McLaurin* v. *Oklahoma State Regents for Higher Education* the Supreme Court held that McLaurin, who was admitted to the university in 1948, was handicapped in being taught in segregated conditions. The Court ordered that he receive the same treatment as white students.

1951: A federal court order in *McKissick* v. *Carmichael* opened the University of North Carolina Law School to Negroes.

1952: The University of Tennessee under court order admitted Negroes to its graduate, professional, and special schools.

1953: Friona University in West Texas voluntarily opened its doors to Negroes.

The Arden and Claymont districts in Delaware desegregated.

Segregation in the use of dining-car facilities had been decreed illegal by the Court in 1950 in the case of *Henderson v. United States.*[2] In 1955 the Interstate Commerce Commission, in response to a petition of the NAACP, outlawed segregation of passengers in all railroad terminals. Since the early 1920's the NAACP had been waging a battle against segregated housing and restrictive covenants. It was never successful in the courts against segregated housing, but in 1948 the United States Supreme Court ruled that while restrictive covenants could stand in voluntary agreements, they could not be enforced by the state courts.

Nevertheless, as America reached the mid-century point in 1950, American Negroes generally had run out of patience with the restrictive, insulting, and degrading segregation laws and practices in existence throughout the country. In the South, wherever a Negro turned, in the public parks and swimming pools, in the hotels, motels, and restaurants, and even in the churches, his entrance was regarded as a trespass. He could travel ten miles or a thousand miles on a highway in the South and would not find a motel that would put him up for the night nor even a "greasy spoon" that would sell him a meal. But the most grievous of all affronts to him was the denial of the opportunity of a decent elementary and secondary education for his children. As a citizen the Negro paid the same rate of taxation as did the white. Yet in every Southern state, the per capita expenditure annually for the Negro child was only a fraction of that spent on the white child. Moreover, in a great many Southern counties there were no tax-supported schools for Negro children at all. For these reasons, among others, Negro parents initiated the several suits that culminated in *Brown v. the Board of Education of Topeka.*

The first of these cases involved a suit brought by Harry Briggs, Jr., and other Negroes against Clarendon County, South Carolina, School District No. 22. The complaint was that the county's schools for Negroes were abysmally inferior to the schools for white children. In a second case, Dorothy E. Davis and others sued the school board of Prince Edward County demanding that Virginia's constitutional and statutory provisions imposing segregation be nullified or that the county's Negro and white high schools be equalized. In Delaware Negro parents filed a suit in the Court of Chancery to desegregate public schools in Claymont and Hockessin. On April 1, 1952, Chancellor Collins J. Sutz ordered the Negro plaintiffs admitted to the schools. The Delaware Supreme Court affirmed the decision and on appeal the case went to the United States Supreme Court.

In Kansas, Oliver Brown brought suit against the Board of Education in Topeka because his daughter had been refused entrance to the white elementary school only five blocks from his home and was required to attend an all-Negro school a mile away. In Washington, D.C., where the Fourteenth Amendment does not apply, Spottswood Bolling sued under the Fifth Amendment, charging that his children were unlawfully excluded from Sousa Junior High School. He maintained that nothing in the statutes of the District of Columbia, as enacted by Congress, empowers the Board of Education to operate separate schools for Negroes and whites. The Supreme Court decided to lump all five cases under the title of *Brown* v. *the Board of Education of Topeka*. What the plaintiffs in all five cases were asking was that the Supreme Court apply the qualitative test of the *Sweatt* case and outlaw segregation in elementary and secondary schools.[3]

During the summer of 1950, a national conference of lawyers associated with the NAACP met in New York and plotted an all-or-nothing attack upon segregation in the American public school system.[4] Any compromise with, or consideration of, gradualism was rejected out of hand. It was, they insisted, entirely unreasonable and unjust to expect Negro children to wait indefinitely for the Jim-Crow school to disappear. The evil of segregation transcended the physical inadequacies and pitiful curriculum of the Southern black school. The damage committed upon the personality of the Negro child by segregation was incalculable.[5]

Their contentions were amply supported during the same year in the *Report of the Midcentury White House Conference on Children and Youth*. Regarding the detrimental effects of segregation on minority group members the report stated:

1. Special stresses are created for individuals by the discrepancy between democratic teachings with respect to equality and the practice of enforced segregation.
2. Segregation is a special source of frustration.
3. Feelings of inferiority and of not being wanted are induced by segregation.
4. Submissiveness, martyrdom, feelings of persecution, withdrawal tendencies, self-ambivalence, and aggression are likely to develop.
5. Distortion in the sense of reality may occur as a consequence of enforced segregation.

6. A few individuals gain psychologically from being members of segregated groups, but most are harmed thereby.[6]

Consequently, on one day in February, 1951, Robert L. Carter, a top-ranking member of the NAACP's legal staff, paid a call on Dr. Kenneth B. Clark, a professor and one of the nation's leading psychologists. Carter wanted to know from Clark whether psychologists had any findings which were relevant to the effects of racial segregation on the personality development of Negro children. He revealed that the legal staff of the NAACP was going to challenge the constitutionality of existing state laws which made possible racially segregated public schools. In short, Thurgood Marshall, Robert Carter, and their staff were going to drive directly for a nullification of the separate-but-equal doctrine of *Plessy* v. *Ferguson,* and they wanted the assistance of psychologists and social scientists in the four cases they were preparing. Thus, Clark was invited to share work with the lawyers in the preparation for the court hearings.[7]

Largely through Dr. Clark's efforts, a corps of some of the nation's most eminent authorities in psychology and related fields and social sciences were mobilized. These included Mrs. Mamie Clark, a psychologist in her own right; Gordon Allport and Jerome S. Bruner, of Harvard; Helen Trager and M. Brewster Smith, of Vassar; Isidor Chein, of New York University and the American Jewish Congress; Otto Klineberg, of Columbia; Louisa Holt, of the University of Kansas and the Menninger Clinic; and David Krech, of the University of California.[8]

Dr. Clark himself served as social science consultant to the legal staff of the NAACP. As such, he acted as liaison between the lawyers and the social psychologists called as expert witnesses or as helpers in the preparation of the social science brief. Dr. Clark had the further duty to advise the lawyers about the special areas of competence of the prospective expert witnesses and to approach such persons on behalf of the legal staff. He himself attended conferences of the legal staff of the NAACP in order to familiarize himself with the legal issues, terminology, and arguments involved in the cases. In the *Virginia* case he and others helped

in analyzing the testimony of expert social science witnesses called by the defendants (the State) so that inconsistencies and weaknesses in their testimony could be brought out in cross examination.[9]

Other social scientists testified in the federal district and state courts as expert witnesses on:

1. The effects of segregation on personality development.
2. The effects of school segregation in lowering of motivation and impairing the ability to learn.
3. The social and psychological significance of a state-imposed racially segregated society.
4. The consequences of desegregation.
5. The relationship between desegregation on the graduate and professional school level and the possibilities of desegregating the elementary and high schools.[10]

In three of these cases a leading social psychologist examined Negro children with "appropriate projective techniques and interviews in order to determine whether they showed evidence of personality distortions related to racial discrimination and segregation." [11]

When the United States Supreme Court accepted these cases on appeal under the title *Brown* v. *the Board of Education of Topeka*, the social scientists were given a special and urgent task. For the first argument in the October, 1952, term of the Court, they prepared an *Appendix to Appellants' Briefs* entitled "The Effects of Segregation and the Consequences of Desegregation: A Social Science Statement." This was prepared by Stuart Cook, Isidor Chein, and Kenneth B. Clark. Thirty-two "outstanding" American social scientists reviewed and endorsed it for presentation to the United States Supreme Court.[12]

At the beginning of 1954 all Southern states had completed detailed studies of the appalling discrepancies in their dual school system. Up to then they had not seriously considered making the Negro schools *really* equal although separate. Many of the legal officials in these states seemed to think that they were still being protected by the hoary decisions in *Plessy* v. *Ferguson* and *Cumming* v. *County Board of Education*. They were rudely awakened from their complacency by the national interest in the case and rumors of the prodigious preparations being made by the NAACP's legal staff. Hence, in an atmosphere of panic and desperation the South pinned its hopes on John W. Davis, a former United States ambassador to Great Britain, Democratic candidate for President of the United States in 1924, and a lawyer who had pleaded more Supreme Court cases than any other man, living or dead.

Of the nine justices on the Supreme Court bench at the time of the *Brown* case, five had been appointed by President Franklin D. Roosevelt. These were: Hugo L. Black, Stanley F. Reed, Felix Frankfurter, William O. Douglas, and Robert H. Jackson. Some had been members of the so-called "new" Court, but they all qualified as "liberals." Three other justices (Thomas Clark, Harold Burton, and Sherman Minton) were Truman appointees. While these men were not conservatives, none of them was as assertive and aggressive in his views as those of the dominant five. The only really unknown quantity on the Court was Chief Justice Earl Warren, whose nomination had just been confirmed by the Senate on March 1, 1954. The *Brown* case was Warren's first major confrontation with the complexities of high court decision making. The segregation laws and practices of the states, as well as those of the federal government, had already taken a bad beating at the hands of these justices. All of them except Warren had been party to the unanimous decisions which struck down desegregation in the four major cases which came before the Court just prior to the *Brown* decision. For the so-called "Supreme Court Watchers," therefore, the big question was not *how* the Court would rule on segregation, but *how far* it would go in its ruling.

On December 9, 1952, when the *Brown* case was first argued, Fred Vinson was still chief justice. As the Court could not reach a decision at that time on the basis of the initial briefs and arguments, six months later on June 8, 1953, the Court restored the cases to the docket for the fall and issued a list of questions upon which it wished that arguments would be made.

The Court asked for enlightenment on the two main points. First, is there historical evidence which shows the intentions of those who framed and ratified the Fourteenth Amendment with respect to the impact of that amendment upon racial segregation in the public school? Second, if the Court finds that racial segregation violates the Fourteenth Amendment, what kind of decree could and should be issued to bring about an end to segregation? Beyond the basic constitutional points, the Court also asked questions concerning the possible implementation of a decision against segregation. Could the Court in the exercise of its equity powers permit a *gradual* transition from segregated to nonsegregated schools?

When the cases were reargued in December, 1953, Chief Justice Earl Warren was presiding. In great detail, extensive briefs described the background of the Fourteenth Amendment and the intentions of its framers and ratifiers. The brief submitted by the United States Attorney General presented suggestions by which the Court could decree a gradual desegregation of the schools. In the matter of the decree, the NAACP's brief said: "In accordance with instructions of this Court we have addressed ourselves to all the plans for gradual adjustment which we have been able to find. None would be effective." [13] In support of its answers on gradualism, the NAACP's brief contained data prepared by the social scientists based upon an objective empirical study of instances of desegregation. It was entitled "Desegregation: An Appraisal of the Evidence." [14] In an oral argument John W. Davis declared:

> . . . we find nothing here on which this Court could formulate a decree, nor do we think the court below has any power to formulate a decree, reciting in what manner these schools are to be altered at all, and what course the State of South Carolina shall take concerning it. Your Honors do not sit, and cannot sit as a glorified board of education for the State of South Carolina or any other state.[15]

At exactly forty-nine minutes past twelve on May 17, 1954, before a packed courtroom, Chief Justice Earl Warren announced that he had the Court's opinions and decisions in numbers one, two, four, and ten, *Oliver Brown* v. *the Board of Education*. For the next thirty minutes Warren proceeded to demolish the separate-but-equal doctrine of *Plessy* v. *Ferguson* as a standing principle of American constitutional law and to remove the legal props from segregated public education in the United States. Using the words of the decision in the *Kansas* case, Warren declared:

> Segregation of white and colored children in public schools has a detrimental effect upon the colored children. The impact is greater when it has the sanction of the law; for the policy of separating the races is usually interpreted as denoting the inferiority of the negro group. A sense of inferiority affects the motivation of a child to learn. Segregation with the sanction of law, therefore, has a tendency to [retard] the educational and mental development of negro children and to deprive them of some of the benefits they would receive in a racial[ly] integrated school system. Whatever may have been the extent of psychological knowledge at the time of *Plessy v. Ferguson* this finding is amply supported by modern authority. Any language in *Plessy v. Ferguson* contrary to this finding is rejected.[16]

One writer commented that in view of the extreme importance of the decision, the supporting arguments were not very well organized. Chief Justice Warren admitted that the historical background of the Fourteenth Amendment provided no definite conclusions about this issue. However, Warren could have written a much stronger argument that the amendment was meant to provide an elastic general standard. Such an explanation would justify an interpretation of the Constitution based on conditions in 1954 which were far different from conditions in 1868. If this had been done, and other available precedents claimed for the 1954 decision, much of the criticism that the decision was "judicial legislation" would have been undermined.[17]

Other more or less objective critics of the *Brown* decision viewed with concern the Court's apparent reliance upon sociological data rather than upon law. Typical of these were the remarks of James Reston of the *New York Times:*

> The Court's opinion read more like an expert paper on sociology than a Supreme Court opinion. It sustained the arguments of experts in education, sociology, psychology, psychiatry, and anthropology in the Gebbart case, namely, that even with equal school buildings, segregated Negro children receive a substantially inferior education.[18]

This was one of the first of the many critical allusions that would be made to the famous "eleventh footnote" given in the citations to the *Brown* decision. In this footnote the Court cited seven social science documents, six of which were presented in the *Appendix to Appellants' Briefs* submitted by the NAACP lawyers in the first argument of the case. On the impact of the social scientists in the case, the noted legal scholar Edmund Cahn observed that the practice of segregation was so obviously cruel that the attempt to prove such cruelty scientifically was hardly necessary.[19]

In the South, however, opinion on the decision ranged from outright defiance and chagrin to mild predictions that peaceful adjustment would be made. Governor James T. Byrnes, who had served on the Supreme Court from 1941 to 1942, defended the doctrine of "separate but equal" but urged the South to preserve order. Governor Robert Kennon, of Louisiana, declared that the state would enact legislation that would provide a school system segregated in fact if not in law. Herman Talmadge, of Georgia, proclaimed that there would be no mixed schools in Georgia so long as he was governor. In Virginia under the monolithic power of Senator Byrd's political machine, John C. Calhoun's hoary doctrine of "interposition" was resurrected.[20] The Virginia legislature passed a resolution condemning the *Brown* decision as an attempt by the Court to usurp the power that lies solely with the states. Following suit, seven other states adopted interposition. These were Alabama, Florida, Georgia, Louisiana, Mississippi, South Carolina, and Arkansas.[21] A new order known as the White Citizens Council was formed in the South to sustain the region in defiance of the Supreme Court.

On March 12, 1956, a group of senators and representatives from eleven Southern states presented to Congress a document entitled "The

Southern Manifesto: Declaration of Constitutional Principles." Part of it reads as follows:

> We regard the decision of the Supreme Court in the school cases as a clear abuse of judicial power. It climaxes a trend in the Federal Judiciary undertaking to legislate, in derogation of the authority of Congress, and to encroach upon the reserved rights of the states. . . .
>
> Without regard to the consent of the governed, outside agitators are threatening immediate and revolutionary changes in our public-school systems. If done, this is certain to destroy the system of public education in some of the States.
>
> With the gravest concern for the explosive and dangerous condition created by this decision and inflamed by outside meddlers: We reaffirm our reliance on the Constitution as the fundamental law of the land.
>
> We decry the Supreme Court's encroachments on rights reserved to the States and to the people, contrary to established law, and to the Constitution.
>
> We commend the motives of those States which have declared the intention to resist forced integration by any lawful means.[22]

The *Manifesto* required no congressional action and as such it had no legal standing. It was signed by one hundred and one southern members of Congress among whom some of the more prominent were: William Fulbright, Richard B. Russell, Strom Thurmond, Allen J. Ellender, Harry F. Byrd, Sam J. Ervin, and John L. McClellan.[23]

Usually austere and generally imperturbable, several members of the Court were privately stung by the irresponsible remarks of some supposedly responsible people with regard to the *Brown* decision. In defense of the decision, Professor Charles L. Black noted that a Court that refused to see inequality in the deliberately segregated society of the South "would be making the only kind of law that can be warranted outrageous in advance — law based on self-induced blindness, on flagrant contradiction of known fact." [24]

In the decision of May 17, 1954, the Court had not discussed the matter of decrees or possible methods or procedures for implementing that decision. Hence, from April 11 to 14, 1955, the Court heard arguments on these matters from counsels from the states involved and others, as well as from the United States Attorney General. In its opinion of May 31, 1955, the Court recognized that local situations would require locally devised programs to implement the court decision. Consequently, the Supreme Court referred to the district courts the responsibility for determining whether or not school districts were acting in good faith to carry out the steps necessary to open "public schools on a racially nondiscriminatory basis with all deliberate speed. . . ."[25]

The phrase "with all deliberate speed" was duly appreciated by the recalcitrant South, which made the most of it. The typical Southern school board postponed devising a plan of desegregation until it was threatened into doing so. Then it pieced together subterfuges, shams, and evasions of every conceivable nature. Some plans proposed integrating elementary schools from first grade upward at one grade a year to be followed by a period of waiting and evaluation. Others featured pupil placement, school selection by students, or community plebiscites. None of the devices, if even workable, could produce more than sheer "tokenism." Counting on the legal delays, many Southern counties literally forced Negro parents to go back to the federal court. Thus, during the five-year period following the 1954 decision, 226 suits were filed in state and federal courts on school segregation, desegregation, and related issues. Every state in the South was involved in litigation on the school issue. Of the Negro children of the South, 92 percent were still attending all-black schools in 1960.

The federal courts, confronted with massive resistance to their decrees on desegregation, could look for little assistance from the executive branch of the national government. Indeed, President Eisenhower's record on integration while he was Army Chief of Staff would not bear scrutiny. Because President Eisenhower did not strongly endorse the Court decision on integration but merely accepted it as the law to be enforced, Marquis Childs described him as "a police officer who must wait for a riot call before he can interfere in a family quarrel." [26]

There can be little doubt that the virtual nullification of the Supreme Court's decision in the South, plus the hands-off attitude of the Eisenhower administration, caused a desperation among Negroes out of which arose the resolve to challenge the unconstitutional structure of the Southern system with either extralegal means or sheer defiance. This resolve sparked the Negro social revolution. A few days after the *Brown* decision was handed down, Channing Tobias, chairman of the NAACP Board of Directors, said:

> It is important that calm reasonableness prevail, that the difficulties of adjustment be realized, and that without any sacrifice of basic principles, the spirit of give and take characterize the discussions. Let it not be said of us that we took advantage of a sweeping victory to drive hard bargains or impose unnecessary hardships upon those responsible for working out the details of adjustment.[27]

After more than five years of frustration, the NAACP had to report back to the Negro people that legal efforts at desegregation were an abject failure and that there seemed little hope for the future.

> Negro children denied their rights are indeed injured parties, but to require them to bear the whole burden of seeking redress of their injury through costly and prolonged litigation, to compete against the massive weight of official state opposition, is to deny justice . . . . even under the most liberal interpretation, this can hardly be deemed to meet the test "of deliberate speed." [28]

In the mid-fifties Negroes were in the grip of a crisis. For almost one hundred years they had looked toward the day when the promises made in the Civil War amendments would be fulfilled. For more than forty years they had faithfully supported the NAACP in its valiant efforts to have the federal judiciary read and interpret the Fourteenth Amendment in the manner intended by its framers. But the victory won in the majestic chamber of the United States Supreme Court in 1954 turned to ashes on the dusty streets of Dixie. To men such as Bull Connor, of Birmingham, the *Brown* decision was a bad, if not dangerous, joke to play on Negroes, especially in the South. Yet the advice to the Negro from all corners, and especially from the unrealistic white moderates, was "allow the Southern whites time to adjust as the forces of moderation and fair play do their work." It was to such counselors that Martin Luther King, Jr., addressed his "Letter from Birmingham Jail."

> Wait? . . . when you have seen hate-filled policemen curse, kick and even kill your black brothers and sisters; when you see the vast majority of your twenty million Negro brothers smothering in an airtight cage of poverty in the midst of an affluent society; . . . when you are humiliated day in and day out by nagging signs reading "white" and "colored"; when your first name becomes "nigger," your middle name becomes "boy" (however old you are) and your last name becomes "John," and your wife and mother are never given the respected title "Mrs."; when you are harried by day and haunted by night by the fact that you are a Negro, living constantly at tiptoe stance, never quite knowing what to expect next, and are plagued with inner fears and outer resentments; when you are forever fighting a degenerating sense of "nobodiness" — then you will understand why we find it difficult to wait. There comes a time when the cup of endurance runs over, and men are no longer willing to be plunged into the abyss of despair. [29]

On December 1, 1955, Mrs. Rosa Parks, a Negro, boarded a bus in Montgomery, Alabama. She and twenty-four other Negro passengers were seated in the Negro section of the bus as it pulled up in Court Square to take on six white passengers. Since all seats for white passengers were already filled, the driver ordered those among the front row of the Negro section to yield their seats to white passengers. This was a time-honored procedure in the South and one that was never challenged by Negroes. Three Negro passengers surrendered their seats, but Mrs. Parks remained seated. After twice asking her to obey the law as well as the custom, the driver summoned the police, who promptly arrested Mrs. Parks. She was charged with violating the city's segregation ordinance. Word of Mrs. Parks' arrest quickly spread throughout the community. Three young and obscure Negro preachers, among whom were Martin Luther King, Jr., and Ralph Abernathy, picked up the story and moved immediately to organize Montgomery's Negroes in support of Mrs. Parks.[30]

During a meeting held at Mr. King's church on the very next evening, it was decided that Negroes in Montgomery would stage a one-day boycott of all Montgomery's buses on Monday, December 5. What began as a one-day boycott lasted for 382 days. It was the first and most effective extralegal campaign ever waged by American Negroes against racial injustice. It was the first battle in the Negro social revolution and the initial step in what the young Martin Luther King was to call a *Stride Toward Freedom*. Indeed, King's own destiny was irrevocably charted during this period. Even before the successful conclusion of the boycott had been achieved, King had become a national figure. On December 5, 1955, Negro leaders in Montgomery organized the Montgomery Improvement Association with Martin Luther King, Jr., as its first president.

The lesson of Montgomery was not lost on the nation's Negroes. The more alert among them realized that if the walls of segregation could not successfully be assailed by litigation alone, perhaps the technique employed in Montgomery could fill the breach. If passive resistance as a medium of social protest had never been employed on a broad scale in America, it would now be introduced with devastating effect in the South. Thus, in the years immediately following Montgomery, the youthful Martin Luther King set for himself the task of fashioning passive resistance, or "nonviolence" as he would call it, into a program with a philosophy. As King himself put it, "It was in this Gandhian emphasis on love and nonviolence that I discovered the method for social reform that I had been seeking for so many months."[31] By 1962 the Southern Christian Leadership Conference, with Martin L. King, Jr., as its head, had become preeminent in the Negro's quest for social justice.

Meanwhile, Negro college students in the South, easily the ones most impatient with the status quo, began to violate local segregation laws and mores deliberately and directly. Seeking to dramatize the injustice of these ordinances, the student demonstrators offered no resistance to violence and actually courted arrest. The chief targets of this movement in the South were department stores which maintained segregated lunch counters while welcoming Negro trade in other sections of the store. Many of these stores maintained "white" and "colored" water fountains. Negro students also concentrated on segregated downtown restaurants. The first of these sit-in demonstrations occurred on February 1, 1960, in Greensboro, North Carolina. Within six months NAACP lawyers were busy representing sixteen hundred students who had been arrested all over the South. The demonstrators had been spat upon, jeered, chased, beaten, and even stomped. They were arrested for violating local ordinances, trespassing, or disturbing the peace. But the movement continued and soon bore successful results. Department stores and chains in dozens of Southern communities desegregated their lunch counters during 1960 and 1961.

Soon the virus of the Negro social revolution in the South was to spread to other sections of the country. White students on the campuses of Northern colleges and universities evinced their support of the Negro's cause by staging sympathetic sit-in demonstrations in their own college towns and nearby cities. Ultimately, much of America's white, middle-class youth, disillusioned and appalled at the true dimensions of white racism, would begin to question the entire value structure of American society, and this evaluation would lead to yet another revolt. Finally, the Negro in the North, amazed at the courage of his Southern brethren, would enlist in the race's revolution. In the metropolis, however, nonviolence would be rejected in favor of the Molotov cocktail and the sniper's rifle.

NOTES

CHAPTER 1

[1] William E. B. Du Bois, *Black Reconstruction in America* (New York: Russell & Russell Publishers, 1935), p. 681.

[2] *Ibid.*

[3] *Ibid.*, p. 685.

[4] Paul Lewinson, *Race, Class and Party: A History of Negro Suffrage and White Politics in the South* (New York: Oxford University Press, 1932, and Russell & Russell Publishers, 1963), p. 55.

[5] C. Vann Woodward, *Reunion and Reaction: The Compromise of 1877 and the End of Reconstruction* (Boston: Little, Brown and Company, 1951), pp. 4-8. See Rayford W. Logan, *The Negro in American Life and Thought: The Nadir 1877-1901* (New York: The Dial Press, Inc., 1954), pp. 13-25.

[6] Logan, *ibid.*, p. 27.

[7] C. Vann Woodward, *Tom Watson, Agrarian Rebel* (New York: Rinehart & Company, Inc., 1938), p. 137.

[8] John D. Hicks, *The Populist Revolt* (A Bison Book: University of Nebraska Press, 1961), p. 115; *National Economist*, March 14, 1889, p. 409.

[9] *National Economist*, December 14, 1889.

[10] Lewinson, *op. cit.*, p. 214 (appendix 2, table 1).

[11] Anna Rochester, *The Populist Movement in the United States* (New York: International Publishers Co., 1943), p. 59.

[12] Woodward, *Tom Watson . . .*, p. 222.

[13] *Ibid.*, pp. 239-240.

[14] *Ibid.*, p. 221.

[15] Roscoe Martin, "The Peoples Party in Texas," *University Texas Bulletin* (No. 3308, 1933), p. 94.

[16] Jamie L. Riddick, "The Negro and the Populist Movement in Georgia" (Unpublished Master's thesis, Atlanta University, 1937), p. 45.

[17] Helen Blackburn, "Populism in the South" (Unpublished Master's thesis, Howard University, Washington, D.C., 1941), p. 22.

[18] Woodward, *Tom Watson . . .*, p. 370.

[19] Lewinson, *op. cit.*, p. 86.

[20] *Ibid.*, p. 81.

[21] Ray Stannard Baker, *Following the Color Line* (New York: Harper Torchbooks, Harper & Row, Publishers, Inc., 1964), p. 246.

[22] 16 Wall. 36 (1873).

[23] *Ibid.*

[24] 109 U.S. 3 (1883).

[25] *Ibid.*

[26] 163 U.S. 537 (1896).

[27] *Ibid.*

[28] Loren Miller, *The Petitioners: The Story of the Supreme Court of the United States and the Negro* (New York: Random House, Inc., 1966), p. 170.

[29] 163 U.S. 537 (1895).

[30] Du Bois, *Black Reconstruction in America*, p. 726.

[31] John W. Burgess, *Political Science and Comparative Constitutional Law* (Boston: Ginn and Company, 1890), vol. 1, p. 48.

[32] Paul H. Buck, *The Road to Reunion, 1865-1900* (Boston: Little, Brown and Company, 1947), p. 296.

[33] James Weldon Johnson, *Along This Way* (New York: The Viking Press, Inc., 1933), p. 158.

[34] Booker T. Washington tells how he came to receive this invitation to speak in his autobiography, *Up from Slavery* (New York: Dodd, Mead & Co., 1965), p. 131.

[35] *Ibid.*, pp. 139-142.

[36] *Ibid.*, p. 146.

[37] Booker T. Washington, "Should Negro Businessmen Go South?" *The Negro in the Cities of the North* (New York: Charity Organization Society, 1905), p. 19.

[38] Emmett J. Scott and Lyman Beecher Stowe, *Booker T. Washington Builder of Civilization* (New York: Doubleday, Page & Company, 1916), pp. 95-96.

[39] Booker T. Washington, "The Negro and the Labor Unions," *Atlantic Monthly*, vol. 111 (June, 1913), pp. 756-757.

[40] Ridgely Torrence, *The Story of John Hope* (New York: The Macmillan Company, 1948), p. 159. For the full story on the financing of Sale Hall, see Edward A. Jones, *A Candle in the Dark, A History of Morehouse College* (Valley Forge: Judson Press, 1967), pp. 89-90.

[41] *Ibid.*, pp. 162-163.

[42] Scott and Stowe, *op. cit.*, pp. 50-56.

[43] Samuel R. Spencer, *Booker T. Washington and the Negro's Place in American Life* (Boston: Little, Brown and Company, 1955), p. 167.

[44] Anderson to Washington, October 12, 1905, Washington Papers, Booker T. Washington Collection in the Manuscript Division of the Library of Congress.

[45] August Meier, "Booker T. Washington and the Negro Press," *Journal of Negro History*, vol. 38 (January, 1953), pp. 67-68. Used by permission of the publisher, The Association for the Study of Negro Life and History, Inc.

[46] Kelly Miller, *Race Adjustment: Essays on the Negro in America* (New York: The Neale Publishing Company, 1908), pp. 22-23. Now available as *Radicals and Conservatives: And Other Essays on the Negro in America* (New York: Schocken Books, 1968).

CHAPTER 2

[1] John Daniels, *In Freedom's Birthplace: A Study of the Boston Negroes* (Boston: Houghton Mifflin Company, 1914), pp. 104, 122.

[2] William V. Simmons, *Men of Mark: Eminent, Progressive and Rising* (New York: Arno Press, 1968), pp. 833-842.

[3] William Harrison, "Phylon Profile IX: William Monroe Trotter — Fighter," *Phylon*, vol. 7 (1946), pp. 238-240.

[4] William E. B. Du Bois, *Dusk of Dawn: An Essay Toward an Autobiography of a Race Concept* (New York: Harcourt, Brace & World, Inc., © 1940), p. 75.

[5] Kelly Miller, *Race Adjustment: Essays on the Negro in America* (New York: The Neale Publishing Company, 1908), p. 14.

[6] Anderson to Washington, October 16, 1905, Washington Papers. Booker T. Washington Collection in the Manuscript Division of the Library of Congress.

[7] Charles Alexander to Emmett J. Scott, June 10, 1905, Washington Papers.

[8] August Meier, *Negro Thought in America 1880-1915* (Ann Arbor: The University of Michigan Press, 1963), pp. 225-226.

[9] Charles Puttkammer and Ruth Worthy, "William Monroe Trotter 1872-1934," *Journal of Negro History*, vol. 43 (1958), pp. 300-301.

[10] Daniels, *op. cit.*, pp. 122-123.

[11] Du Bois states that Trotter "was arrested, according to the careful plans which William L. Lewis, Washington's Attorney had laid." See William E. B. Du Bois, "William Monroe Trotter," *Crisis*, May, 1934, p. 134.

[12] *New York Times*, July 31, 1903, p. 1.

[13] W. E. B. Du Bois, *The Souls of Black Folk* (Chicago: A. C. McClurg & Co., 1903)

[14] Du Bois, *Dusk of Dawn* . . ., pp. 87-88.

[15] *Ibid.*, p. 64.

[16] Though the "Call" was issued by Du Bois, he acknowledged that most of the platform of the new movement was written by Trotter. See Ralph V. Bunche, "The Programs, Ideologies, Tactics and Achievements of Negro Betterment and Interracial Organizations," *The Negro in America* (Unpublished manuscript, Carnegie-Myrdal Study), vol. 1, 1940, pp. 15-17.

[17] For copy of the "Call," as well as other assorted printed material on the Niagara Movement, see folder designated "Niagara Movement" in the Joel E. Spingarn Papers, Moorland Foundation, Library of Howard University.

[18] Kelly Miller, *Race Adjustment* . . ., p. 16.

[19] *Outlook*, September 14, 1907, p. 45.

[20] Washington to Anderson, October 12, 1905, Washington Papers.

[21] Washington to Anderson, December 30, 1905, Washington Papers.

[22] Elliott M. Rudwick, "The Niagara Movement," *Journal of Negro History*, vol. 42 (1957), p. 181.

[23] *Ibid.*, p. 193.

[24] Puttkammer and Worthy, *op. cit.*, p. 304.

[25] *New York Times*, April 18, 1915, sec. 2, p. 15.

[26] Puttkammer and Worthy, *op. cit.*, p. 308.

[27] Arthur S. Link, *Wilson: The New Freedom* (Princeton, N.J.: Princeton University Press, 1956; Princeton Paperback, 1967), p. 252; Used by permission of Princeton University Press. *New York Times*, November 13, 1914, p. 1.

[28] Puttkammer and Worthy, *op. cit.*, pp. 308-309.

[29] James Weldon Johnson, *Along This Way* (New York: The Viking Press, 1933), p. 314.

[30] Charles Flint Kellogg, *NAACP, A History of the National Association for the Advancement of Colored People* (Baltimore: The Johns Hopkins Press, 1967), pp. 9-11.

[31] Mary White Ovington, *The Walls Came Tumbling Down* (New York: Harcourt, Brace & World, Inc., 1947), p. 103.

[32] Oswald Garrison Villard to Francis Jackson Garrison, April 28, 1898, in The Oswald Garrison Villard Papers, Houghton Library, Harvard University.

[33] For the most authoritative discussion on the background of the "Call," see Kellogg, *op. cit.*, pp. 12-16, 298-299.

[34] *Ibid.*, pp. 19-20.

[35] Villard to Garrison, June 4, 1909, Villard Papers.

[36] Villard to Garrison, November 21, 1910, Villard Papers.

[37] Villard to Garrison, June 4, 1909, Villard Papers.

[38] Trotter to Spingarn, January 2, 1913, Spingarn Papers.

[39] Minutes of the Board of Directors of the National Association for the Advancement of Colored People, May 14, 1910, in the Manuscript Division of the Library of Congress. (This citation will hereafter read: Board Minutes, NAACP.)

[40] Robert H. Brisbane, "The Rise of Protest Movements Among Negroes Since 1900" (Ph.D. Dissertation, Harvard University, 1949), pp. 46-47.

[41] Gunnar Myrdal, *An American Dilemma, the Negro Problem and Modern Democracy* (New York: Harper & Row, Publishers, Inc., 1944), vol. 2, p. 830.

[42] *Ibid.*, p. 820.

[43] Board Minutes, NAACP, June 28, 1910.

[44] Du Bois, *Dusk of Dawn . . .*, p. 95.

[45] Elliott M. Rudwick, "W. E. B. Du Bois: in the Role of *Crisis* Editor," *Journal of Negro History*, vol. 43 (January, 1958), p. 218.

[46] Villard to Spingarn, March 20, 1913, Spingarn Papers.

[47] J. Saunders Redding, "Portrait . . . W. E. Burghardt Du Bois," *American Scholar*, vol. 18 (1948-1949), p. 96.

[48] Rudwick, "W. E. B. Du Bois . . .," p. 222.

[49] Du Bois to Villard, March 18, 1913, Villard Papers.

[50] Ovington to Villard, November 21, 1913, Villard Papers.

[51] Meier, *op. cit.*, pp. 235-236.

[52] Villard to Garrison, August 18, 1913, Villard Papers, as quoted in Kellogg, *op. cit.*, p. 164.

[53] Emmett J. Scott, "Letters of Negro Migrants of 1916-1918," *Journal of Negro History*, vol. 4 (October, 1919), pp. 419-420.

[54] Myrdal, *op. cit.*, vol. 1, p. 194.

[55] *Ibid.*, pp. 194-195.

[56] Du Bois, *Dusk of Dawn . . .*, p. 233.

[57] Jane Addams, "The Progressive Party and The Negro," *Crisis*, November, 1912, pp. 30-31.

[58] Du Bois, *Dusk of Dawn . . .*, p. 234.

[59] *Crisis*, November, 1912, p. 29.

[60] Du Bois, *Dusk of Dawn . . .*, p. 235.

[61] Link, *op. cit.*, p. 246.

[62] *Ibid.*, p. 247.

[63] *Ibid.*, pp. 240-248.

[64] Villard to Wilson, July 21, 1913, Villard Papers, as quoted in Kellogg, *op. cit.*, p. 163.

[65] Wilson to Villard, July 23, 1913, *ibid.*

[66] Link, *op. cit.*, p. 250.

[67] *Ibid.*, p. 251.

[68] Board Minutes, NAACP, October 9, 1916; Kellogg, *op. cit.*, p. 179.

[69] Kellogg, *op. cit.*, p. 181.

[70] Board Minutes, NAACP, April 9, 1917.

[71] Board Minutes, NAACP, September 17, 1917.

[72] James Weldon Johnson, *Black Manhattan* (New York: Arno Press and the New York Times, 1968), p. 236.

[73] Kellogg, *op. cit.*, pp. 260-262.

[74] Johnson, *Black Manhattan*, pp. 241-243.
[75] Board Minutes, NAACP, June 10, 1918.
[76] *Crisis*, July, 1918, p. 111.
[77] *Messenger*, November, 1917, p. 31.
[78] Rudwick, "W. E. B. Du Bois . . .," p. 227.
[79] Board Minutes, NAACP, July 8, 1918, quoted in Kellogg, *op. cit.*, pp. 272-273.
[80] *Guinn v. United States*, 238 U.S. 347 (1915).
[81] *Ibid.*
[82] 245 U.S. 60 (1917).
[83] 271 U.S. 323 (1926).
[84] Johnson, *Along This Way*, p. 361; see also William Pickens, "The American Congo—Burning of Henry Lowry," *Nation*, March 23, 1921, pp. 426-428.
[85] *New York Times*, July 3, 1917, p. 1.
[86] *Congressional Record*, 65th Congress, 2nd Session, vol. 56, part 1, p. 638.
[87] *Ibid.*
[88] Board Minutes, NAACP, September 17, 1917.
[89] *Congressional Record*, 67th Congress, 1st Session, vol. 61, part 1, p. 87.
[90] Johnson, *Along This Way*, p. 371.
[91] Brisbane, *op. cit.*, p. 64.
[92] Myrdal, *op. cit.*, vol. 2, p. 834.
[93] Du Bois, *Dusk of Dawn . . .*, p. 290.
[94] Mary White Ovington, *Half a Man, The Status of the Negro in New York* (New York: Longmans, Green and Co., 1911), pp. 75 ff. See also Johnson, *Black Manhattan*, pp. 126-145.
[95] Myrdal, *op. cit.*, vol. 2, pp. 837-839.
[96] Sterling D. Spero and Abram L. Harris, *The Black Worker: The Negro and the Labor Movement* (New York: Columbia University Press, 1931), p. 129.
[97] *Ibid.*, p. 131.
[98] *Proceedings*, Annual Conference of the National Urban League, Detroit, Michigan, October 15-19, 1919.
[99] T. Arnold Hill, "Open Letter to Mr. William Green, President, American Federation of Labor," *Opportunity*, February, 1930, p. 57.
[100] *Ibid.*
[101] Spero and Harris, *op. cit.*, p. 140.
[102] *Ibid.*
[103] *Ibid.*, p. 141.
[104] Horace R. Cayton and George S. Mitchell, *Black Workers and the New Unions* (Chapel Hill: University of North Carolina Press, 1939), p. 407.
[105] *Messenger*, February, 1926, p. 56.
[106] Spero and Harris, *op. cit.*, p. 142.

CHAPTER 3

[1] *New Republic*, vol. 8 (October 14, 1916), p. 262.
[2] James Weldon Johnson, *Black Manhattan* (New York: Arno Press and the New York Times, 1968), p. 151.
[3] Kenneth T. Jackson, *The Ku Klux Klan in the City, 1915-1930* (New York: Oxford University Press, 1967), p. 22.
[4] Herbert J. Seligmann, *The Negro Faces America* (New York: Harper & Row, Publishers, Inc., 1920), p. 296.
[5] "Opinion of W. E. B. Du Bois," *Crisis*, May, 1919, pp. 10-11.

[6] "Investigation Activities of the Department of Justice," 66th Congress, 1st Session, 1919, *Senate Documents*, vol. 12, p. 162.

[7] Walter F. White, "The Work of a Mob," *Crisis*, September, 1918, p. 222.

[8] Claude McKay, *Selected Poems of Claude McKay* (New York: Bookman Associates, 1953), p. 36.

[9] Arthur Waskow, *From Race Riot to Sit-In, 1919 and the 1960's* (Garden City, N.Y.: Doubleday & Company, Inc., 1966), p. 12.

[10] *Ibid.*, pp. 12-16.

[11] "The Riot at Longview, Texas," *Crisis*, October, 1919, pp. 297-298.

[12] Waskow, *op. cit.*, pp. 105-110.

[13] *Crisis*, October, 1919, pp. 297-298.

[14] *Ibid.*, pp. 23-33.

[15] Board Minutes, NAACP, November 10, 1919.

[16] See Walter F. White, "Chicago and Its Eight Reasons," *Crisis*, October, 1919, pp. 293-297. See also St. Clair Drake and Horace R. Cayton, *Black Metropolis* (New York: Harcourt, Brace & World, Inc., 1945), pp. 65ff.

[17] Waskow, *op. cit.*, pp. 121-140.

[18] Johnson, *Along This Way*, p. 342.

[19] Charles Flint Kellogg, *NAACP, A History of the National Association for the Advancement of Colored People*, p. 242.

[20] Board Minutes, NAACP, February, 1925, quoted in Kellogg, *op. cit.*, pp. 244-245.

CHAPTER 4

[1] Editorial Introduction to Truman H. Talley, "Marcus Garvey — The Negro Moses?" *Worlds Work*, vol. 41 (December, 1920), p. 153.

[2] Edmund D. Cronon, *Black Moses: The Story of Marcus Garvey and the Universal Negro Improvement Association* (Madison: The University of Wisconsin Press, 1966), p. 7.

[3] Robert H. Brisbane, "The Rise of Protest Movements Among Negroes Since 1900" (Ph.D. Dissertation, Harvard University, 1949), p. 84.

[4] Robert H. Brisbane, "Some New Light on the Garvey Movement," *Journal of Negro History*, vol. 36 (1951), pp. 56-57.

[5] Amy Jacques Garvey, ed., *Philosophy and Opinions of Marcus Garvey or Africa for the Africans* (2nd. ed.; London: Frank Cass & Co. Ltd., 1967), part 2, p. 126.

[6] *Ibid.*

[7] *Ibid.*

[8] *Ibid.*, p. 127.

[9] James Weldon Johnson, *Black Manhattan* (New York: Arno Press and the New York Times, 1968), p. 253.

[10] Garvey, *op. cit.*, p. 82.

[11] *Ibid.*, p. 43.

[12] W. E. B. Du Bois, "Back to Africa," *Century*, February, 1923, p. 538.

[13] Gunnar Myrdal, *An American Dilemma, the Negro Problem and Modern Democracy* (New York: Harper & Row, Publishers, Inc., 1944), vol. 1, p. 696.

[14] Du Bois, "Back to Africa," p. 548.

[15] Garvey, *op. cit.*, p. 84.

[16] *Ibid.*, p. 129.

[17] *Ibid.*, pp. 357-358.

[18] Cronon, *op. cit.*, p. 51.

[19] Brisbane, "The Rise of Protest Movements . . .," p. 95.
[20] Claude McKay, *Harlem: Negro Metropolis* (New York: E. P. Dutton & Co., Inc., 1940), p. 154.
[21] *New York Times*, August 3, 1920, p. 7.
[22] Garvey, *op. cit.*, pp. 135-142.
[23] *Ibid.*, p. 140.
[24] McKay, *op. cit.*, pp. 162-163.
[25] Roi Ottley, '*New World A-Coming': Inside Black America* (Boston: Houghton Mifflin Company, 1943), p. 76.
[26] *New York Times*, August 3, 1920, p. 7.
[27] Johnson, *Black Manhattan*, p. 254.
[28] Cronon, *op. cit.*, pp. 60-61, 175.
[29] Columbia Records, No. 14024D.
[30] Charles D. Kepner, *Social Aspects of the Banana Industry* (New York: Columbia University Press, 1936), pp. 180-181.
[31] Garvey, *op. cit.*, pp. 128-129.
[32] For the most accurate and complete account of financial transactions and other involvements of the Black Star Line, see Cronon, *op. cit.*, pp. 54-59, 78-99, 121-124.
[33] Brisbane, "Rise of Protest Movements . . .," p. 101.
[34] *Ibid.*, p. 102.
[35] McKay, *op. cit.*, p. 157.
[36] *Ibid.*, p. 160.
[37] Garvey, *op. cit.*, p. 90.
[38] For the entire document, see Garvey, *op. cit.*, pp. 293-308.
[39] Department of Justice agents did, however, uncover a Negro "Anarchist Plot" in New Orleans, involving some of Garvey's followers. See *New York Times*, January 20, 1923, p. 6.
[40] *Garvey* v. *U.S.*, 4 Federal (2nd) 975 (1923).
[41] *Ibid.*, p. 976.
[42] *New York Times*, July 3, 1923, p. 12.
[43] Garvey, *op. cit.*, p. 131.
[44] *New York Times*, April 7, 1923, p. 5
[45] See letter from Commissioner Garcia (UNIA) to President King of the Republic of Liberia, June 8, 1920, in Garvey, *op. cit.*, pp. 363-364.
[46] This was the Cavalla River Region of Cape Palmas, Liberia.
[47] For full information, see Garvey, *op. cit.*, pp. 362-385.
[48] For a rather humorous account of this incident, see McKay, *op. cit.*, p. 164.
[49] Brisbane, "Rise of Protest Movements . . .," pp. 107-108.
[50] *New York World*, June 25, 1924.
[51] *New York Times*, August 5, 1924, p. 21.
[52] Garvey, *op. cit.*, p. 389.
[53] *New York Times*, August 28, 1924, p. 10; August 29, 1924, p. 4.
[54] For the text of this agreement, as well as all correspondence relating to it, see *Papers Relating to the Foreign Relations of the United States*, vol. 2 (1925), pp. 367-495.
[55] *New York Times*, August 13, 1925, p. 40.
[56] *New York Times*, August 5, 1924, p. 21; August 6, 1924, p. 4.
[57] "The Opinion of W. E. B. Du Bois," *Crisis*, May, 1924, p. 8.
[58] McKay, *op. cit.*, p. 170.
[59] *Garvey* v. *United States*, 267 U.S. 604 (1925).
[60] *New York Times*, November 24, 1927, pp. 1, 23, 27.
[61] McKay, *op. cit.*, pp. 170-179.

258 : THE BLACK VANGUARD

[62] Roi Ottley, *The Lonely Warrior, The Life and Times of Robert S. Abbott* (Chicago: Henry Regnery Company, 1955), p. 218.
[63] *New York Times,* June 21, 1920, p. 1.
[64] For the most recent and probably the best work on the Negro Renaissance, see Blanche E. Ferguson, *Countee Cullen and the Negro Renaissance* (New York: Dodd, Mead & Co., 1966).
[65] Quoted in the *Journal of Negro History,* vol. 36 (1951), p. 60.
[66] Countee Cullen, "Heritage," *Color* (New York: Harper & Row, Publishers, Inc., 1925), pp. 36-44.
[67] Brisbane, "Some New Light on the Garvey Movement," pp. 60-62.
[68] Ottley, *The Lonely Warrior . . .,* p. 218.

CHAPTER 5

[1] *The Hilltop* (Howard University Student Publication), February 4, 1924.
[2] See "Enrollment in Negro Universities and Colleges," *School and Society,* vol. 28 (September 29, 1928), pp. 401-402.
[3] Kelly Miller, "The Higher Education of the Negro Is at the Crossroads," *Educational Review,* vol. 72 (December, 1926), p. 276.
[4] *Ibid.,* p. 277.
[5] G. Victor Cools, "Why Negro Education Has Failed," *Educational Review,* vol. 68 (December, 1924), p. 258.
[6] "Opinion of W. E. B. Du Bois," *Crisis,* October, 1924, p. 252.
[7] *Atlanta Constitution,* February 5, 1925, p. 1.
[8] "Opinion of W. E. B. Du Bois," *Crisis,* April, 1925, p. 249.
[9] *Ibid.*
[10] *New York Times,* January 28, 1925, p. 8.
[11] Du Bois, *Crisis,* p. 250.
[12] *The Hilltop,* May 8, 1925, p. 1.
[13] *Washington Post,* May 8, 1925, p. 1.
[14] "Opinion of W. E. B. Du Bois," *Crisis,* October, 1925, p. 270.
[15] *Ibid.,* August, 1925, p. 164.
[16] "The Durkee-Turner Incident," *Crisis,* May, 1926, p. 38.
[17] W. E. B. Du Bois, "Negroes in Colleges," *Nation,* March 3, 1926, p. 228.
[18] As quoted in "Interpretation," *Crisis,* July, 1925, pp. 146-147.
[19] "Opinion of W. E. B. Du Bois," *Crisis,* August, 1926, p. 164.
[20] For full coverage of the strike and its background, see *Crisis,* December, 1927, pp. 345-346.
[21] "Opinion of W. E. B. Du Bois," *Crisis,* May, 1925, p. 11.
[22] As quoted in *Daily Press* editorial, *Crisis,* May, 1925.
[23] *Ibid.*
[24] "Opinion of W. E. B. Du Bois," *Crisis,* June, 1925, p. 60.
[25] *New York Times,* October 15, 1927, p. 4.
[26] *Crisis,* December, 1927, pp. 345-346.
[27] W. E. B. Du Bois, "Postscript," *Crisis,* December, 1927, pp. 347-348.
[28] "Opinion of W. E. B. Du Bois," *Crisis,* May, 1926, p. 8.
[29] Francis J. Grimke, "Lincoln University," *Crisis,* August, 1926, pp. 196-197.
[30] Du Bois, "Negroes in Colleges," *Nation,* March 3, 1926, pp. 228-229.
[31] Ridgely Torrence, *The Story of John Hope* (New York: The Macmillan Company, 1948), pp. 114-115.
[32] *Ibid.,* p. 149; Edward A. Jones, *A Candle in the Dark, A History of Morehouse College* (Valley Forge: Judson Press, 1967), pp. 83-84.

CHAPTER 6

[1] W. E. B. Du Bois, "The Black Voter and the Republican Party," *Nation*, July 10, 1920.
[2] See Ira D. Reid, *The Negro Immigrant: His Background, Characteristics and Social Adjustment, 1899-1937* (New York: Columbia University Press, 1939), pp. 233-249.
[3] Claude McKay, *Harlem: Negro Metropolis* (New York: E. P. Dutton & Co., Inc., 1940), pp. 132-135.
[4] The adoption of the Cumulative Voting Rule by Illinois in 1870 made it possible for Negroes to achieve these results. See Harold F. Gosnell, *Negro Politicians* (Chicago: The University of Chicago Press, 1935), pp. 65-66. Used by permission of The University of Chicago Press.
[5] *Ibid.*, pp. 40, 41, 55.
[6] Dixon Ryan Fox, "The Negro Vote in Old New York," *Political Science Quarterly*, vol. 32 (1917), pp. 252-275.
[7] James Weldon Johnson, *Black Manhattan* (New York: Arno Press and the New York Times, 1968), pp. 129-131; Mary White Ovington, *Half a Man* (New York: Longmans, Green and Company, 1911), pp. 199-203.
[8] McKay, *op. cit.*, pp. 124-125.
[9] *New York Times*, October 3, 1921, p. 2.
[10] *Ibid.*, July 11, 1923, p. 40.
[11] *Ibid.*, November 16, 1927, p. 24.
[12] "Report on the Needs of the Negro," Unpublished Manuscript, Republican Program Committee, Washington, D.C., 1939.
[13] Norman P. Andrews, "The Negro in Politics," *Journal of Negro History*, vol. 5 (1920), p. 434.
[14] Quote from Editorial Research Reports, June 14, 1927, pp. 466, 469ff., in Paul Lewinson, *Race, Class and Party* (New York: Oxford University Press, 1932, and Russell & Russell Publishers, 1963), p. 171.
[15] Monroe N. Work, ed., *Negro Year Book, an Annual Encyclopedia of the Negro, 1931-1932* (Tuskegee: The Negro Year Book Publishing Company, 1938), p. 92.
[16] *Ibid.*, *1937-1938*, pp. 111-112.
[17] *New York Times*, July 21, 1923, p. 3.
[18] "The N.A.A.C.P. and Parties," *Crisis*, September, 1924, p. 199.
[19] W. E. B. Du Bois, "Is Al Smith Afraid of the South?" *Nation*, October 17, 1928, p. 393.
[20] *New York Times*, October 20, 1928, p. 15.
[21] Gosnell, *op. cit.*, p. 30.
[22] *Ibid.*, p. 30, as quoted in *Chicago Tribune*, October 31, 1928.
[23] *New York Amsterdam News*, November 7, 1928, p. 2.
[24] *New York Times*, March 28, 1929, p. 15.
[25] *New York Amsterdam News*, April 4, 1928, p. 20.
[26] From the *Greensboro Daily News*, April 19, 1920. Quoted in the *National Association for the Advancement of Colored People, Twenty-first Annual Report* (January, 1930), p. 8.
[27] Heywood Brown, "It Seems to Heywood Brown," *Nation*, May 21, 1930, p. 591.
[28] Lewinson, *op. cit.*, pp. 84-85.
[29] *Guinn and Beal* v. *United States*, 238 U.S. 347 (1915).
[30] *Newberry* v. *United States*, 256 U.S. 232 (1921).
[31] "The White Primary," *Crisis*, February, 1925, p. 156.

[32] *Ibid.*

[33] *Nixon* v. *Herndon,* 273 U.S. 536 (1927).

[34] "National Association for the Advancement of Colored People," *Crisis,* May, 1925, p. 33.

[35] "The White Primary, the N.A.A.C.P. Attack on Disfranchisement," *Crisis,* March, 1927, pp. 9-10.

[36] 273 U.S. 536 (1927).

[37] Walter F. White, *A Man Called White* (New York: The Viking Press, Inc., 1948), p. 86.

[38] *Nixon* v. *Condon,* 286 U.S. 89 (1932).

[39] *Grovey* v. *Townsend,* 295 U.S. 45 (1935).

[40] *Ibid.*

[41] White, *op. cit.,* p. 88.

CHAPTER 7

[1] This document caused quite a stir in the United States Senate when it was read in that body by Senator Henry Cabot Lodge. See *Congressional Record,* 68th Congress, 1st Session, vol. 65, part 1, p. 609.

[2] *New York Times,* November 30, 1922, p. 23.

[3] *Ibid.*

[4] Benjamin Gitlow, *I Confess* (New York: E. P. Dutton & Co., Inc., 1940), pp. 479-480.

[5] *New York Times,* August 10, 1925, p. 14.

[6] The Congress met for six days (October 25-31). See James W. Ford, *The Negro and the Democratic Front* (New York: International Publishers Co., 1938), p. 200.

[7] As quoted in "Bolshevizing the American Negro," *Independent,* vol. 115 (December 5, 1925), p. 631.

[8] Ford, *op. cit.,* p. 82.

[9] *Ibid.*

[10] For the plans for the establishment of the Black Belt Republic, see Monroe N. Work, ed., *Negro Year Book, An Annual Encyclopedia of the Negro, 1937-1938,* pp. 70-71.

[11] Gitlow, *op. cit.,* p. 482.

[12] *Ibid.*

[13] Amy J. Garvey, ed., *Philosophy and Opinions of Marcus Garvey or Africa for the Africans* (London: Frank Cass & Co. Ltd., 1967), p. 69.

[14] W. E. B. Du Bois, *Dusk of Dawn: An Essay Toward an Autobiography of a Race Concept* (New York: Harcourt, Brace & World, Inc., 1940), pp. 302-303.

[15] See *Herndon* v. *Lowry,* 301 U.S. 242 (1937).

[16] For a detailed discussion of the background of the case, see Zecharia Chaffee, *Free Speech in the United States* (Cambridge, Mass.: Harvard University Press, 1942), pp. 388ff.

[17] Gitlow, *op. cit.,* p. 480.

[18] See Frank R. Crosswaith, "Meeting the Crisis," *New York Amsterdam News,* August 11, 1934, p. 8.

[19] Roi Ottley, *'New World A-Coming'; Inside Black America* (Boston: Houghton Mifflin Company, 1943), p. 114.

[20] Adam Clayton Powell, *Marching Blacks* (New York: The Dial Press, Inc., 1945), pp. 108-109.

[21] John A. Davis, "We Win the Right to Fight for Jobs," *Opportunity*, August, 1938, pp. 230-237.

[22] See *New Negro Alliance* v. *Sanitary Grocery Co.*, 303 U.S. 552 (1938).

[23] The New York Mayor's Commission on Conditions in Harlem, "The Negro in Harlem: A Report on Social and Economic Conditions Responsible for the Outbreak of March 19, 1935," *New York Amsterdam News*, July 18, 1936.

[24] Carl Offord, "Slave Markets in the Bronx," *Nation*, June 29, 1940, pp. 780-781.

[25] "Harlem," *Fortune*, vol. 20 (July, 1939), pp. 168, 170.

[26] Ottley, *New World . . .*, p. 119.

[27] See Lunabelle A. Wedlock, "The Reaction of Negro Publications and Organizations to German Anti-Semitism," *The Howard University Studies in the Social Sciences*, vol. 3, no. 2, (Washington, D.C.: Howard University, 1942), pp. 120-136.

[28] Ottley, *New World . . .*, *pp.* 117-118.

[29] Claude McKay, *Harlem: Negro Metropolis* (New York: E. P. Dutton & Co., Inc., 1940), p. 203.

[30] See Mayor's Commission on Conditions in Harlem.

[31] *Ibid.*

[32] Powell, *op. cit.*, pp. 72ff.

[33] Sterling D. Spero and Abram L. Harris, *The Black Worker: The Negro and the Labor Movement* (New York: Columbia University Press, 1931), pp. 388, 397.

[34] Brailsford R. Brazeal, *The Brotherhood of Sleeping Car Porters* (New York: Harper & Row, Publishers, Inc., 1946).

[35] Walter F. White, *A Man Called White* (New York: The Viking Press, Inc., 1948), p. 115.

[36] Walter F. White, *Rope and Faggot, A Biography of Judge Lynch* (New York: Alfred A. Knopf, Inc., 1929).

[37] Powell, *op. cit.*, p. 73.

[38] John T. Gillard, "The Negro Challenges Communism," *Commonweal*, vol. 16 (May 25, 1932), p. 97.

[39] McKay, *op. cit.*, p. 234.

[40] Walter White, of the NAACP, was one of the first to become alarmed. See the *New York Times*, July 6, 1931, p. 21.

[41] Michael Gold, "The Communists Meet," *New Republic*, vol. 71 (June 15, 1932), p. 117.

[42] Arthur E. Holt, "Communist Do Not Segregate," *Christian Century*, vol. 49 (September 9, 1931), p. 1114.

[43] Gillard, *op. cit.*, p. 96.

[44] *National Association for the Advancement of Colored People, Twenty-Second Annual Report, 1931*, pp. 11-13.

[45] *Ibid.*, p. 12.

[46] *New York Times*, December 30, 1931, p. 16.

[47] *Ibid.*, June 21, 1931, sec. 3, p. 5.

[48] *Powell* v. *Alabama*, 287 U.S. 45 (1932).

[49] Ottley, *New World . . .*, *p.* 244.

[50] "Negro Editors on Communism," *Crisis*, April, 1932, pp. 117-118.

[51] *National Association for the Advancement of Colored People, Twenty-Fourth Annual Report, 1933*, p. 7.

[52] *Ibid.*

[53] Ralph Bunche, "The Program, Ideologies, Tactics and Achievements of Negro Betterment and Interracial Organizations," *The Negro in America*, (Unpublished manuscript, Carnegie-Myrdal Study), vol. 2, p. 319.

[54] The late Dean Kelly Miller of Howard University offers the following version of the Congress idea: "The original suggestion for such a Congress was made by James W. Ford, Vice-Presidential candidate on the Communist ticket, at a session of the Co-ordinating Committee held at Howard University last May [1935]. The suggestion was ardently espoused and seconded by A. Philip Randolph, sometime editor of the *Messenger*, a radical Negro magazine, which heads toward Moscow." Quoted in Horace R. Cayton and George S. Mitchell, *Black Workers and the New Unions* (Chapel Hill: The University of North Carolina Press, 1939), p. 421.
[55] Bunche, *op. cit.*, pp. 319-320.
[56] Cayton and Mitchell, *op. cit.*, p. 417.
[57] *Ibid.*, p. 421.
[58] Bunche, *op. cit.*, pp. 337-339.
[59] *Atlanta Daily World*, February 19, 1936, pp. 1, 6.
[60] The financial report is taken from Bunche, *op. cit.*, p. 352.
[61] *Ibid.*, p. 372.
[62] *Ibid.*, p. 378.
[63] *Ibid.*, pp. 378-379.
[64] *New York Times*, April 27, 1940, p. 1.
[65] Bunche, *op. cit.*, p. 358.
[66] *Ibid.*, p. 359.
[67] *Ibid.*, p. 360.
[68] *New York Times*, April 29, 1940, p. 17.
[69] James Weldon Johnson, *Negro Americans, What Now?* (New York: The Viking Press, Inc., 1934), p. 68.
[70] Martin Ebon, *World Communism Today* (New York: McGraw-Hill Book Company, Inc., 1948), p. 290.

CHAPTER 8

[1] James Weldon Johnson, *Along This Way* (New York: The Viking Press, Inc., 1933), p. 239.
[2] "How Will Negroes Vote?" *Life*, October 16, 1944, p. 94.
[3] William A. H. Birnie, "Black Brain Trust," *American Magazine*, January, 1943, pp. 36-37.
[4] Roi Ottley, *'New World A-Coming': Inside Black America* (Boston: Houghton Mifflin Company, 1943), p. 256.
[5] Birnie, *op. cit.*, p. 37.
[6] Ottley, *'New World . . .'*, p. 37.
[7] Walter F. White, *A Man Called White* (New York: The Viking Press, Inc., 1948), p. 187.
[8] *Ibid.*, p. 191.
[9] *Ibid.*, p. 223.
[10] Langston Hughes, *Fight for Freedom, The Story of the NAACP* (New York: W. W. Norton & Company, Inc., 1962), pp. 94-95.
[11] As quoted in *ibid.*
[12] *Ibid.*, pp. 233-240.
[13] *Ibid.*, pp. 96-97.
[14] White, *A Man . . .*, p. 229.
[15] For a short but authentic treatment of the problem of discrimination against Negroes in war industries, see Charles S. Johnson, *To Stem This Tide* (Boston: The Pilgrim Press, 1943), pp. 1-30.

[16] For Randolph's version of the Movement, see Rayford W. Logan, *What the Negro Wants* (Chapel Hill: The University of North Carolina Press, 1944), pp. 133ff.
[17] See Malcolm Ross, *All Manner of Men* (New York: Reynal & Company, Inc., 1948), p. 20.
[18] Executive Order 8802, June 25, 1941, *Code of Federal Regulations: Title 3 — The President*, 1938-1943 Compilation, p. 957.
[19] Executive Order 9346, May 27, 1943, *ibid.*, pp. 1280-1281.
[20] John Beecher, "8802 Blues," *Negro Digest*, May, 1943, p. 53, condensed from *New Republic*, February 22, 1943.

CHAPTER 9

[1] John Beecher, "8802 Blues," *Negro Digest*, May, 1943, p. 55.
[2] Carey McWilliams, *Brothers Under the Skin* (Boston: Little, Brown and Company, 1943), p. 45.
[3] *Ibid.*, p. 314.
[4] Roi Ottley, *'New World A-Coming': Inside Black America* (Boston: Houghton Mifflin Company, 1943), p. 303.
[5] Florence Murray, *The Negro Handbook; 1944* (Current Reference Publications, 1944), p. 212.
[6] *Commonweal*, January 29, 1943, p. 363.
[7] *Hearings Before the Committee on Labor, House of Representatives*, Seventy-eighth Congress, Second Session, vol. 1 (1944), p. 235.
[8] *President's Committee on Fair Employment Practice, First Report*, July, 1943 to December, 1944 (Washington, D.C.: U.S. Government Printing Office, 1945), p. 33.
[9] *Hearings before the Special Committee to Investigate Executive Agencies, House*, Seventy-eighth Congress, First and Second Sessions, part 2, 1944, pp. 1459ff.
[10] *Hearings before the Subcommittee of the Committee on Appropriations, United States Senate*, National War Agencies Appropriations Bill, 1945, Senate, Seventy-eighth Congress, Second Session, p. 177.
[11] *Ibid.*
[12] *Ibid.*, p. 63.
[13] *Time*, December 27, 1943, p. 19.
[14] For a review of the entire case, see *Hearings, House, Special Committee to Investigate Executive Agencies*, Seventy-eighth Congress, First and Second Sessions, 1944, pp. 2110-2192.
[15] *Ibid.*, p. 2126.
[16] For a summary of these directives and findings, see *Hearings on the National War Agencies Appropriations Bill*, 1945, Senate, pp. 172-175.
[17] *New York Times*, December 3, 1943, p. 12.

CHAPTER 10

[1] George S. Schuyler, "What's Wrong with the NAACP?" *Negro Digest*, September, 1947, p. 29.
[2] W. E. B. Du Bois, "Marxism and the Negro Problem," *Crisis*, May, 1933, p. 103.

264 : THE BLACK VANGUARD

3 "Postscript by W. E. B. Du Bois," *Crisis*, January, 1934, p. 20.
4 *Ibid.*, April, 1934, p. 115.
5 *Ibid.*, June, 1934, p. 183.
6 Board Minutes, NAACP, June 11, July 9, 1934.
7 "Dr. Du Bois Resigns," *Crisis*, August, 1934, p. 245.
8 Board Minutes, NAACP, May 14, 1934.
9 *Ibid.*, November 14, 1938.
10 *Missouri Ex Rel. Gaines* v. *Canada*, 305 U.S. 337 (1938).
11 *Ibid.*, p. 352.
12 *Alston* v. *School Board of the City of Norfolk, Virginia*, 112 Fed. 2nd 992 (1940).
13 Board Minutes, NAACP, April 14, 1930.
14 Walter F. White, *A Man Called White* (New York: The Viking Press, Inc., 1948), p. 114.
15 Langston Hughes, *Fight for Freedom, The Story of the NAACP* (New York: W. W. Norton & Company, Inc., 1962), p. 136.
16 321 U.S. 649 (1944).
17 313 U.S. 299 (1941).
18 *Smith* v. *Allwright*, 321 U.S. 665 (1944).
19 Hughes, *op. cit.*, pp. 127-129.
20 White, *op. cit.*, p. 145.
21 *Sipuel* v. *Board of Regents of the University of Oklahoma*, 332 U.S. 631 (1948).
22 White, *op. cit.*, p. 146.
23 *McLaurin* v. *Oklahoma State Regents*, 339 U.S. 637 (1950).
24 White, *op. cit.*, p. 151.
25 *Ibid.*
26 *Sweatt* v. *Painter*, 399 U.S. 634 (1950).
27 Within recent years the functions of the SREB have broadened considerably. See Redding S. Sugg, Jr., and George Hilton Jones, *The Southern Regional Education Board* (Baton Rouge: Louisiana State University Press, 1960), pp. 122ff.
28 *To Secure These Rights, The Report of the President's Committee on Civil Rights* (Washington, D.C.: U.S. Government Printing Office, 1947), p. 146.
29 *New York Post*, October 17, 1947, p. 18.
30 *New York Times*, December 3, 1947, p. 11.
31 George S. Schuyler, "Betraying the Negro Case," *Plain Talk*, December, 1947, p. 16.
32 *New York Herald Tribune*, October 28, 1947, p. 12.
33 *The Report of the President's Committee on Civil Rights*, p. 151.
34 *Ibid.*, pp. 1-178.
35 *Higher Education for American Democracy, A Report of the President's Commission on Higher Education* (Washington, D.C.: U.S. Government Printing Office, December, 1947), vol. 2, pp. 31-32.

CHAPTER 11

1 Much of the data on the National Urban League given in this chapter is based upon a paper prepared especially for the author by Lester Granger, former Executive Secretary of the National Urban League. (Hereafter cited as Granger to author.)
2 Granger to author.
3 National Urban League, *The Urban League Story, 1910-1960* (New York: The National Urban League, Inc., 1961), p. 8.

[4] *Ibid.,* p. 23.
[5] Granger to the author.
[6] *Ibid.*
[7] Horace R. Clayton and George S. Mitchell, *Black Workers and the New Unions* (Chapel Hill: The University of North Carolina Press, 1939), p. 409.
[8] Quoted in *ibid.,* pp. 409-410 from Lester B. Granger, "New Trade Union Movement of the Negro," *Workers' Council Bulletin,* No. 18.
[9] Granger to the author.
[10] National Urban League, *op. cit.,* p. 8.
[11] Granger to the author.
[12] National Urban League, *op. cit.,* p. 24.
[13] *Ibid.,* p. 23.
[14] Granger to the author.
[15] National Urban League, *op. cit.,* p. 19.

CHAPTER 12

[1] C. Eric Lincoln, *The Black Muslims in America* (Boston: Beacon Press, 1961), pp. 88-89.
[2] *Ibtd.,* p. 14.
[3] *Ibid.,* p. 106.
[4] Malcolm X, *The Autobiography of Malcolm X* (New York: Grove Press, Inc., 1964), p. 2.
[5] Lincoln, *op. cit.,* p. 191.
[6] *Ibid.,* pp. 29-30.
[7] *Ibid.,* p. 3, n. 1.
[8] *Ibid.,* p. 18.
[9] *Ibid.,* pp. 22-27.
[10] *Ibid.,* p. 24, as quoted in E. D. Beynon, "The Voodoo Cult Among Negro Migrants in Detroit," *The American Journal of Sociology,* vol. 43 (July, 1937 – May, 1938), p. 905.
[11] Louis E. Lomax, *When the Word Is Given* (Cleveland: The World Publishing Company, 1963), p. 34.
[12] Lincoln, *op. cit.,* p. 200.
[13] *Ibid.,* p. 92.
[14] Frances L. Broderick and August Meier, *Negro Protest Thought in the Twentieth Century* (Indianapolis: The Bobbs-Merrill Company, Inc., 1965), p. 211.
[15] *Ibid.,* p. 212.
[16] *Ibid.,* pp. 212-213.
[17] *Ibid.,* pp. 221-222.
[18] *Ibid.,* p. 224.

CHAPTER 13

[1] Florence Murray, ed., *The Negro Handbook, 1942* (New York: Wendall Malliet and Company, 1942), p. 168.
[2] *Ibid.*
[3] Robert E. Cushman, "Our Civil Rights Become a World Issue," *New York Times Magazine,* January 11, 1948, p. 12.

[4] Paul N. Lazarsfeld, "The Negro Vote," *Nation*, September 30, 1944, p. 379.
[5] The Negro contingent at the Democratic National Convention went down fighting for Wallace. See Florence Murray, ed., *The Negro Handbook, 1946-1947* (New York: Current Books, Inc., 1947), p. 294.
[6] For a good description of this drive, see Henry Lee Moon, "How Negroes Voted," *Nation*, November 25, 1944, p. 641.
[7] *New York Times*, July 15, 1948, p. 3.
[8] *Ibid.*, pp. 1, 9.
[9] Robert H. Brisbane, "The Negro's Growing Political Power," *Nation*, September 27, 1952, pp. 248-249.
[10] *Ibid.*
[11] Walter White, "Will the Negro Elect Our Next President?" *Collier's*, November 22, 1947, p. 26.
[12] Murray, *Negro Handbook, 1946-1947*, pp. 16-17.
[13] *New York Times*, June 10, 1948, p. 16.

CHAPTER 14

[1] Walter White, *How Far the Promised Land?* (New York: The Viking Press, Inc., 1955), p. 35.
[2] 339 U.S. 816 (1950).
[3] 347 U.S. 483 (1954).
[4] Board Minutes, NAACP, October 9, 1950.
[5] Langston Hughes, *Fight for Freedom, The Story of the NAACP* (New York: W. W. Norton & Company, Inc., 1962), p. 138.
[6] Helen L. Witmer and Ruth Kotinsky, eds., *Personality in the Making: The Fact-Finding Report of the Midcentury White House Conference on Children and Youth* (New York: Harper & Row, Publishers, Inc., 1952), p. 139.
[7] Kenneth B. Clark, *Prejudice and Your Child* (Boston: Beacon Press, 1963), appendix 5.
[8] Kenneth B. Clark, "The Background: The Role of the Social Scientists," *Journal of Social Issues*, vol. 9, no. 4 (1953), pp. 4-5.
[9] *Ibid.*
[10] *Ibid.*, p. 3.
[11] *Ibid.*
[12] *Ibid.*, pp. 5-6.
[13] Quoted in Harry S. Ashmore, *The Negro and the Schools* (Chapel Hill: The University of North Carolina Press, 1954), p. 106.
[14] *Journal of Social Issues*, vol. 9, no. 4 (1953).
[15] Ashmore, *op. cit.*, p. 106.
[16] 347 U.S. 483 (1954).
[17] Robert G. McCloskey, *The American Supreme Court* (Chicago: The University of Chicago Press, 1960), p. 216.
[18] *New York Times*, May 18, 1954, p. 14.
[19] Carl A. Auerbach, Lloyd K. Garrison, Willard Hurst, and Samuel Mermin, *The Legal Process* (San Francisco: Chandler Publishing Co., 1961), p. 117.
[20] Robert H. Brisbane, "Interposition: Theory and Fact," *Phylon*, vol. 17, p. 12.
[21] Don Shoemaker, ed., *With All Deliberate Speed* (New York: Harper & Row, Publishers, Inc., 1957), pp. 99-102.
[22] Hubert H. Humphrey, ed., *Integration vs. Segregation* (New York: Thomas Y. Crowell Company, 1964), pp. 32-35.
[23] *Ibid.*

[24] *Ibid.*, p. 66. As quoted in Charles L. Black, *The Occasions of Justice* (New York: The Macmillan Company, 1963).

[25] *Brown v. Board of Education of Topeka*, 349 U.S. 294 (1955).

[26] As quoted in Leo Katcher, *Earl Warren, A Political Biography* (New York: McGraw-Hill Book Company, 1967), p. 384.

[27] Hughes, *op. cit.*, p. 139.

[28] *Ibid.*, pp. 145-146.

[29] As quoted in Martin Luther King, Jr., *Why We Can't Wait* (New York: Signet Books, New American Library, Inc., 1963), pp. 76-95.

[30] Martin Luther King, Jr., *Stride Toward Freedom* (New York: Harper & Row, Publishers, Inc., 1958), pp. 41ff.

[31] *Ibid.*, p. 79.

BIBLIOGRAPHICAL NOTES

While the literature on the Reconstruction and post-Reconstruction periods of American history is vast in quantity, qualitatively most of it reproduces the stereotypes so familiar to the American mind. An exception to this pattern, however, is the work of C. Vann Woodward, especially his *Origins of the New South, 1877-1913* (Baton Rouge: Louisiana State University Press, 1951). From a narrower view, but of equal importance, on this period are William E. B. Du Bois, *Black Reconstruction in America* (New York: Russell & Russell Publishers, 1935), and Rayford W. Logan, *The Negro in American Life and Thought; The Nadir 1871-1901* (New York: The Dial Press, Inc., 1954). For Negro disfranchisement during the post-Reconstruction period, Paul Lewinson, *Race, Class and Party* (New York: Russell & Russell Publishers, 1963) is still a standard work; and there is the superb treatment of the period in John Hope Franklin, *From Slavery to Freedom: A History of American Negroes* (New York: Alfred A. Knopf, 1956). For what is perhaps the best discussion of the Negro and the United States Supreme Court there is Loren Miller, *The Petitioners: The Story of the Supreme Court of the United States and the Negro* (New York: Random House, Inc., 1966). For the Negro's part in the Populist Revolt, see John D. Hicks, *The Populist Revolt* (Lincoln: A Bison Book: University of Nebraska Press, 1961); Anna Rochester, *The Populist Movement in the United States* (New York: International Publishers Co., 1943); and C. Vann Woodward, *Tom Watson, Agrarian Rebel* (New York: Rinehart & Company, Inc., 1955).

The running battle between Booker T. Washington on the one hand and W. E. B. Du Bois and William Monroe Trotter on the other constitutes the background of Negro history in the twentieth century.

269

The major source for Washington's part in the controversy is the Booker T. Washington Collection in the Manuscript Division of the Library of Congress. A good single volume on Washington is Samuel R. Spencer, *Booker T. Washington and the Negro's Place in American Life* (Boston: Little, Brown and Company, 1955). Of special value are the monographs by August Meier on several phases of Washington's life. There apparently does not exist any significant collection of papers of William Monroe Trotter. For his origins as well as for his major activities, see John Daniels, *In Freedom's Birthplace: A Story of Boston Negroes* (Boston: Houghton Mifflin Company, 1914); William Harrison, "Phylon Profile IX: William Monroe Trotter — Fighter", *Phylon*, vol. 7 (1946), and Charles Puttkammer and Ruth Worthy, "William Monroe Trotter, 1872-1934," *Journal of Negro History*, vol. 43 (1958). For the Niagara Movement, which was originally Trotter's idea, see Elliot M. Rudwick, "The Niagara Movement," *Journal of Negro History*, vol. 42 (1957).

The National Association for the Advancement of Colored People was partly an outgrowth of the Niagara Movement. The basic sources for the origins of the NAACP are the personal papers of Oswald Garrison Villard at the Houghton Library at Harvard University and the Joel Elias Spingarn Collection on deposit at the Moorland Foundation at Howard University. The best single volume on the NAACP is Charles Flint Kellogg, *NAACP: A History of the National Association for the Advancement of Colored People* (Baltimore: The Johns Hopkins Press, 1967). Available at the Manuscript Division of the Library of Congress are Minutes of the Board of Directors of the National Association for the Advancement of Colored People (1909-1960). For W. E. B. Du Bois' involvement with Washington and Trotter and his activities with the Niagara Movement and the NAACP, see Francis L. Broderick, *W. E. B. Du Bois, Negro Leader in a Time of Crisis* (Stanford: Stanford University Press, 1959) and Du Bois' own book, *Dusk of Dawn: An Essay Toward an Autobiography of a Race Concept* (New York: Harcourt, Brace & World, Inc., 1940). An indispensable source on Du Bois, as well as for Negro history in general, is the magazine, *Crisis*, from 1910 to 1940. The difficulty with using this source is that the collected volumes do not yet have a general index.

The most definitive work on the race riot of 1919 is Arthur Waskow, *From Race Riot to Sit-In, 1919 and the 1960's* (New York: Doubleday & Company, Inc., 1966). Valuable discussions of the riots are to be found also in James Weldon Johnson, *Along This Way* (New York:

The Viking Press, Inc., 1933) and Herbert J. Seligmann, *The Negro Faces America* (New York: Harper & Row, Publishers, Inc., 1920). Unfortunately for students of Negro history, there is no collection of Marcus Garvey papers. The best sources on Garvey today are the two volumes entitled *The Philosophy and Opinions of Marcus Garvey* (London: Frank Cass & Co. Ltd., 1962). The University Publishing House published Volume 1 in 1923 and Volume 2 in 1926. The best biography of Marcus Garvey is Edmund D. Cronon, *Black Moses: The Story of Marcus Garvey and the Universal Negro Improvement Association* (Madison: The University of Wisconsin Press, 1955). Incomplete files of Garvey's newspaper, the *Negro World*, are on deposit at the Moorland Foundation of Howard University and the Schomburg Collection of the New York Public Library. Claude McKay presents an interesting and valuable picture of Garvey in his book, *Harlem: Negro Metropolis* (New York: E. P. Dutton & Company, Inc., 1940).

For a good description of the conditions of Negroes in New York City prior to World War I, see James Weldon Johnson, *Black Manhattan* (New York: Alfred A. Knopf, Inc., 1930) and Mary White Ovington, *Half a Man: The Status of The Negro in New York* (New York: Longmans, Green and Company, 1911). Ira D. Reid deals brilliantly with the conditions of black West Indians in New York during this same period in his *The Negro Immigrant: His Background, Characteristics and Social Adjustment, 1899-1937* (New York: Columbia University Press, 1939). Very little of significance has been written on Negro political activity in the North during the first three decades of this century. The activities of the Chicago Negro during this period are well covered in Harold F. Gosnell, *Negro Politicians* (Chicago: The University of Chicago Press, 1935) and in St. Clair Drake and Horace Cayton, *Black Metropolis* (New York: Harcourt, Brace & World, Inc., 1945). For two good articles on the subject, see Dixon Ryan Fox, "The Negro Vote in Old New York," *Political Science Quarterly*, vol. 32 (1917), and Norman P. Andrew, "The Negro In Politics," *Journal of Negro History*, vol. 5 (1920).

The first Negro flirtations with radical ideologies occured during and immediately following World War I. For some light on the personalities involved, see "Investigation Activities of the Department of Justice," 66th Congress, 1st Session, 1919, *Senate Documents*, vol. 12, and a New York State document entitled *Report of the Joint Legislative Committee Investigating Seditious Activities*, part 1, vol. 2, Senate of the State of New York, Albany, N. Y., 1920. Communist Party activity

among American Negroes began as early as 1919. A most vivid and reliable account of this activity is given in Benjamin Gitlow, *I Confess*
(New York: E. P. Dutton & Co., Inc. 1940). William Ford, *The Negro
and the Democratic Front* (New York: International Publishers Co.,
1938) is good as a supplement. For the official line of the Communist
Party vis-à-vis the American Negro, see The Communist Party of
America, *Manifesto and Program Report to the Communist International* (Chicago: Communist Party of America, 1923). The Communist
Party's infiltration and capture of the National Negro Congress, 1936-
1940, is vividly told by Ralph J. Bunche in "The Programs, Ideologies,
Tactics and Achievements of Negro Betterment and Interracial Organizations," *The Negro in America* (Unpublished manuscript, Carnegie-
Myrdal Study, 1940), vol. 2, on deposit at the Schomburg Collection
of the New York Public Library.

The subject of organized labor and the Negro is superbly treated in
several volumes. These include Sterling D. Spero and Abram L. Harris,
The Black Worker and the Labor Movement (New York: Columbia
University Press, 1931) and Horace Cayton and George S. Mitchell,
Black Workers and New Unions (Chapel Hill: The University of North
Carolina Press, 1939). Of a more specialized nature, but valuable
nonetheless, is Brailsford R. Brazeal, *Brotherhood of Sleeping Car
Porters* (New York: Harper & Row, Publishers, Inc., 1946). For the
best description of the so-called "Black Brain Trust" of the early
1940's, see Roi Ottley, *'New World A-Coming': Inside Black America*
(Boston: Houghton Mifflin Company, 1943). Discrimination against
Negroes in the war industries during the early years of World War II
is dealt with adequately in Charles S. Johnson, *To Stem This Tide*
(Boston: Pilgrim Press, 1943) and Carey McWilliams, *Brothers Under
the Skin* (Boston: Little, Brown and Company, 1943). For the 1941
March On Washington and specifically for A. Philip Randolph's account, see Rayford Logan, *What the Negro Wants* (Chapel Hill: The
University of North Carolina Press, 1944). Supplemental to this is Malcolm Ross, *All Manner of Men* (New York: Reynal & Company, Inc.,
1948). For the best description of the Harlem and Detroit riots of 1943,
see Walter F. White, *A Man Called White* (New York: The Viking
Press, Inc., 1948). Langston Hughes also treats the riots in his *Fight
for Freedom: The Story of the NAACP* (New York: W. W. Norton
and Company, Inc., 1962).

Among the major Negro organizations in existence today, none
presents a greater problem for study and research than the National

Urban League. Unlike the founders of the NAACP, none of the people who participated in the establishment of the League left any available papers and letters. There is not, at this writing, a single volume in print dealing entirely with the League. For the early history of the League one must rely principally on the periodical *Opportunity*, which was the official publication of the body. For more recent years, some useful information about the League can be gleaned from *The Urban League Story, 1910-1960* (The National Urban League, 1961). For this study the writer was indeed fortunate in obtaining a six-page memorandum from Dr. Lester Granger dealing with his twenty-year tenure as Executive Director of the National Urban League. The original copy of this document is in possession of Dr. Granger, who at this writing is residing in Denver, Colorado.

The story of the Black Muslims in America is well told in several good volumes. First among these, of course, is Malcolm X, *The Autobiography of Malcolm X* (New York: Grove Press, Inc., 1940). Next to this the best and most scholarly treatment of the Black Muslims is given in C. Eric Lincoln, *The Black Muslims in America* (Boston: Beacon Press, 1961). Supplemental to this is Louis E. Lomax, *When the Word Is Given* (Cleveland: The World Publishing Company, 1963). Not very much has yet been written about the Congress of Racial Equality. However, some important letters and memoranda written by James Farmer, a founder of CORE, are reproduced in Francis L. Broderick and August Meier, *Negro Protest Thought in the Twentieth Century* (Indianapolis: The Bobbs-Merrill Company, Inc., 1965).

The historic *Brown v. Board of Education of Topeka* decision of the U.S. Supreme Court in 1954 has been discussed in innumerable volumes in recent years. However, in the vital matter of the background and preparation of the briefs for the plaintiffs, two publications by Kenneth B. Clark are still indispensable for research on the matter. These are Dr. Clark's article, "Desegregation: An Appraisal of the Evidence," *Journal of Social Issues*, vol. 9, no. 4 (1953), and appendix 5 to his book, *Prejudice and Your Child* (2nd ed., Boston: Beacon Press, 1963). As the years pass, undoubtedly a vast literature on the great life and tragic end of Martin Luther King, Jr., will appear. Not much of it, however, will surpass two volumes written by King himself on his activities, his hopes, and his faith. These are his *Why We Can't Wait* (New York: Harper & Row, Publishers, Inc., 1964), which includes his famous "Letter From Birmingham Jail," and his *Stride*

Toward Freedom: The Montgomery Story (New York: Harper & Row, Publishers, Inc., 1958), in which King discusses the beginning of the nonviolence crusade in America.

INDEX